FLR
17.95

Making an Impact

of related interest

Childhood Experiences of Domestic Violence
Caroline McGee
Foreword by Hilary Saunders
ISBN 1 85302 827 4

Domestic Violence
Guidelines for Research-Informed Practice
Edited by John P. Vincent and Ernest N. Jouriles
ISBN 1 85302 854 1

The Child's World
Assessing Children in Need
Edited by Jan Horwath
ISBN 1 85302 957 2

Approaches to Needs Assessment in Children's Services
Edited by Harriet Ward and Wendy Rose
Foreword by Professor Al Ainsley-Green
ISBN 1 85302 780 4

Child Welfare Policy and Practice
Issues and Lessons Emerging from Current Research
Edited by Dorota Iwaniec and Malcolm Hill
ISBN 1 85302 812 6

Effective Ways of Working with Children and their Families
Edited by Malcolm Hill
ISBN 1 85302 619 0
Research Highlights in Social Work 35

Social Work with Children and Families
Getting into Practice
Ian Butler and Gwenda Roberts
ISBN 1 85302 365 5

Child Welfare Services
Developments in Law, Policy, Practice and Research
Edited by Malcolm Hill and Jane Aldgate
ISBN 1 85302 316 7

Making an Impact:
Children and Domestic Violence

A Reader

Marianne Hester, Chris Pearson and Nicola Harwin

Jessica Kingsley Publishers
London and Philadelphia

Acknowledgements

Many thanks to everyone who read and commented on the material in the Reader. Thanks in particular to Elaine Farmer, Gill Hague and Ellen Malos (Domestic Violence Research Group and University of Bristol); and to members of the Advisory Group – Chris Atkinson (NSPCC), Bruce Clark (NSPCC), David Johnston (Social Services Inspectorate, Welsh Office), Caroline McGee (NSPCC) and Helen Roberts (Barnardo's).

First published in the United Kingdom in 2000 by
Jessica Kingsley Publishers
116 Pentonville Road, London
N1 9JB, UK

and

400 Market Street, Suite 400
Philadelphia, PA USA

www.jkp.com

© Copyright 2000 Making an Impact

Second impression 2000
Third impression 2002
Printed twice in 2004

Library of Congress Cataloging in Publication Data

Hester, Marianne, 1955–
    Making an impact – children and domestic violence : a reader /
Marianne Hester, Chris Pearson and Nicola Harwin.
        p.   cm.
    Includes bibliographical references and index.
    ISBN 1 85302-844-4 (alk. paper)
    1. Family violence--Great Britain. 2. Children and violence-
-Great Britain. 3. Child welfare--Great Britain. I. Pearson,
Chris, 1960–   . II. Harwin, Nicola. III. Title.
HV6626.23.G7H47   1999   99-41639
362.76'8'0941--dc21   CIP

British Library Cataloguing in Publication Data

A CIP catalogue record for this book is available from the British Library

ISBN 1 85302 844 4 pb

Printed and Bound in Great Britain by
Athenaeum Press, Gateshead, Tyne and Wear

CONTENTS

Making an
Impact

**children and
domestic violence**

PREFACE

It is mainly women who experience domestic violence and it is largely men who perpetrate such violence. But children are frequently caught in the middle. They often witness the violence directly or they are aware that it is happening in the home. As a result, they also may be damaged both emotionally and physically. Indeed, they may be directly caught in the violence, suffering similar abuse to their mother. Research suggests that women who experience domestic violence are on average, beaten 35 times before they ask for help and then make between 5–12 different contacts in an effort to end the violence. Such contacts may be to a wide range of agencies spanning statutory, voluntary and private provision. Crucial to the effectiveness of response must be the quality of staff in those agencies. Such effectiveness will in turn be influenced by agency policy and practice – and here training has a vital role to play.

Making an Impact – Children and Domestic Violence Training Pack has been designed to ensure that training materials for front line staff dealing with domestic violence are more readily available than has been the case in the past. The quality of advice, support and information offered by professionals across the country is believed to be varied and inconsistent. More thorough training will help staff deal more effectively with families where domestic violence is occurring. They should be proactive in asking whether violence is a factor rather than offer excuses, such as "she never told me". Trained staff will have greater knowledge of this important and complex subject. Training will also develop and improve their levels of skill and combine these with greater sensitivity and confidence. Such training should also help change that social work practice which has tended to play down or ignore altogether the dimension of domestic violence when addressing child protection concerns. The protection and wellbeing of the mother has a direct bearing on the safety and welfare of the child and, as such, should form a key element in any plan to offer support and protection.

Making an Impact brings together a wealth of experience. Commissioned by the Department of Health, it has been written by a consortium of practitioners, trainers and researchers from NSPCC, Barnardo's and the University of Bristol. An Advisory Group of wide ranging membership has played an invaluable contributory role. In the hands of competent trainers, *Making an Impact* will certainly be making a difference.

The publication of the training pack in June 1998 comes at an important time. During its first year in office, the new Government has repeatedly stressed its determination to tackle domestic violence urgently and comprehensively. Across Government there are a number of Departments with vital roles to play in the development of strategic policies. These need drawing together to ensure an integrated and complete picture. There is an increased recognition that central and local government must work closely together to translate such policies into tangible achievements. The practical effects of the new legal framework provided by Part IV of the *Family Law Act 1996* which was implemented in the Autumn of 1997 are beginning to emerge.

And the whole framework for interagency co-operation in child protection, known in short as "Working Together", is the subject of current public consultation. In launching that consultation earlier in the year, the Under-

Secretary of State, Paul Boateng wrote: "we believe that more needs to be
done to break down barriers and to promote a wider, more holistic view of
the needs of children and their families". Such ambition entirely mirrors the
aims of *Making an Impact*. It will raise issues about dealing with perpetrators.
It will also help ensure that domestic violence is fully recognised in planning
services for a wide range of people who, as adults or children, experience
such abuse.

Arran Poyser
Social Services Inspector
Department of Health

April 1998

INTRODUCTION

> The Department of Health commissioned the development of this Reader and an associated Training Resource to increase awareness about the impact on children of domestic violence and to develop professional understanding of how best to offer help and support.
>
> Please note that the Training Resource, which was devised by Barnardo's, the NSPCC, the Domestic Violence Research Group of the University of Bristol, and with the assistance of a multi-disciplinary Advisory Group, can be obtained from the NSPCC at the NSPCC National Training Centre, 3 Gilmour Close, Beaumont Leys, Leicester LE4 1EZ. The Training Resource provides detailed training materials for use with single- and multi-agency groups, including guidance to trainers.

The 1990s have seen considerable public, policy and professional concern about domestic violence, as the scale of the problem and its consequences for women and children have increasingly been recognised. Domestic violence has a significant impact on children's lives and on their current and future well-being. We know that many women experience domestic violence and that when a women is being abused not only is her parenting capacity likely to be affected, there is also a high probability that her children may be abused.

The Farmer and Owen study (1995) *Child Protection Practice: Private Risks and Public Remedies* found that in three out of five cases where children had suffered physical abuse, neglect or emotional abuse, the mothers were also subject to violence from their male partners. Domestic violence was a feature of most of the cases with the worst outcomes for children, and professionals were found to give little attention to the fact that children were witnessing and living with high levels of violence.

Traditionally the abuse of women and the abuse of children have been examined as separate issues, with services and policies being developed at different stages by different groups. Children's experiences and voices have largely been ignored in contexts of domestic violence. This Reader, and the associated Training Resource, seek to respond to the experiences of children and of the many women who are striving to care for and protect their children. They also aim to build on the existing skills and understanding both in social work and in the wider professional community, and to encourage collaboration and the effective use of resources and expertise across professions and agencies in the interests of children.

experience domestic violence – both the women and children concerned.
The second part details the key pieces of legislation, both criminal and civil,
which have a bearing on children and their carers who experience domestic
violence, in particular the *Children Act 1989, Family Law Act 1996, Protection
from Harassment Act 1997* and *Housing Act 1996*. There is a focus on the
relevant aspects of the legislation and discussion regarding the implications for
practice. The third part provides detailed overviews and discussion of practice
issues with regard to children who have experienced domestic violence, their
carers and the domestic violence perpetrators. There is also discussion of
developments in multi-agency approaches to both domestic violence and
child protection.

It is hoped that the material in the Training Resource and Reader together will
enable professionals working with children to develop informed and
appropriately sophisticated child protection responses where children are
living in circumstances of domestic violence.

Language

Throughout the training pack the term 'black' is used to describe African,
Caribbean and Asian people. There are more specific references in some case
studies.

The term 'victim' is not used within these training exercises as it is seen to be
negative. 'Survivor of domestic violence' conveys a more positive outcome for
women and children and, as such, is the preferred terminology.

Part One

Children and
Domestic Violence

We begin the Reader by examining the interrelationship between domestic violence and the abuse of children. Increasingly it has been found that in circumstances where the carer (usually the mother) is experiencing domestic violence and abuse from her male partner, the children are also likely to be abused by the same man. The children may suffer direct physical, sexual or emotional abuse, or the abusive impact of witnessing or being aware of, abuse to their mothers.

In order to examine these issues in detail, Chapter One provides an overview of the research and issues which relate to 'domestic violence' – what it is, who it involves, what the dynamics are, the impact of parenting, and so on. That allows us to move, in Chapter Two, to a discussion of what the research shows with regard to the links between domestic violence and abuse of children. Chapter Three examines the impact of domestic violence on children living in such a context.

CHAPTER ONE: DOMESTIC VIOLENCE – WHAT IT IS

Having knowledge and understanding of what domestic violence is about and the effect it has on those involved is crucial for practitioners to be able to work with 'children and domestic violence'. Without knowledge about the dynamics of domestic violence the actions of those concerned can be difficult to understand, and the behaviour of mothers may appear contradictory or unreasonable.

1.1 Terminology

A variety of terms have been used to talk about domestic violence, such as 'family violence', 'domestic abuse', 'violence to women from known men'; as well as 'domestic violence'. To different degrees all of these terms have their limitations. We have decided to use the term 'domestic violence', not because it most accurately reflects the phenomenon we are discussing, but because it is the most commonly used. Consequently a number of issues need to be considered in relation to the term:

- the word 'domestic' might appear to limit the context for the violence to those who live together, whereas violence from male partners often continues after women leave (Evason 1982; Binney, Harkell & Nixon 1988; Hester and Radford 1996).

- the word 'violence' may indicate exclusively physical abuse, whereas individuals subject to domestic violence experience a range of different forms of abuse from their partners, not all of which are, in themselves, inherently 'violent' (Barron, Harwin and Singh 1992; Hague and Malos 1993). When we talk about 'violence' in this Reader and in the Training Resource we are including both 'directly' violent and more 'indirectly' abusive behaviours such as physical, sexual, emotional, and verbal abuse.

- 'domestic violence' masks the issue of gender, the fact that perpetrators tend to be men and their victims usually women (Dobash and Dobash 1980; Abrahams 1994; Mooney 1994).

- 'domestic violence' is violence or abuse from one adult to another which takes place within the context of a close relationship (Home Affairs Select Committee 1993). It masks the interrelationship between such abuse and abuse experienced by children (see Chapter Two in this Reader).

1.2 What is domestic violence?

By domestic violence we mean any violent or abusive behaviour (whether physical, sexual, psychological, emotional, verbal, financial etc.) which is used by one person to control and dominate another with whom they have or have had a relationship. Most studies have focused on domestic violence in heterosexual relationships, where it has been found that the vast majority of cases involve violence from men to women (Dobash and Dobash 1992; Mooney 1994; British Crime Survey 1996). For instance, NCH Action for Children, in their study on domestic violence and children, suggest that 90-97% of domestic violence is from men to women (Abrahams 1994: 6). Where women are violent to male partners it is often as a means of self-defence and in response to long term violence and abuse from their partners (Hague and Malos 1993; Dobash and Dobash 1992).

Domestic violence can also take place in same sex relationships, although the limited research in this area suggests that there may be differences in comparison with the way domestic violence manifests in heterosexual relationships (Taylor and Chandler 1995; Lobel 1986; Radford, Kelly, and Hester 1996). Moreover, domestic violence may involve the wider family network, for instance abuse by in-laws (Bhatti-Sinclair 1994).

In this Reader the main focus is on violence in relationships between men and women and the abuse of children in this context. We largely talk about 'men as perpetrators' and 'women on the receiving end of the violence and abuse'.

1.3 Is domestic violence 'mutual'?

It is sometimes argued that domestic violence is *mutual* between male and female partners, or even a phenomenon *mainly directed by women towards their male partners*. Many practitioners are probably aware of this perspective, but do not know its origins. Straus, Gelles and Steinmetz (1980) in the United States, carried out research into domestic violence using an instrument called the Conflict Tactics Scale (CTS) and involving self-report questionnaires. It led to results that suggested that men and women were equally violent in heterosexual relationships, and that a 'battered husband syndrome' existed of at least a similar extent to domestic violence against women. However, the original CTS relied on a hierarchy of behaviours which omitted the context and anticipated effect of a particular violent act – ignoring that in reality a threat to use physical violence may be more controlling than the physical act itself, and failing to distinguish whether an act of violence is used to control or as a means of self-defence (see Nazroo 1995; Saunders 1988; Dobash and Dobash 1992). The CTS, without examining the context of the replies, therefore provided an inaccurate picture of the main direction and impact of the violence. Moreover, the focus of the CTS was only on physical acts of violence, thus omitting sexual or psychological or other forms of abuse. Straus and Gelles now themselves acknowledge that there are problems with the instrument and some modifications have been made (Gelles and Loseke 1993; Hyden 1994). However, it continues to be used quite widely, especially in the US.

1.4 How much?

There are no national data in the UK concerning general incidence of domestic violence, or which show how many women with children separate from male partners because of domestic violence. Findings from the British Crime Surveys and other studies none the less indicate that violence to women from male partners is widespread, is a feature in a significant proportion of divorces, and provides the most common context for homicide of women. There is an emphasis in the studies, especially the British Crime Survey, on physical violence and a consequent under-representation of sexual and psychological abuse (see Smith 1989; Mirrlees-Black 1995).

Despite the detrimental effects on the individuals experiencing domestic violence which the studies highlight, the behaviours involved may not necessarily be deemed to amount to the commission of a criminal offence. Physical assault and rape may in some instances be deemed to constitute

'actual bodily harm' or 'grievous bodily harm' and ongoing harassment after a woman is no longer with her violent partner may be considered under the recent *Protection from Harassment Act 1997* (see Chapter Five for details of the legislation)

■ From a GP surgery and health projects survey in Hammersmith and Fulham, of 281 women who completed questionnaires 133 (47%) indicated that they had experienced domestic violence (McGibbon, Cooper and Kelly 1989).

■ In England and Wales 45% of female homicide victims – two women per week – are killed by their present or former partners (e.g. Criminal Statistics, 1992), compared to about 10% of male victims (in Mullender and Morley 1994: 5).

■ The Exeter Family Study (Cockett and Tripp 1994) found that one in four separated women with children had separated from partners because of domestic violence, and earlier research suggested that one in three marriages may have broken down partly as a result of domestic violence (Borkowski, Murch and Walker 1983). Anywhere between 40 and 60% of separated or divorced women have experienced violence in their relationships (Hughes 1992).

■ In a random sample-survey in London of 100 men and women, 30% of women reported to having been subject at some time to physical violence 'more severe' than being grabbed, pushed or shaken from a (current or former) boyfriend or male partner; 27% had been injured; 27% threatened with violence; 23% raped; and 37% had suffered mental cruelty (Mooney 1994).

■ Figures extrapolated from the British Crime Survey (which excludes both sexual and emotional abuse) suggest that one in ten women who have lived with a male partner have experienced domestic violence from their partners at some time in their lives. Over one third of these incidents happen after separation when the couple are no longer living together (Mirrlees-Black 1995).

■ Studies that include a range of abusive behaviours indicate that domestic violence occurs in anything between 30–50% of male–female relationships (Kelly 1996; Ball 1995).

■ A total of 63,699 women and children were accommodated in UK refuges in 1995/96, of whom at least two-thirds were children (WAFE 1997).

■ Twenty five percent of the assaults recorded by the police are cases of domestic violence (British Crime Survey 1996; Dobash & Dobash 1980).

■ A survey of 484 women in Surrey's shopping centres found that one in four defined themselves as having experienced domestic violence from a male partner/ex-partner since the age of 18 years (Dominy and Radford 1996).

■ A study of domestic violence and the impact on costs in Hackney, estimated that one in nine women in the borough in 1996 had experienced domestic violence (Stanko, Crisp, Hale and Lucraft 1998).

1.5 Accounts of survivors, abusers and witnesses

Our knowledge about domestic violence comes from the accounts of
survivors and to a lesser extent from the accounts of perpetrators of
domestic violence and witnesses (e.g. Dobash and Dobash 1980, 1992; Pahl
1985; Kelly 1988; WAFE 1989; Homer, Leonard and Taylor 1984; Hanmer and
Saunders 1993; Hoff 1990; Straus, Gelles and Steinmetz 1980; Thurston and
Beynon 1995; Dobash, Dobash, Cavanagh and Lewis 1995; Hearn 1996a;
Hearn 1996b). We know from these accounts that the perception of the
perpetrator and the perception of the woman he has abused often differ –
perpetrators may not see their behaviour as abusive or controlling, in the way
the individual on the receiving end does (Dobash, Dobash, Cavanagh and
Lewis 1995; Hearn 1996a; Hearn 1996b). Jeff Hearn points out, based on his
interviews with men who have been violent to women they know:

> Men generally define violence in much narrower terms than do women.
> The paradigm form of violence for men is physical violence. But even here
> certain kinds of physical violence are often excluded or referred to in
> passing. (Hearn 1996a: 27-28)

Perpetrators are likely to deny and cover up their abusive behaviour, and may
therefore appear as quite a different person in public than at home. Many
women have described their violent partners as appearing very 'charming' at
work, to the police, in court and so on, but generally aggressive and abusive at
home. An Asian woman, whose marriage had been arranged, describes how
her husband appeared 'charming' to others but was 'violent and cruel' to her:

> My family and the people who arranged the marriage did not know that
> he was violent and cruel. We were led to believe that the family he
> belonged to, including him, were all good respectable people, which is why
> I married him. We married very quickly once introduced, and I was not
> able to get to know him beforehand, but he was a 'charmer' able to
> convince people into believing he was nice. (Bowstead, Lall and Rashid
> 1995: 11)

In the report of the Bridge Consultancy Service, on the death of 5-year-old
Sukina Hammond by her father, who was also a domestic violence
perpetrator, it is pointed out that many apparently conflicting descriptions
were attributed to him by the professionals involved:

> In meeting with professionals at the centre of the case, we were struck by
> the very wide range of descriptions given of Sukina's father. For example
> we heard him described as 'gentle, vicious, flamboyant, withdrawn,
> aggressive, deferential, caring, cold'. It is quite an extraordinary range of
> descriptions in respect of one individual. (in Harris Hendriks, Black and
> Kaplan 1993: 31)

The accounts of survivors provide the nearest we will get to the 'truth' about
what domestic violence involves, how it feels, and what the implications are
(Kelly 1988; Kelly and Radford 1996). It is, therefore, important to take the
experiences of survivors of domestic violence as the starting point for
definition, understanding and for the development of realistic practice, bearing
in mind that 'experience' is a complex phenomenon, perhaps remembered
selectively or in stages, perhaps presented as various versions. This means
including in any definition of domestic violence the wide range of behaviours

children and
domestic violence

MAKING AN IMPACT – CHILDREN AND DOMESTIC VIOLENCE

which women have described as abusive and controlling (what Kelly, 1988, has described as a 'continuum' of violence). It also means taking into account the impact of such violence on the individuals concerned, and how that impact may be influenced by, for example, social, cultural or religious contexts (Mama 1996; Bhatti-Sinclair 1994).

Domestic violence includes physical assault, sexual abuse, rape, threats and intimidation, humiliating and controlling behaviour, withholding of finances, deprivation, isolation, belittling and constantly criticising. That domestic violence involves a possible range of behaviours is echoed in the definition used by the Department of Health (Department of Health 1997: 3). Perpetrators may use any one of these behaviours, and usually use a mixture of these, to achieve control. Perpetrators may also be aided in their abuse by other family members or friends, or even agencies. As Amina Mama outlines, talking in this instance about Black women:

> Many women are in fact multiply abused; at the hands of their partners and the police, or their partners and his relatives, or their partners and their employers. (1996: 11)

Domestic violence is not limited to any particular class, ethnic or social group, but is perpetrated by men against women across the social spectrum (Smith 1989; Hague and Malos 1993). However, the experience of domestic violence may differ as a result of these different contexts (Mama 1996; Kelly 1994; Hester, Kelly and Radford 1996). For instance:

> The economic and power relations are very different when one is considering domestic violence against a middle class but financially dependent wife, as compared to domestic violence against a single mother of three in a local authority flat, or violence against a professional working woman. (Mama 1996: 46)

It can be particularly shocking to hear women describe the often gross physical and/or sexual abuse which they have been subjected to by their male partners. It has to be recognised, however, that the less obvious behaviours – the emotional abuse, constant criticism, undermining, humiliation, isolation and living in fear – may have equally detrimental consequences upon the health and well being of women as the physical and sexual violence. These more psychological forms of abuse may serve to destroy a woman's sense of self, or can be used to allude to even worse abuses, often involving (verbal or non-verbal) threats to kill.

> ... mental torture can be just as bad. Not being able to have any friends or freedom or just being totally put down that you almost believe that you're such a bad person really. (Hester and Radford, unpublished interview)

> It was a look... and if he looked at me I knew, you know, it was just a look. [Previously] he had followed me up and threw me on the bed and had his hands round my throat, and he said 'you know I can kill you'. And that was the look in his face... that's from where the look came... (Hester and Radford, unpublished interview)

The abusive behaviour usually escalates over time, and in particular escalates when women attempt to leave or in other ways assert their individuality and strength. As one woman survivor describes:

I was becoming myself again... I had moved away from the kind of person he had all this control over. And as he was losing his control over me, his violence was getting worse. (Hester and Radford, unpublished interview)

1.6 When does it begin?

While domestic violence can begin at any time during a relationship, most studies indicate that violence tends to start early on – in particular once the relationship has become 'formalised' through the couple living together or through marriage (see Pahl 1985; Hester and Radford 1992; Kelly 1988). This may be explained in terms of the woman now being perceived to 'belong' to the man. This is exemplified by Kiranjit Ahluwalia's description of her own violent relationship, where her husband-to-be was charming and nice until the moment they were married. As soon as the marriage had taken place he started to be physically, psychologically and eventually also sexually violent towards her in his quest to control all aspects of her life (Ahluwalia and Gupta 1997).

For many women, violence from their husbands or male partners is also likely to begin at the time of pregnancy, or when the children are small. Or violence may increase at this time (Hoff 1990; Pahl 1985; Mezey and Bewley 1997). Abrahams (1994), for example, outlines how this was very much the case for the women in the NCH Action for Children survey, and increased their vulnerability as a result:

> The majority of the respondents in this survey were... not only young women but young mothers when they first experienced violence from their partners. Being young themselves and having one or more small children of their own means that they were vulnerable emotionally... they were also vulnerable materially.... A significant number of the mothers who were interviewed said that the violence had begun around the time of pregnancy or babyhood, and others claimed that it had started once their children had become toddlers. (1994: 23)

1.7 Domestic violence is often ongoing

It is easy to assume that once a domestic violence perpetrator is no longer living with his wife/partner then the violence will stop. However, that is unlikely to be the case. It has to be recognised that violent male partners may continue to abuse and harass their ex-partners, and will use any situation where both are present, or in contact with one another (e.g. via contact arrangements for the children), to do so (Kelly 1988; Hester & Radford 1992 & 1996; Johnston 1992). In Kelly's study of 60 women, 70% of the women who had left violent men were harassed after separation. In Hester and Radford's study (1996) of child contact arrangements in circumstances of domestic violence, all but three of the fifty-three mothers interviewed had been assaulted or further abused during child contact negotiations and arrangements after separation. Malos and Hague (1993) also provide instances of continued violence and abuse after families had been rehoused.

Violence may escalate and thus become especially apparent around the time of separation. As a result it may appear that such 'separation violence' is a one-off. As Peter Jaffe points out, 'Men's violence may be minimised as only an

emotional reaction to the separation' (Jaffe 1996: 24). Instead, physical violence at the time of separation is likely to be an extension of abusive behaviour which the perpetrator was already using during the relationship. Professionals may want to emphasise 'separation violence' because that feels easier to deal with or to dismiss. As a family court welfare officer pointed out in a recent survey, there may be a comfort in thinking that the violence is 'merely' a product of the immediate separation and that as professionals they therefore do not have to cope with any history or further instances of violence (Hester, Pearson and Radford 1997).

1.8 The impact of domestic violence

Domestic violence may have a considerable impact on both women and children. The impact on children will be discussed in Chapter Three.

Violence from male partners may leave women with severe and permanent physical damage, and can affect their mental health. There are large cost implications (both monetary and social), yet little has been done in the UK to support abused women via contact with medical services. Studies that have been carried out in the UK indicate that:

■ Abused women are more likely to have internal injuries than accident victims (Burge 1989).

■ Over half the women interviewed in Northern Ireland, in a Department of Health and Social Services sponsored study, said they needed medical treatment for their injuries as a result of domestic violence. 39% required hospital treatment at least once. One third were hit while pregnant (McWilliams and McKiernan 1993).

■ In Mooney's survey in London, 40% of women experiencing domestic violence had difficulty sleeping, and 46% experienced depression and loss of confidence (1994).

■ Individuals experiencing domestic violence are more likely to be injured than other victims of violence. Nearly one third of cases reported to the British Crime Survey required medical attention. 69% of incidents led to an injury. 13% resulted in broken bones (British Crime Survey 1996).

■ Stanko, Crisp, Hale and Lucraft (1998), in a study of domestic violence in Hackney, found that the estimated costs of providing assistance, support and advice for domestic violence were approximately £7.5 million. The real costs were social as much as economic, and borne by children as much as their mothers.

The impact of domestic violence can vary greatly with each individual woman, and may depend on the form and frequency of the violence, although the impacts can be similar whether there is physical violence or more emotional/psychological abuse. As outlined above, the range of impacts from physical abuse can include injuries, disability, and death (Dobash and Dobash 1992: ch1).

Apart from these direct physical forms of harm, many women will also experience psychological effects including loss of self-respect, low self-worth, feelings of hopelessness, depression, loss of confidence, dependence on the

perpetrator and minimisation or even denial of the violence (Kirkwood 1993; Walker 1984). In Maynard's (1985) examination of social work case files all the women who were experiencing domestic violence were referred to as lethargic and lacking in energy, and for some of the women a pattern emerged of depression, committal to mental hospital and sometimes attempted suicide. The possible impact of domestic violence on women's mental health was echoed by McGibbon, Cooper and Kelly's London study (1989) where some women indicated they were feeling depressed and isolated, and that they were not coping, especially as they were often deprived of any family support. Women may be prescribed tranquilisers in order to live through the abuse (see Mullender 1996a).

There is a tendency by professionals to see incidents of domestic violence in relation to a 'hierarchy of severity' where physical violence is perceived as the most extreme and emotional or psychological abuse is rated as less severe. Clearly this echoes what the courts perceive as actual evidence (Hester and Radford 1996; Hester, Pearson and Radford 1997). This is similar to the development of knowledge over the last couple of decades concerning child protection, which started with the 'battered baby' and is now beginning to explore the impact of emotional abuse (Glaser and Prior 1997). Yet, it has to be recognised that where actual impact of the violence and abusive behaviour is concerned, it is often the emotional and psychological abuse that women talk about as having the greatest and longest lasting impact. (This may similarly be the case for children – see Chapters Three and Nine). The psychological effects can be even more difficult to deal with than physical injury, partly because they are so hidden and therefore difficult to prove and have taken seriously:

> ... it was only bruises I could show .... I can't show my insides and say like, I'm totally messed up, the children are messed up, I can't do that. (Hester and Radford, unpublished interview)

But also because, while bruises and broken bones fade and mend, the emotional impacts, especially the sense of worthlessness and fear, can be very long-lasting and much more difficult to overcome (Dobash and Dobash 1992; Hoff 1990; Hague and Malos 1993). The psychological impact of domestic violence has been found to have parallels with the impact of torture and imprisonment on hostages. Graham, Rawlings and Rimini (1988) suggest that women's experiences in violent relationships can be understood through the model of the Stockholm Syndrome, 'which has been developed to account for the paradoxical psychological responses of hostages to their captors' (p 218). While the model does not explain why it is largely women who experience domestic abuse and men who are the perpetrators, it does to some extent explain women's resultant behaviour:

> The model shows how the psychological characteristics observed in battered women resemble those of hostages, suggesting that these characteristics are the *result* of being in a life-threatening relationship rather than the *cause* of being in the relationship. Second, the model uses a power analysis that shows how extreme power imbalances between an abusive husband and battered wife, as between captor and hostage, can lead to strong emotional bonding. (Graham, Rawlings and Rimini 1988: 218)

The model may to some extent help us to see what is going on when women behave in a seemingly contradictory way, unable to leave a violent relationship and often returning even after they have left. In particular the way perpetrators often isolate and undermine women thus rendering them dependent, the way perpetrators terrorise through unpredictable threat of violence and death leading women to be ever watchful and appeasing, and the way perpetrators at times appear nice or kind thus creating the hope that it will be possible to rescue the relationship. Women attempting to survive and cope in such circumstances may feel that staying with their violent partner will appease him and thus lessen the violence, or they might be optimistic about the future of their loving life together and thereby minimise the danger that they are in.

1.9 The impact of domestic violence on parenting

For mothers living with violent and abusive partners protection of their children is often a prime concern, although their actions may not necessarily be perceived as protective by professionals. This can lead to inappropriate and punitive interventions. Milner (1996) provides an example of how a mother's attempt to keep her 3-month-old son quiet in order to prevent violence to him led the mother, and not the abuser, to be prosecuted:

> One man with convictions for violence regularly beat his partner, including hitting her with a spade, and attacked his 3-month-old son when he was fretful. The mother gave the son a sleeping pill to keep him quiet and safe from assault before reporting matters to the police. Remarkably, the man was not prosecuted while the mother was charged with ill-treating her child. Her child was taken into care and she was sentenced to a two-year probation order. (Milner 1996: 121)

In Hester and Radford's (1996) study of child contact arrangements, mothers generally wanted contact between children and their fathers to take place, but would attempt to stop contact if they felt this posed a danger to the child. Rather than seeing this as protective, however, the courts and child welfare professionals would tend to see the women as merely obstructive or manipulative. Women may also contact social services in order to obtain help with protection of their children, yet might not disclose the domestic violence in the fear that their children will then be taken away. As Kelly (1994) points out, women will instead suggest that they are 'unable to cope', leading to them being seen as inadequate mothers.

For some women the physical and emotional effects of the domestic violence can have a detrimental impact on their mothering and relationships with their children. Mothers may therefore appear to professionals as inadequate or as unable to cope. It has to be recognised, however, that this is likely to be a direct effect of the domestic violence and that with support, and in particular help to be safe, mothers can resume parenting of their children (this is discussed further in Chapter Eight).

Holden and Ritchie (1991), in their US study, found that mothers might be inconsistent in their parenting due to the abuse they were experiencing from their partners. In some cases the abuse prevented them from maintaining standards of care and/or led them to perceive child care as more stressful

than those women not experiencing violence. Some mothers were also found to act in more punitive ways towards the children in the presence of violent men. (This was a finding echoed by Brandon and Lewis, 1996.) A number of the mothers in the NCH study (Abrahams 1994) described the effect of domestic violence on them as mothers, including losing their self-confidence as mothers, being emotionally drained with little to give to their children, taking out their frustrations on the children, and experiencing an emotional distance between themselves and their children. The mothers pointed out how these effects could be compounded by the difficult behaviour of the children at a time when they too could be trying to come to terms with the violence they were witnessing and experiencing.

Kelly (1996) has similarly suggested that the impact of domestic violence on mothering might include women being forced to make difficult choices, such as leaving without the children in order to protect themselves or their children. Violence against the children from mothers can at times be understood as a means of protecting the children from harsher treatment from their male partners and/or because of their own sense of frustration or distress. Kelly also points out that the abuse of the woman and her daily caring for the children might in some instances be so closely connected that the impact of the violence on her mothering could be especially powerful. This might include situations where:

- children are conceived through rape

- pregnancies are used as a means of control

- children are encouraged or choose to side with the man

- children join in the abuse and/or replicate the man's behaviour (1996: 130)

All of these can lead women to feel ambiguities and contradictions about their children, and Kelly argues that it is therefore essential for women to be given time and space to explore these issues.

1.10 Parenting by violent and abusive fathers

Another aspect that needs to be taken into account is parenting by violent and abusive fathers. Holden and Ritchie (1991) found that children were more likely to have to cope with negative fathering from the domestic violence perpetrator than other children. In their study of women and children in American refuges and a comparison group of women, the violent men were reported as being more irritable, less involved in child rearing, less physically affectionate, and used more negative control techniques such as physical punishment than men in the comparison group. In Hester and Radford's (1996) study of child contact arrangements fathers were often reported to lack parenting skills or interest in caring for children, leading in some instances to dangerous or even deadly situations for the children concerned. Yet they also found that professionals are often very optimistic about men's parenting skills, while scrutinising women's parenting in much greater detail (see also Farmer and Owen 1995 – discussed further in Chapter Eight).

1.11 Staying/leaving

Despite the impact of domestic violence as described above, some professionals still find it difficult to understand why women do not leave a violent partner, or why they return to the violent relationship once they have left. The research points to two main ways of understanding the decision-making processes of women who are being abused by their male partners. These are:

1.   learned helplessness and the cycle of battering

2.   use of active strategies for survival and coping

Learned helplessness

In a highly contentious approach, it has been argued by Lenora Walker (1984) that the reason women stay in violent relationships is because they become locked into a 'cycle of battering' through 'learned helplessness'. Walker describes this 'cycle of battering' as having three stages which are repeated over and over again. There is the initial build-up of tension, which is released by a violent episode, and followed by reconciliation and sweetness – until tension builds up again, and so on. Women end up merely responding to the different phases of the cycle, victimised into helplessness, and ever hopeful that the reconciliation and sweetness phase will predominate. This model has led to the so-called 'battered women's syndrome', used as a defence in criminal and other proceedings in the US (Dobash and Dobash 1992).

While Walker's model may seem to reflect the experience of some of the women abused by male partners, it misses out many of the aspects that women describe. 'Learned helplessness' presents a passive view of the victimised wife, yet women in violent relationships are seldom 'passive':

> Generally, they were always scheming about how to stop the battering, e.g. by examining their own behaviour or ways of escaping the situation, by considering how they could get and keep some money. They took steps to please their mates and to satisfy their demands; they protected and took care of their children. (Hoff 1990:64)

> For most women, active pursuit of assistance is a continual aspect of their lives, ebbing and flowing with their experiences at the hands of violent men and of the institutions from which they seek assistance. (Dobash and Dobash 1992: 232)

Furthermore, the 'cycle of battering' presents the violence as part of a regular or regularised pattern, yet women describe their experiences of abuse from their male partners as often unpredictable or irregular (and therefore even more controlling) and the outcome as neither reconciliation nor sweetness. As Lee Ann Hoff found in her interviews with women who had experienced domestic violence:

> Some beatings occurred in the middle of the night when totally unanticipated. After the first beating there were no routine pleas for forgiveness, but rather diminishing remorse by the man. Also, some incidents were not remembered by the man because he was drunk, or they were denied outright. (Hoff 1990: 65)

And finally, 'learned helplessness' presents women's situation as a form of individualised psychological trait, where it is the woman who ends up as the

problem rather than her circumstances and the violence and abuse she faces. Consequently, professional intervention is likely to focus on enabling *her* to change, for instance by offering her assertiveness training, rather than dealing with her need for real material support in the form of housing, finance and stopping her partner from being able to continue his violence and abuse against her. As the Dobashes point out:

> An explanation of the behaviour of women trapped in violent relationships does not require the specification of unique psychological traits associated with learned helplessness and a battered woman syndrome. (Dobash and Dobash 1992:233)

Use of strategies for survival and coping

Women are faced with complex choices when they are making decisions about leaving violent partners. For each woman those decisions are dependent on the particular circumstances she faces, such as:

■ perceived dangerousness (he will kill her if she leaves; or he will kill her if she does not leave)

■ her access to money, housing and other resources

■ the (anticipated or actual) reaction of family and friends

■ the (anticipated or actual) reaction of the agencies she approaches

■ emotional attachment to her partner.

The potential outcomes of some or all of these aspects are crucial to women's attempts to survive and cope in the immediate and/or longer term. At the same time a particular event, a 'final straw', may precipitate that she leaves, and she may realise that 'solutions to the man's violence do not reside in a change of [her] own behaviour' (Dobash and Dobash 1992:230). In relation to the women in Lee Ann Hoff's study, these 'final straw' events included:

> fear that he would kill her; that she would kill herself; fear for her children or family; recognition that there is no hope for change; the shock of a particular beating; the horror of being beaten while pregnant. (1990: 63)

In the NCH Action for Children survey (Abrahams 1994) mothers gave the following reasons why they found it difficult to leave their violent partner permanently:

Table 1.1

reasons women find it difficult to leave violent partner permanently (in rank order) N=102	%
thought he would change	72
afraid of what he might do	63
didn't want to leave the home	58
didn't want to upset the children	54
nowhere to go	49
couldn't afford to leave	44

too much in love with him	37
didn't want to end the relationship	31
thought the violence was a 'once off'	23
family pressure not to leave	22

For some women, the fear of being killed stops them attempting to leave – as one women in a refuge said, whose husband had put his hands round her neck until she passed out, 'I was too scared to leave' (Elizabeth in WAFE 1989: 17). Almost two-thirds of the women in the NCH survey were discouraged from leaving their violent partner 'for fear of what he might do to them if they did' (Abrahams 1994: 68 and see Table 1), and had experience of the threats being acted upon. As outlined earlier, it has to be recognised that violence continues post-separation and that the period after a woman leaves a violent man is an extremely dangerous time for her as the man is likely to attempt to find her. The homicide statistics show us that most women are killed in the period after they leave (Mullender and Morley 1994; Jones 1980). As a result some women might (realistically) feel it is actually safer, despite all the terrible problems, to go back once more. They may also feel that if they go back, that may appease the man, making him less violent. For some Black and particularly Asian women the pressures to stay, or to go back if they have managed to leave, may be especially great where the family (his and/or hers) are hostile or take part in the abuse, or where 'bounty hunters' have been hired to find them (Mama 1996; Bhatti-Sinclair 1994). Moreover, immigrant women face problems leaving violent men as they are unable to claim any public support if they have only arrived in Britain during the previous year (see also Chapter Seven).

Women may also see staying in a refuge or with family and friends as a means of indicating to the perpetrator that his behaviour must change, in the hope that they can continue to live together as a couple or family in the future. As indicated in Table 1.1, nearly three-quarters of the women in the NCH survey thought that the man would change. While research shows that this view is clearly unrealistic, the underlying sentiment is perhaps not surprising considering the public pressures to keep families together and the negative light in which single-parent families are seen.

Not having access to alternative accommodation, or having to stay with friends and family – in other words, having nowhere to go – is a fundamental reason for many women staying (Malos and Hague 1993; Mama 1996). Also, some women are reluctant to uproot themselves and their children from home, school and friends when it is the man's violent and abusive behaviour which is at issue. In the NCH survey 'not wanting to leave the home' (58%) ranked higher than 'nowhere to go' (49%) (see Table 1.1). The *Family Law Act 1996* now provides means for abusers to be ousted from the family home (see Chapter Six). However, the *Housing Act 1996* curtails women and children's access to safe and permanent accommodation (see Chapter Seven).

The children are also an important part of the equation. Many women make decisions about staying or leaving on the basis of the children and only leave a violent relationship once they feel the children are affected, or if the children disclose that they are also being abused by their father or the mother's

partner (Kelly 1988; Hilton 1992; Hester, Humphries, Pearson, Qaiser, Radford and Woodfield 1994). Some women decide not to leave violent relationships because they feel the children would be materially worse off if they left, and in the NCH survey over half the mothers stayed because they did not want to upset their children (see Table 1.1). Violent and abusive men are also likely to use threats concerning the children in order to make women stay, especially threats that women will lose their children because they will be reported to social services as bad mothers (especially powerful when the men appear charming and capable) or because the children will be abducted (Abrahams 1994; Hester and Radford 1996).

The added impact of racism on Black children also needs to be recognised in relation to women's decisions. Imam, in one example where a woman decided to return to live with her violent husband, describes how the children's experience of racism in a refuge created greater pressures on their mother to return. The children said that they were frightened of their father and 'hated what he was doing to Mum', but they found the racism from other children and mothers in the refuge was worse (Imam 1994: 190).

Disclosing domestic violence

The ease with which women are able to disclose violence and abuse they are experiencing is subject to the same coping and survival strategies as outlined above in relation to staying and leaving. Women are concerned that if they disclose, the response they get might be hostile, indifferent or will blame them for the violence. Moreover, they have no guarantee that disclosure will make them safe. Women also find sexual abuse and rape especially difficult to talk about. For practitioners to enable individuals who have experienced domestic violence to disclose the details of their experience, and to elicit information regarding the particular impacts for the individual, it is very important to respond positively and to believe what is being said. It is also crucial to focus on how women themselves perceive their own and their children's safety. (The issue of disclosure will be looked at again in relation to adults in Chapter Eight and in relation to children in Chapter Nine).

Agency support

Women often contact numerous agencies for help regarding the violence and abuse they face, including social services, general practitioners, and the police.

The Dobashes argue that women are only being realistic if they are wary of the support offered by agencies:

> ... research and experience in both [Britain and the US] reveals that traditional agency response has often been inadequate and sometimes detrimental. In the past and still today, members of the helping professions have often remained 'neutral', offered sympathetic advice and/or concentrated on the needs of children and reconciliation, or offered therapy to the woman. Women have often been blamed for the violence, asked to change their behaviour in order to meet their husband's demands, and had their own concerns and requests deflected or ignored. (Dobash and Dobash 1992: 232)

Research indicates that women are often not provided with the response or help that they need, although the response from many agencies is improving:

- In Homer, Leonard and Taylor's (1984) study of women leaving violent relationships in Cleveland, over half of the 80 women had contacted between six and eight agencies and a sizeable proportion (13%) had contacted between nine and eleven agencies (often a number of times, and apart from the refuge where they ended up staying).

- Mama (1996) in her survey of a 100 Black women's experiences of domestic violence and support services found a wide variation between ethnic minority groups in the access to and/or support provided by social services. 33% of the women had made contact with social services, with Asian women more likely than African or African Caribbean women to do so.

- Hanmer and Saunders (1993), in their West Yorkshire study, found that women on average contacted eleven agencies before they obtained the help they needed, with Black women contacting an average of 17 agencies.

We have to understand the many complexities outlined above, and in particular women's attempts to optimise their own and their children's safety and survival, if we are also to understand the seemingly contradictory (but in reality safety-oriented) choices that women in violent relationships are seen to make with regard to their children and themselves.

1.12 Summary

- Domestic violence is taken to mean any violent or abusive behaviour (e.g. physical assault, sexual abuse, rape, threats and intimidation, humiliating and controlling behaviour, withholding of finances, deprivation, isolation, belittling and constantly criticising) which is used by one person to control and dominate another with whom they have or have had a relationship. The vast majority of cases involve violence from men to women. Perpetrators may also be aided in their abuse by other family members or friends, or even agencies.

- Domestic violence is not limited to any particular class, ethnic or social group, but is perpetrated by men against women across the social spectrum. The experience of domestic violence may differ as a result of these different contexts.

- Violence to women from male partners is widespread, is a feature in a significant proportion of divorces, and provides the most common context for homicide of women.

- The perpetrator and the perception of the woman he has abused often differ – perpetrators may not see their behaviour as abusive or controlling, in the way the individual on the receiving end does. Perpetrators are likely to deny and cover up their abusive behaviour, and may therefore appear as quite a different person in public than at home.

- While domestic violence can begin at any time during a relationship, most studies indicate that violence tends to start early on – in particular once the relationship has become 'formalised' through the couple living together or through marriage.

- The abusive behaviour usually escalates over time, and in particular escalates when women attempt to leave or in other ways assert their individuality and strength.

- Violence from male partners may leave women with severe and permanent physical damage, and can affect their mental health. There are large cost implications, both monetary and social.

- The impact of domestic violence can vary greatly with each individual woman, and may depend on the form and frequency of the violence, although the impacts can be similar whether there is physical violence or more emotional/psychological abuse.

- There is a tendency by professionals to see incidents of domestic violence in relation to a 'hierarchy of severity' where physical violence is perceived as the most extreme and emotional or psychological abuse is rated as less severe. Yet, it is often the emotional and psychological abuse that women talk about as having the greatest and longest lasting impact. The psychological impact of domestic violence has been found to have parallels with the impact of torture and imprisonment on hostages.

- For mothers living with violent and abusive partners protection of their children is often a prime concern, although their actions may not necessarily be perceived as protective by professionals.

- For some women the physical and emotional effects of the domestic violence can have a detrimental impact on their mothering and relationships with their children. Mothers may therefore appear to professionals as inadequate or as unable to cope. It has to be recognised, however, that with support, and especially with help to be safe, mothers can usually resume parenting of their children.

- Some women may feel ambiguities and contradictions about their children as a result of the domestic violence, and it is therefore essential for women to be given time and space to explore these issues.

- Children are more likely to experience negative fathering from domestic violence perpetrators than other children.

- Women are faced with complex choices when they are making decisions about leaving violent partners. For each woman those decisions are dependent on the particular circumstances she faces.

- The ease with which women are able to disclose violence and abuse they are experiencing is subject to coping and survival strategies. Women are concerned that if they disclose, the response they get might be hostile, indifferent or will blame them for the violence. Moreover, they have no guarantee that disclosure will make them safe.

- Women often contact numerous agencies for help regarding the violence and abuse they face, including social services, general practitioners, and the police. They are often not provided with the response or help that they need, although the response from many agencies is improving.

CHAPTER TWO: DOMESTIC VIOLENCE AND THE ABUSE OF CHILDREN

An increasing variety of research has highlighted that children are likely to be at risk of physical, sexual and/or emotional abuse in the context of domestic violence. From the research it is apparent that *domestic violence is an important indicator of risk of harm to children.*

Much of the initial research was carried out in the United States, Australia and Canada but more recently a number of studies in the UK have echoed the findings from elsewhere. The evidence concerning the abuse of children in circumstances of domestic violence has arisen both from research focusing on domestic violence, and from that focusing on child abuse and protection. The studies have often included accounts of women survivors of domestic violence, and examination of records from social services or health. Recently there have been an increasing number of accounts from children who have lived in circumstances of domestic violence.

From the research a number of aspects are apparent:

■ that the domestic violence perpetrator may also be directly – physically and/or sexually – abusive to the child;

■ that witnessing violence to their mothers may have an abusive and detrimental impact on the children concerned; and

■ that the perpetrators may abuse the child as a part of their violence against women.

The studies regarding child protection and domestic violence often separate out, and focus on merely one aspect of, abusive behaviour to children, and also separate the experiences of mothers from those of children. Many of the studies have taken a somewhat narrow look at abuse of children in the context of domestic violence, often focusing only or primarily on physical abuse of children and carers. There has been a more limited incorporation of the sexual abuse of children, and a smaller number of studies examining the emotional abuse associated with children living with or witnessing violence to their mothers.

Overall, however, the research indicates that in order to develop professional understanding of and practice in relation to child abuse we need to recognise that children often experience a mixture of physical, sexual and/or emotional abuse, and that focusing on only one aspect of these different forms of abuse can therefore be false. Similarly, where there is both domestic violence and child abuse, we need to examine the whole picture. Moreover, child abuse in the context of domestic violence has to be understood as gendered, that is, not as 'family violence' carried out by 'family members' or 'parents' but specifically as violence and abuse primarily carried out by men against their children and female partners.

2.1 Domestic violence as an abusive context for children – 'direct' abuse

Research from the US was some of the first to suggest that abuse of children was likely to take place in circumstances of domestic violence, and that domestic violence might thus be an indicator of child abuse. The studies were

often carried out in very different ways and using different types of samples, which makes it harder to make direct comparisons. Even so, the studies provide clear indications of a link between the direct abuse of children and living in a context where there is domestic violence to mothers.

A couple of American studies from the late 1960s and early 1970s indicated that men who sexually abused their children were in many instances also physically abusing their wives. For instance, Tormes (1972) found that 13 out of 20 fathers who sexually abused their daughters were physically violent to their wives (as well as to other members of their families). Similarly, Browning and Boatman (1977) found that a majority of fathers who sexually abused their children were physically abusive to other family members.

This link between sexual abuse of children and violence to wives (let alone other family members) was somewhat lost in the consequent debates and practice concerning child sexual abuse (see Dietz and Craft 1980). Studies in the US examining links between child abuse and domestic violence have tended to focus on physical abuse of both children and mothers. In an overview of the later American studies, Edleson (1995) indicates that in 32% to 53% of all families where women are being physically beaten by their partners, the children are also the victims of direct abuse by the same perpetrator.

Stark and Flitcraft (1988), in one of the later US studies, examined a sample of 116 children who had been identified as subject to abuse or neglect in the records of a hospital. They also examined medical records in order to look for incidents of physical injury to the mother. It was found that 45% of the children had mothers who were also being physically abused and another 5% had mothers whose relationships were full of conflict. Stark and Flitcraft conclude that:

> ...[wife] battering is the most common context for child abuse, [and] the battering male is the typical child abuser. (Stark and Flitcraft 1988: 97)

In another US study, Bowker, Arbitell and McFerron (1988), also found that there was a direct link between 'wife beating' and abuse of children. Their sample of 1000 battered women was not representative of the population generally. None the less a clear link between abuse of children and the context of domestic violence emerges. From the 775 women in the sample who had children with their violent partners it was reported that 70% of their husbands also physically abused the children. The more frequent the violence to wives, including physical violence and marital rape, the more extreme the physical abuse of the children. The authors conclude that

> the severity of the wife beating is predictive of the severity of the child abuse. (Bowker, Arbitell and McFerron 1988: 165)

A more recent study in the US, again focusing on physical abuse, concludes that 'marital violence is a statistically significant predictor of physical child abuse' (Ross 1996: 589). The study, based on a representative sample of 3,363 parents, examined violence by both men and women against their partner using the Conflict Tactics Scale – and is therefore likely to have over represented violence by women against their husbands and children (see Chapter One). Even so, the study showed that male perpetrators are more likely to be violent to both wife and children. As Ross concludes:

> ...even women who are the most chronically violent have only a 38%
> probability of physically abusing a male child, whereas the most chronically
> violent husbands are almost certain to physically abuse their children.
> (Ross 1996: 595)

As indicated, many of the recent US studies have tended to focus on physical
abuse of children and physical domestic violence. Other forms, especially
sexual abuse, have been excluded and Ross's study in particular is also likely
to have underestimated the level of abuse by husbands relative to that by
wives. However, Truesdell, McNeil and Deschner (1986), who examined the
incidence of domestic violence in child sexual abuse cases concluded that (as
in the case of child physical abuse):

> ... wife abuse is more common in families in which incest occurs than in
> the general population. (p 140)

A study by Goddard and Hiller (1993) in Australia has examined different
types of violence and abuse to children in order to examine wider
implications. They surveyed 206 cases of child abuse presenting at the child
protection unit of a hospital. Domestic violence was a feature in over half
(55%) of the physical child abuse cases, and in slightly less (40%) of the child
sexual abuse cases. The physical abuse cases involved mainly boys (63%) while
the sexual abuse cases involved primarily girls (82%). Moreover, in almost all
of the cases involving both child sexual abuse and domestic violence, the
siblings were also being emotionally, sexually, and/or physically abused.

2.2 Domestic violence as an abusive context for children – living with and witnessing violence

Alongside the work examining direct physical and sexual abuse of children in
contexts of domestic violence, attention has also been focused on the
experiences of children living in such contexts but who might not be being
'directly' abused. In a sense this development parallels the studies concerning
women's experiences of domestic violence, where physical violence from
male partners was initially focused on, but with an increasing recognition that
the psychological effects of living with the fear and threat of possible violence
often had a greater impact on the women concerned (see Chapter One).

In recognition of the potential impact on children of witnessing domestic
violence a number of local authorities in the UK have defined witnessing
domestic violence as abuse of children, for instance, Strathclyde Regional
Council Social Services Department (Hague, Kelly, Malos, and Mullender 1996).

A wide range of research has found that witnessing violence to their mothers
can have a detrimental impact on children, tantamount to emotional abuse or
psychological maltreatment (Saunders, Epstein, Keep and Debbonaire 1995;
Abrahams 1994; Jaffe, Wolfe and Wilson 1990; Christensen 1990; Carroll
1994). As Kolbo, Blakely and Engleman (1996) conclude, in their review of the
research literature concerning children who witness domestic violence:

> Two decades of empirical research indicate that children who witness
> domestic violence are at increased risk for maladaptation. (Kolbo, Blakely
> and Engleman 1996: 289)

Harris Hendriks, Black and Kaplan (1993) express concerns about the abusive effect on children of witnessing violence to their mothers especially gross acts of violence, including murder. As they state, very many of the children in their study of a clinical sample involving 160 children from 62 families had 'witnessed often horrific violence from their father to their mother. From this they could and should be protected' (p 33). (The impacts on children of witnessing domestic violence is discussed in greater detail in Chapter Three.)

'Witnessing' domestic violence may suggest that the child is present in the room or location when an incident takes place. However, children can 'witness' domestic violence in a number of ways which extend beyond direct observation of violent and abusive acts to their mothers or other carers. Where children do not directly witness the violence or abuse, they might still overhear incidents or in other ways be aware that violence or abuse has occurred. Hughes (1992) found that in 90% of cases children are in the same or the next room when domestic violence takes place. In the NCH Action for Children study (Abrahams 1994), for example, 73% of the children had directly witnessed violent assaults on their mothers, including 10% of the children whose mothers had been sexually abused or assaulted by violent partners in front of them, nearly two thirds (62%) had overheard violent incidents, and about half (52%) saw the injuries resulting from domestic violence (p 30). Children interviewed in the study recounted some of these incidents:

> He would come in and rip my mother's clothes off. He tried to strangle her, just to beat her up like... We were always watching it... he used to tell us to get back to bed...' (Child – in Abrahams: 1994: 31)

> A lot of times I just heard it from the bedroom, and once (my sister) and I heard it, and we were just crying our eyes out for my Mum, you know, she just sounded so desperate downstairs... crying and screaming. (Child – in ibid.: 31-32)

> It was depressing. My mother was always on edge, scurrying around... And I was frightened as well, every time he was there, thinking, 'Oh, what's he going to do today? Is he going to knife her or what?'. (Child – in ibid.: 33)

While much of the research has focused on the witnessing by children of physical violence to mothers, McGee (1996 and forthcoming) points out that witnessing other ongoing abusive behaviour is at least as important because:

> ... many children may not directly witness the physical assaults but will be exposed to other forms of violence and abuse directed at their mother.

In interviews with children and young people a 12-year-old girl told her:

> I've never seen Dad hit her , but I've seen him get very angry and like once when Mum was really ill, she had to be taken to hospital in fact, he said 'No, just leave her, leave her'. And then I was the one who had to phone the doctor. (McGee 1996)

2.3 Domestic violence as a context for child deaths

Domestic violence was also found to be an important feature in the highly publicised death of Maria Colwell at the hands of her father in 1974. During

the late 1980s cases involving child deaths again highlighted the importance of domestic violence as a context for child abuse. In the backgrounds to the fatal abuse of five-year-old Sukina Hammond by her father, and of three-year-old Toni Dales by her step-father, was the ongoing violence and abuse from these men to the children's mothers (O'Hara 1994; Bridge Child Care Consultancy 1991; National Children's Bureau 1993; and see also report on death of Kimberley Carlile, London Borough of Greenwich 1987). Yet in these, and many other cases where children have been killed, the significance of violence to the mothers as an indicator of potential risk to the children have in practice tended not to be understood nor acknowledged (James 1994; O'Hara 1994). As a consequence, the assessment of danger from the perpetrators has been unrealistic. As O'Hara explains:

> In both [the Dales and Hammond] cases the professionals involved with the children suspected that they were being physically abused and knew that their mothers were being subjected to violence by their partners, and in both cases there was a failure to appreciate the danger to the children represented by the men concerned. (O'Hara 1994: 59)

However, despite the earlier research findings and the child deaths that had been found to have occurred in contexts of domestic violence, and despite knowledge from refuges about links between domestic violence and abuse of children, it is only during the 1990s that these links have emerged in the public and social work debates in the UK. The Dartington overview of the research into child protection, *Messages from Research*, (Department of Health 1995) has been particularly important in this respect.

2.4 UK research on child abuse and protection

Child protection studies have probably provided the largest body of research in the UK to indicate, if incidentally, that domestic violence is an important feature in the background of children who have been subject to abuse or risk of harm. There are certain limitations to the use of child protection data, in particular that it provides a narrow 'clinical' sample which is unlikely to be representative of the population as a whole. Only a small proportion of incidents of child abuse come to the attention of agencies, with under-reporting in relation to middle class sectors of the population and over-representation of ethnic minorities (Hooper 1995; Kelly, Regan and Burton 1991).

None the less, from the child protection studies it is apparent that domestic violence is often a significant and consistent feature, no matter what the form of abuse a child is deemed to have suffered, whether physical, sexual or emotional abuse. While most of this research did not set out to examine domestic violence, it none the less indicates that in instances of child abuse between a fifth and nearly two-thirds of the children were also living in circumstances of domestic violence. The more detailed the studies the more likely they were to find that domestic violence was also an issue:

■ Moore (1975) in an in-depth study of 23 'violent matrimonial cases' referred to the NSPCC found that children had been adversely affected by this context.

■ Hyman (1978) found in relation to 85 cases of non-accidental injury to children that social workers described 41% of mothers and 19% of fathers as having been 'violently treated' by the other partner.

- Maynard's (1985) examination of 103 social services case files found that one in three of these mentioned domestic violence.

- A study by the Social Services Department of the London Borough of Hackney indicated that the mothers of at least one third of children on the Child Protection Register were experiencing domestic violence. Of allocated social services cases, 1 in 5 involved domestic violence (Miller, London Borough of Hackney 1994).

- Cleaver and Freeman (1995) in a detailed study of 30 families undergoing the early stages of child abuse enquiries, found that 12 of the cases (nearly 50%) also involved domestic violence.

- Gibbons, Conroy and Bell (1995) found that in 27% of 1,888 referrals with child protection concerns, across a number of authorities, domestic violence was also recorded.

- Farmer and Owen (1995), in their study of outcomes of child protection practice, found that 52% of 44 sample cases involved domestic violence.

- Brandon and Lewis (1996), examining significant harm of children (that is, maltreatment and neglect) found that 21 out of 54 children in the background sample and 28 out of 51 children in the intensive interview sample had witnessed domestic violence.

- Humphreys (1997) in a study of Coventry Social Services child protection cases found that in 11 out of 32 cases, women were also reported to have severe injuries as a result of incidents of domestic violence.

- Examination by Hester and Pearson (1998) of NSPCC case files revealed that, in at least a third of 111 cases accepted for service, domestic violence was also an issue. This rose to nearly two-thirds (62%) after the team included a more detailed focus on domestic violence in their work.

- In Farmer and Pollock's (1998) study of substitute care for sexually abused and abusing children, 2 in 5 children (39%) in a case file sample of 250 newly looked after children had lived in families where there was violence between their parents – mainly violence by the man to the mother. This rose to over half (55%) in the more detailed follow-up sample of 40 sexually abused and/or abusing young people in care.

- Skuse (forthcoming) has found in a small clinical sample, links between sexual abuse of boys and living in a context of domestic violence. There was a stronger correlation where the boys were both victims and perpetrators of sexual abuse.

During the 1970s a small number of child protection oriented studies in the UK began to examine the effect on children of domestic violence. Two studies were carried out under the auspices of the NSPCC, one examining the impact on children living in a context of 'violent marital conflict' (Moore 1975) and the other drawing on social workers' perceptions of families where children had been injured non-accidentally (Hyman 1978). Both indicate the existence of links between some form of abuse of children and a context of 'marital violence'. The studies are problematic, however, in that they present the mothers in a very negative light, and hint that they are the central cause of both the child abuse and marital violence, despite the examples given in

the studies, which indicate that it is men who are being violent and abusive to children and their mothers.

Farmer and Owen (1995) provide one of the more detailed studies linking child protection work and domestic violence. In their study of the outcomes for children of child protection practice, they found that domestic violence (mainly involving violence from the male to female partner) was a feature 'across the full range of households and categories of abuse in the study' (p 138), with abuse of children including physical, sexual, and emotional abuse as well as neglect. In cases of child *sexual abuse* they found that 'some form of family violence had been evident at the time of the abuse in two-fifths' (that is 40%) of the cases (p 223). With regard to cases of *physical abuse, neglect and emotional abuse*, 29 cases in all, 'there were 17 instances (59%) in which there was also other current violence in the family apart from the child abuse which had brought the case to conference. This was usually a man's violence to a woman...' (p 224). They concluded that the children with the worst outcomes were especially likely to have mothers who were being abused by their male partners, although the domestic violence tended to be ignored by the professionals involved.

Another, more recent, study by Glaser and Prior (1997 and forthcoming) examined the cases of 94 children registered with local authorities solely or partly for *emotional abuse*. Minutes from child protection conferences were looked at, and interviews were carried out with social work managers. It was found that over 60% of the emotional abuse of children was taking place in contexts where there was domestic violence and of parental mental ill-health, and/or alcohol/drug abuse. Domestic violence was the main feature in relation to 28% of the children. (It should also be recognised that for many women mental ill-health or alcoholism is often a *result* of ongoing violence from male partners – Stark and Flitcraft 1988; Humphreys 1997; Cleaver, Unell and Aldgate forthcoming; and see Chapter One).

A number of recent studies have focused more specifically on domestic violence in child abuse cases. Brandon and Lewis (1996), for example, examined significant harm in relation to children who had witnessed domestic violence. 54 children were in a 'background sample' and 51 in an 'intensive interview sample' which included information from parents, teachers and from some of the children themselves. Overall, approximately half (49%) the children from each sample group had witnessed violence. About half (28 out of 51) of the intensive interview sample, 'warranted inclusion as cases of harm or potential harm from domestic violence' (p 36). Brandon and Lewis conclude that the abusive consequences of witnessing domestic violence generally need to be recognised by social workers and other professionals:

> ... the evidence points to the possibility that the cumulative harm from witnessing violence will affect the child's emotional and mental health in future relationships.... Until professions recognise that when the child sees violence at home there is a likelihood of significant harm, it will not be possible to act to prevent long-term damage. (1996: 41)

Humphreys (1997) examined the cases of 32 families, with 93 children, who were the subject of case conferences in Coventry, with a deliberate over-sampling of (12) Asian families. Nearly half the women (11 of 32) were reported to have sustained severe injuries from their male partners, with a

further 3 women apparently experiencing other more psychological forms of domestic violence. The research echoes the findings from Maynard (1985) that women who have experienced domestic violence are at particularly high risk of having their children accommodated. Two-thirds of the women (24 of 32) 'were either "threatened" with the accommodation of their children or did in fact have their children accommodated in situations where they were also the subject of abuse from violent men' (p 13; and see Chapter Eight for further discussion of this issue). Humphreys also found that issues of mental ill-health and alcohol abuse were important features in the domestic violence cases. In particular, mental health issues were of relevance for women in 13 of the 32 cases (and for 5 of the 12 Asian women). Yet generally connections were not made by the professionals involved between depression or psychosis and the domestic violence the women experienced. In 18 of the 32 cases alcohol abuse was seen to be a problem for the woman's partner. Child protection conferences appeared to find it easier to name alcohol as a problem rather than the men's violence to their partners, and the issue of domestic violence was consequently 'lost'.

Hester and Pearson's (1998) practice-related study looked specifically at domestic violence in child abuse cases referred to the NSPCC. The study highlighted the direct links between *sexual abuse* of children and living in a context of domestic violence. Moreover mothers and children were found to be most likely to be abused by the same perpetrator, who was usually the children's natural father. The study used a multi-method approach, which included analysis of case records over a two-year period. Most of the 111 cases accepted for service by the NSPCC team during this period involved sexual abuse as the main concern (n=83, 77%), with the children also experiencing a range of other abusive behaviours including physical and emotional abuse. Social services were involved in some way in 61% of the cases. Over half the sexual abuse cases involved domestic violence (almost exclusively male to female violence). With regard to the perpetrator, in over half (53%) of the child sexual abuse cases the abusers were the children's fathers or father figures. This rose to over two-thirds (69%) in instances where domestic violence was also identified.

2.5 UK research on women's experiences of domestic violence and the link with child abuse

Research in the UK focusing on domestic violence, in particular women's experiences, has consistently revealed a link between domestic violence and physical and/or sexual abuse of children. It has also shown that the majority of children living in circumstances of domestic violence witness the violence and abusive behaviour to their mothers:

- Levine (1975), in a study of 50 families with 117 children seen in a general medical practice found that the 'children who observed their parents in violent conflict' were in danger of physical harm and/or detrimentally affected by observing the violence.

- Dobash and Dobash (1984) interviewed 109 mothers from refuges, and found that over half (58%) of their children had been present when there was violence to the women from male partners.

■ A representative study of 286 married working class mothers and single mothers from all social classes in Islington, London, found that many women experiencing domestic violence reported more severe violence when pregnant than at other times, and women experiencing violence were twice as likely to experience miscarriage (Andrews and Brown 1988).

■ Women's Aid statistics estimate that between 22% and 33% of the children of women coming to refuges are physically and/or sexually abused by the mother's husband or cohabitee (Hanmer 1989).

■ In the study by NCH Action for Children (Abrahams 1994), involving a questionnaire survey of 108 mothers who had experienced domestic violence, via NCH's family centres, at least 27% of the children were said to be physically abused by the domestic violence perpetrator (who was usually the father). Almost three-quarters (73%) of the children witnessed violent assaults on their mothers, and almost two thirds (62%) overheard violent incidents.

■ In Hester and Radford's (1996) study of contact arrangements in circumstances of domestic violence, 21 of the 53 women interviewed in England reported that their children had been physically and/or sexually abused by fathers. In eleven instances there was social services involvement with regard to abuse of the children by fathers. In six instances, all involving child abuse, no contact was formally ordered between fathers and children, and in a further two cases social services demanded that there be no contact in order to protect the children. The majority of children were also reported to be adversely affected by witnessing violence to their mothers.

■ Mezey and Bewley (1997) examined domestic violence in relation to pregnancy. They found that the risk of moderate to severe violence appears to be greatest in the period after women have given birth.

2.6 UK research on children's experiences of domestic violence

Children's experiences of living with domestic violence have been examined in a number of ways, incorporating clinical samples and children who have decided to call helplines. A more systematic study is under way, which looks at how children make sense of their experiences of living with domestic violence, and their coping strategies (Mullender, Kelly, Hague, Malos and Imam forthcoming).

■ Epstein and Keep (1995) examined a random sample of 126 of Childline's callers who talked about living with domestic violence. Over a third (38%) said their mother's partner (mostly the child's biological father) also physically abused them or their siblings.

■ In Harris Hendriks, Black and Kaplan's (1993) clinical sample involving 160 children from 62 families where (mostly) mothers had been murdered by violent partners, one in ten of the children had experienced physical abuse from a parent and 'very many' had witnessed violence from their father to their mother.

■ McGee (1996 and forthcoming) in interviews with mothers and children who had experienced domestic violence found a direct link between domestic violence of mothers and abuse of children.

2.7 UK research on mothers of sexually abused children

In the UK there have been a couple of studies focusing on mothers of sexually abused children. They found that nearly all the mothers had also experienced violence from the same abuser as their children:

- In her study of 15 mothers of sexually abused children, Hooper (1992) found that in 9 out of 11 instances involving the father (or father figure) as the abuser the woman had also experienced physical, verbal and/or sexual abuse from the same perpetrator.

- Forman's (1995) interviews with a self-selected sample of 20 mothers of sexually abused children with social services involvement revealed that all the mothers had also experienced violence or abuse from the same men. Of the alleged abusers, most (seventeen in all) were the natural fathers, one a step-father, one an adoptive father, and one a cohabitee.

2.8 Child abuse as part of the perpetrators' violence against the mothers and vice versa

Men's abuse of their children and partners may be difficult to separate into discrete categories of 'child abuse' and 'domestic violence' because in some instances the intention of the abuser is that the violence or abuse of a child will have a directly abusive impact on the woman. Kelly (1996) explains this as a 'double level of intentionality':

> That an act directed against one individual is at the same time intended to affect another/others. (Kelly 1996: 123)

Hester and Pearson's (1998) study of NSPCC child abuse cases involving domestic violence provides examples where abuse of the woman and of the child(ren) by the same man was so closely inter-connected that they were simultaneous expressions of both domestic violence and child abuse. This included an example where the father held a 6 week-old baby over a first floor balcony in order to try and prevent the mother from leaving after he had hit her. In another example the mother was unable to intervene to protect her children from the man's physical abuse of them because she was too frightened of the repercussions of this for herself. In their earlier study concerning child contact arrangements, Hester and Radford (1996) also found instances where the children had become implicated in the violence against their mothers through being forced to further the father's abuse. One father made his seven year old son kick and punch his mother despite the child's protestations and crying.

> He made them kick and punch me and they did because they were so frightened of him. [Son] kicked me, he punched me in the face. But, when he had done it his father told him he hadn't done it hard enough, and he was to go and put his shoes on and do it harder. (in Hester and Radford 1996: 10)

Some of the men used the children to force the women to stay within the relationship. One father ensured he always had one of the children with him so that the mother could not leave the relationship, as he knew she would not leave without them (in Hester and Radford 1996: ch 2). Similar incidences are discussed in a study by Malos and Hague (1993a: ch3).

Both Hooper (1992) and Forman (1995) argue, on the basis of their studies concerning mothers of sexually abused children, that the sexual abuse of the children could be seen as constituting domestic violence or abuse in relation to the mothers. The violence to the mothers also served to distance them as a source of support for the children, so that the men could more easily continue their sexual abuse. Hooper, for instance, found that the violence to mothers often preceded the sexual abuse of the children and usually continued alongside it, such that the man's abuse of the children was also directly intended to be abusive of his partner:

> Children were used by violent men both to extend means of control over their mothers (for example by battering or verbally undermining women in the presence of children as well as by sexually abusive behaviour) and to extend their domain of control to someone with less power to resist. (Hooper 1992: 355)

Men may also threaten to kill, or actually murder, children as part of their ongoing abuse of women. In a book documenting the killing of women and children in domestic homicides, the Women's Coalition Against Family Violence (1994) provide examples of fathers abusing children in order to control, abuse and torture the mothers. For instance, Kay was threatened with the death of herself and then her children when she tried to leave her violent partner. She had to leave without the children:

> He grabbed me and ran the blade around the front of my neck and then the back of my neck. As he was doing this he was saying that he was going to kill me. He ran the knife around my throat but not heavily enough to cut. He then said he wasn't going to kill me but would go upstairs and get Michael and Laurell [the children] and cut their throats in front of me and let me live to suffer knowing that I would have caused it... I agreed with him that I would not ring or talk to him any more and that I would leave the kids with him and get out of his life. I think that is why he let me go... (Kay in Women's Coalition Against Family Violence 1994: 31)

The interconnectedness of men's abuse of both children and women are important considerations with regard to the conflicts and problems women may face as mothers (outlined in Chapter One) and has direct implications for the ability of children to disclose to their mothers that they are being abused (see Chapter Three).

2.9 Children and post-separation violence – child contact

There is often an expectation in child protection work that women should leave violent partners in order to protect children. Not only does this place undue responsibility on mothers for men's violence and abuse, it also ignores the reality that the violence may not cease despite the separation of the spouses or partners. In their attempt to continue to control 'their' wife and children, violent men will continue to abuse and harass their ex-partners. Child contact is often the major flashpoint for the post-separation violence and provides a context where men may be able to continue to abuse and harass both woman and/or child(ren) (Hester and Radford 1996; Abrahams 1994; Smart 1995; Women's Coalition Against Family Violence 1994; Debbonaire 1997; Hester and Pearson 1998; Anderson 1997; Johnston 1992).

Children may also be murdered by their fathers on contact visits. There are currently no statistics regarding this in the UK or elsewhere, but cases are regularly reported in national newspapers (and see Women's Coalition Against Family Violence 1994).

Abrahams (1994), in the NCH study, describes how problems for the mothers 'often continued when their violent partners maintained some kind of contact with their children after they had left' (p 76). Many of the mothers provided examples of how their ex-partners used contact with the children to 'get back' at them:

> He tried pinching (my daughter) a few times when she was younger... taking her from me, locking himself in his mothers'... just to get at me, it was you know, to get me going and start the police going, because he used to like it when I called the police... he thought it was great to have a fight. (Abrahams 1994: 77)

Hilton (1992) similarly describes, from her study in the US of 20 women who had experienced domestic violence, that children's contact (or access) with fathers post-separation at times led to further abuse of mothers and/or their children. For example, violence and abuse to women, with their children witnessing this:

> One woman was abused when the father came to take the child out. Another woman allowed the father regular visits, but when she refused his sexual advances and told him to leave her house, he choked and stabbed her in front of their 3-year-old son. (Hilton 1992: 82)

In Hester and Radford's (1996) study of 53 post-separation families in England where women had left male partners, the men continued to be violent to their wives/partners in 50 out of the 53 instances and the possibility of further violence to children remained. Failure to address the risks or to make provision for safety meant that for a substantial proportion of children in the study, contact with fathers was reported to have an adverse effect upon their welfare. It was apparent that many of the fathers were merely using parental responsibility and contact as a means of continuing their violence towards, and control over, their ex-partner. Parenting and caring for children was not the main objective. In only seven out of fifty-three cases did contact arrangements 'work', that is there was no further abuse or harassment of the women or children involved. Mothers reported that children had been physically and/or sexually abused or neglected on contact visits with fathers, and children were also being used to collude in ongoing abuse of the mother. Children were used by ex-partners to convey threats and abusive messages to women, were pressurised into carrying out acts of violence against mothers as well as being involved in plans to kill mothers. One of the children interviewed described being physically abused during contact with her father, and how the abuse appeared to be escalating:

> ... he (father) was in a really bad mood... and he just grabbed me and started throwing me around and that ...he'd hit me before but not like that, 'cos he got me and threw me into the door... (Anne, aged 13 in ibid.)

She was also concerned that her father would try to persuade her to let him into the refuge where she and her mother were staying. This she found particularly worrying in view of the father's repeated threats to kill the mother:

> ... sometimes, because my dad like threatened to kill her ... when I'd go over there and see him, he would be like, you've got to let me in the refuge... (Anne, aged 13 in ibid.)

Fifteen of the women who participated in the Hester and Radford study were Black or Asian and two of the white women had Black children. The research showed parallels with Mama's findings (1996), indicating that Black women may experience greater difficulties than white women in gaining protection for child contact arrangements. Asian mothers in particular experienced significantly less support from professionals because assumptions were made about Asian communities:

> Police and social workers were noticeably reluctant to lend support either due to beliefs that the support would be provided from within the community or because of fear of upsetting community leaders. (Hester and Radford 1996: 33)

In their study of domestic violence and NSPCC practice, Hester and Pearson (1998) again found an overlap between domestic violence to mothers and the abuse of children during contact visits with fathers. In eighteen instances where children were suspected of or had been found to have been abused in relation to contact, fifteen of these cases also involved domestic violence. The NSPCC were carrying out work with the children with regard to sexual abuse in nine instances, physical abuse in one instance and emotional abuse in eight instances. In two of the cases the grandfathers had sexually abused the children during the father's contact time.

Forman (1995) also indicates the difficulties mothers and their children may experience in relation to contact, including further abuse. In one example the mother, although reluctant to send her children on contact visits to the father, thought they would be safe because the contact took place at the paternal grandparents' home. However, the children were abused by both father and grandfather. As Forman concludes, in such circumstances children may 'think their mother is "sending" them to be abused' (p 15).

The arrangements made for contact with violent fathers need to be considered in relation to the protection of children from abuse and harm. It is in the arena of contact that the ongoing abuse of children, both directly and indirectly, is likely to continue and yet may be ignored.

2.10 Summary

- Domestic violence is an important indicator of risk of harm to children.

- A wide range of studies have indicated that children are likely to be at risk of actual physical, sexual and/or emotional abuse from perpetrators of domestic violence.

- Domestic violence is often a significant and consistent feature, no matter what the form of abuse a child is deemed to have suffered, whether physical, sexual or emotional abuse.

- Witnessing violence to their mothers can have a detrimental impact on children, tantamount to emotional abuse or psychological maltreatment. Children can 'witness' domestic violence in a number of ways which

extend beyond direct observation of violent and abusive acts. They might overhear incidents or in other ways be aware that violence or abuse has occurred. Most children are in the same or the next room when domestic violence takes place.

- A number of local authorities in the UK have defined witnessing domestic violence as abuse of children, for instance, Strathclyde Regional Council Social Services Department.

- Domestic violence has been an important feature in some instances of child death – e.g. Maria Colwell, Sukina Hammond and Kimberley Carlile. In many cases where children have been killed, the significance of violence to the mothers, as an indicator of potential risk to the children, has often not been understood nor acknowledged by child care professionals.

- Men's abuse of their children and partners may be difficult to separate into discrete categories of 'child abuse' and 'domestic violence' because in some instances the intention of the abuser is that the violence or abuse of a child will have a directly abusive impact on the woman (or vice versa). Violent men may use the children to force the women to stay within the relationship. They may also threaten to kill, or actually murder, children as part of their ongoing abuse of women.

- The interconnectedness of men's abuse of both children and women are important considerations with regard to the conflicts and problems women may face as mothers and has direct implications for the ability of children to disclose to their mothers that they are being abused.

- In order to develop professional understanding of and practice in relation to child abuse, we need to recognise that children often experience a mixture of physical, sexual and/or emotional abuse, and that focusing on only one aspect of these different forms of abuse can therefore be false. Similarly, where there is both domestic violence and child abuse, we need to examine the whole picture.

CHAPTER THREE: THE IMPACT OF DOMESTIC VIOLENCE ON CHILDREN

3.1 How does domestic violence affect children?

Studies outlined in Chapters One and Two have generally found that children who have lived in the context of domestic violence may have more 'adjustment difficulties' than children from non-violent homes. It has to be recognised that there is no uniform response to living with domestic violence. Children's responses vary enormously with some children being affected far more than others, and children within the same family can be affected differently. Each child and each child's experiences and reactions are unique.

It is, therefore, important to find out exactly what each child has experienced in order to gain some understanding of what the possible impact of these experiences might be, rather than to think in terms of a simple checklist of indicators. Even so, it can be hard to discern the specific impact of living with domestic violence on children, especially as some of the resulting behaviours also occur in children experiencing other forms of abuse or neglect (Holden and Ritchie 1991). Of course, for many children the impacts of living with domestic violence will be compounded by, and interwoven with, the impacts of the direct sexual and/or physical abuse they are also experiencing from the same man.

The wide range of effects children might experience in circumstances of domestic violence can include any of the following behavioural, physical and psychological effects, which may be short term and/or long term:

- physical injuries, including bruises, broken bones

- being protective of mother and/or siblings; by physically intervening, withholding information, getting help etc.

- advanced in maturity and in sense of responsibility

- aggression/anger to mother and/or others (including other adults and siblings)

- introversion/withdrawal

- feeling guilty/to blame

- secretive/silent/unable to tell

- self-blame/bitterness

- fear/insecurity/tension

- truanting/running away

- difficulties at school

- disruptions in schooling and living arrangements

- emotional confusion in relation to parents

- bed-wetting

- nightmares

- sleep disturbances

- eating difficulties

- self-harm

- weight loss

- developmental delays in young children

- sadness/depression

- social isolation

- difficulties with trusting others

- low self-esteem

- poor social skills

- highly developed social skills

- ability to negotiate difficult situations

It should be noted that until the mid 1980s many professionals within the fields of psychiatry took the view that children of all ages react only to a 'mild' or 'transient' degree to situations of overwhelming stress, such as that created by living in a context of domestic violence (see Harris Hendriks, Black and Kaplan 1993). Clearly, this view has been superseded by the findings from research into domestic violence and children.

3.2 *How do we know about the impact of domestic violence on children?*

There is clear evidence from various kinds of research that domestic violence can have a detrimental impact on children. We still lack detail, however, about how factors such as age, race, economic status, gender, disability, sexuality and children's resilience influence children's perceptions and reactions, both in the short and longer term. We need studies that look at a wider range of the population, and we especially need to know more about Black women and children who are experiencing domestic violence.

Most research studies have been conducted with samples taken from refuges or from child protection or child support services. As Kelly (1994) has indicated, in refuge samples there may be some confusion of the effects of the domestic violence with the effects of living in a refuge. Refuge samples in the UK are not generally representative in that they tend to over-represent children from lower income families. Those studies which have tended to draw their samples from child protection or child support services, also lead to problems of generality, as most children living with domestic violence do not come to the attention of any services. Such samples, therefore, will be skewed towards lower income families (Hallett 1995). It is also possible that such studies will be focusing on those situations where the violence is likely to have been more prolonged, has escalated over time and involves physical violence (Davis and Carlson 1987; Pagelow 1982).

Fantuzzo and Lindquist (1989) point out that the source of the data about children in most studies is the child's mother. This may ignore differences between children's and adult's perceptions of the impact of living with

domestic violence. In this respect, it is important, as far as is possible and age-appropriate, that children themselves should be allowed to define the impact of their experiences.

This need to understand children's experiences directly from themselves is beginning to be addressed in research in Britain. Caroline McGee (1996 and forthcoming), for instance, has interviewed approximately 50 children about their experiences of domestic violence and of the support they received from the child protection services. Mullender, Kelly, Hague, Malos and Imam (in progress) are currently carrying out a large cross-institutional research project on children and domestic violence in order to explore how children cope and make sense of their experiences of this. Most current research has not raised children's voices in this way. However, some research has included the direct perspective of the child, albeit in relatively small numbers (e.g. Hague, Kelly, Malos and Mullender 1996; Abrahams 1994; Hester and Radford 1996; Saunders 1995).

3.3 UK research indicating the impact of domestic violence on children

Various studies in the UK have indicated the extent of the impact of domestic violence on children from the perspective of child professionals, refuge workers and mothers:

- Moore's (1975) study of 23 'violent matrimonial cases' on the NSPCC's case load, found that in 80% of the cases children had been 'adversely affected' by living in circumstances of matrimonial violence. These effects included children being 'anxious', having difficulties at school and being silent and withdrawn.

- In a study in Northern Ireland (Evason 1982) 72% of the women interviewed felt that the domestic violence they had experienced had adversely affected their children. This included children suffering 'mentally', such as being very nervous and having nightmares.

- In the survey by NCH Action for Children, of 108 women who had experienced domestic violence (who between them had 246 children), 91% believed the violence had a detrimental impact of some sort on their children in the short term. Most (86%) of the mothers considered that these effects had continued in the longer term, as children were growing up and into adolescence. The other 9% who thought there had been no impact mainly consisted of women whose children were still babies at the time of the violence (Abrahams 1994).

- In a study of refuge provision for children (Hague, Kelly, Malos and Mullender 1996) 98% of the child refuge workers felt that children experienced problems and difficulties as a direct result of living with domestic violence. Only one of the children's workers thought that children were not affected, and a further two workers were unsure of the impact.

- All of the 100 women in Mama's (1996) study of Black women experiencing domestic violence reported being aware that their partner's violence was having a negative impact on their children.

3.4 The impact of both 'direct' abuse and the 'indirect' abuse of witnessing domestic violence

As Chapter Two indicated, many children may experience both direct abuse and witness violence to their mother. Where children do not experience direct abuse they are still likely to witness or be aware of the violence to their mothers. Whilst those cases involving the direct abuse of children are more likely to come to the attention of child protection services, there is also a growing recognition that living with or growing up in an atmosphere of violence can have detrimental effects on the children concerned. Despite differences in research methods and in measurement instruments used, in their review of the literature on children witnessing domestic violence, Kolbo, Blakely and Engleman (1996) conclude that there is clear evidence from all these studies to suggest that witnessing violence can have a negative effect on children's emotional and behavioural development

Some earlier research had suggested that children who were abused physically and/or sexually *and* had witnessed domestic violence showed most distress (Hughes 1988; Hughes, Parkinson, and Vargo 1989; Davis and Carlson 1987). Hughes and her colleagues (1989) refer to this as children being 'doubly abused'. Others have suggested that children react more to the stress experienced by their mothers than to the violence itself (Wolfe, Jaffe, Wilson and Zak 1985; Hershorn and Rosenbaum 1985, and more recently in the UK, Thoburn, Lewis and Shemmings 1995). Other research, however, such as the NCH study (Abrahams 1994), found from the mothers' perceptions that there were no great differences in short or long term effects between children who had themselves experienced violence and abuse and those who were witnesses to their mothers being abused. Abrahams concludes that professionals have probably minimised the impact on children of witnessing violence:

> This in turn suggests that living in a home where there is domestic violence may have a much more adverse impact on children.... than might otherwise have been supposed. (Abrahams 1994, p41).

A similar minimisation by social workers of the effects on children of witnessing domestic violence was found by Farmer and Owen (1995) in their child protection study.

The majority of children in Hester and Radford's (1996) study of child contact arrangements were also reported to be adversely affected by witnessing violence to their mothers. Mothers described the many ways in which the children were affected, including having nightmares and their development being delayed:

> ... she had nightmares and everything after [witnessing violent assault on mother]... My eldest daughter is affected very, very badly and I mean, she's tried to settle into senior school this year and her teacher's been really worried because of the effect this is having on her. (Laura)

> ... he saw a lot of violence and his speech is very delayed. (Davina)

Similarly, in a recent study looking at the practice issues raised by focusing on domestic violence in relation to NSPCC child abuse cases, the case files were found to contain several examples of children having witnessed attacks of

physical violence towards their mothers (Hester and Pearson 1998). This included instances of children witnessing their mothers being stabbed in the head, being attacked with a knife or attempts at strangulation. In one example, the father locked the children in the room with him, whilst he physically attacked their mother, thus forcing the children to witness the violence. Some children remembered violence even though their mothers did not realise that they had been aware of it. In one instance an older child recounted the violence she had witnessed as a much younger child (aged 2 or 3), and in another a 5-year-old daughter recounted:

> 'unprompted memories from the past of abuse ... that she observed and which ... (mother) remembers but never thought (daughter) had seen'. (Hester and Pearson 1998)

This replicates the findings from Jaffe, Wolfe and Wilson (1990), that even very young children are aware of violence occurring around them and can be adversely affected, though they cannot necessarily make sense of it at the time. In the NCH study, the mothers who thought there had been no impact on their children because they were still babies at the time of the violence (Abrahams 1994) might have been over optimistic in this way. Mothers may also underestimate the impact of the violence on their children, believing that children are unaware of the violence for instance if they are not present or if the violence occurs at night. Some mothers feel that they have managed to protect their children from the worst of the violence, when, in fact, children are fully aware of what is happening. The findings from Hester and Pearson (1998) also confirm that children tend to keep silent about what they know or have observed and will only disclose this when they are in some way given permission to do so.

3.5 Factors influencing the impact of domestic violence on children

Whilst research has clearly indicated the adverse impact of domestic violence on children, it is also clear that different children react in different ways and that the relationship between the violence and the effect it has on a child can be both complex and multi-faceted (Peled and Davis 1995; Saunders 1995). A range of personal and contextual factors can influence the extent of the impact (Kelly 1996). These 'mediating variables' are often referred to as 'protective' or 'vulnerability' factors in that they can improve or accentuate the child's response to the violence (Moore, Pepler, Weinberg, Hammond, Waddell and Weiser 1990). The factors might include any of the following (not in any rank order):

- age
- race
- socio-economic status
- gender
- culture
- religion
- the emotional/physical development of the child

- issues concerning disability

- issues concerning sexuality

- the child's role and position in the family

- the child's relationship with her/his parent(s)

- the child's relationship with siblings

- the child's relationships outside the family (including with peers, other adults and other family members)

- the degree of maternal stress

- the frequency and form of the violence

- the length of exposure to the violence

There is still much to learn about the ways in which such factors might influence the way children react to living with domestic violence. The current knowledge on the impact of some of these variables is discussed below.

3.6 Age as an influencing factor

At the most fundamental level, age has an influence in terms of the ways that children are able to make sense of their experiences, and the range of options they have to express their distress or anxiety. There are difficulties, however, in assessing and measuring the complexity of the impact of age, and there is still much to learn.

Generally, *pre-school children* are more likely to have physical symptoms of their anxiety, such as stomach aches, bed-wetting and sleep disturbances, while *primary school children* are able to present their fears in broader ways, including behaviourally and emotionally. *Adolescents* may attempt to gain relief through drugs, early marriage or pregnancy (Sinclair 1985 in Mullender 1996b: 142) or they might become involved in criminal activity (Jaffe, Wolfe and Wilson 1990). There is a need for more detailed research to ascertain how far the extent of such behaviour in young people is linked to their experiences of domestic violence. For instance, studies of young homeless people suggest that running away from home is often to escape the violence and abuse they are experiencing or witnessing there. Similarly, the NCH Action for Children research study (Abrahams 1994) on children and domestic violence found that 13% of the mothers in the study reported children having run away from home to escape the violence there (although details about the ages of the children involved are not given).

The impact of domestic violence on pre-school children

Some of the earliest US studies did include differences in children's responses according to age. Hilberman and Munson (1977), for example, found that pre-school children living with domestic violence displayed a range of behavioural and physical problems (although they did not report all the ages of the 209 children in their sample). The problems included, having sleeping difficulties (including insomnia, nightmares and being fearful of going to bed), bed-wetting, headaches, stomach aches, diarrhoea and asthma.

Other early US studies and professional/clinical observations (Alessi and Hearn 1984; Pfouts, Scopler and Henley 1982) suggested that *younger* children, in particular, were most affected by living with domestic violence. Hughes and Barad's (1983) study found that mothers identified their pre-school children as having more behaviour problems than their older children, although school-aged boys also displayed some aggressive behaviour. Moreover, pre-school children recorded lower levels of self-esteem on a self-concept scoring instrument than was the case for school-age children. Younger children may also experience delayed development as a result of living with domestic violence, as was noted by one of the refuge workers in Hague, Kelly, Malos and Mullender's (1996) survey of refuge provision:

> Our worst case was a child which hadn't developed physically – a 6-year-old in nappies and not talking, unable to communicate. But in the refuge that child developed well eventually. (p 32)

The impact of domestic violence on younger school-aged children

The study by Hilberman and Munson (1977), mentioned above, also reported that school age children living with domestic violence experienced difficulties at school, including erratic attendance, poor performance and lack of concentration. In order to measure in more detail the impact of age on the responses of children to domestic violence, some of the subsequent US studies divided their sample into age groups. Their findings are somewhat contradictory, however, and any differences are far from clear-cut.

Hughes' study (1988) suggested that pre-school children displayed more behavioural problems than school-aged children. This was certainly the case in relation to mothers' reports concerning the behaviour of their pre-school children (echoing Hughes and Barad's 1983 findings). It did not hold true in relation to anxiety measures, where the older age groups (6–8 years and 9–12 years) had similar anxiety levels, which were both much higher than the levels recorded by the pre-school children. This was seen to be possibly a result of less accurate self-reporting in the case of pre-school children.

In contrast, other studies have found that school-aged children were likely to have more behavioural problems than pre-school children (Davis and Carlson 1987; Holden and Ritchie 1991; Hughes, Parkinson and Vargo 1989). According to children's refuge workers (Hague, Kelly, Malos and Mullender 1996), younger children generally displayed more behavioural difficulties but were more resilient, whilst older children understood more, were more angry and found trusting others especially problematic.

The impact of domestic violence on older children

There have been very few studies which have either looked at the specific impact of domestic violence on older (teenage) children, or which have been able to chart any possible changes in responses as children develop from being school-aged to being young adults. Studies which have been drawn from refuges have been hampered in this by the fact that teenagers do not tend to constitute a significant proportion of the refuge population (only 15% of 2271 children in refuges in a 1994–5 survey were aged 11–17, Hague, Kelly, Malos and Mullender 1996). Research studies which have drawn samples from a variety of sources have also contained few older children (see, for example, Hester and Radford 1996).

The reasons for this are quite complex, including the fact that most refuges, for instance, have an upper age limit for boys. This applied to almost 90% of the refuges at the time of the survey carried out by Hague and her colleagues (1996). Teenagers are also more able to exert choice about where and who they live with so that some might remain at home rather than endure the disruptions of moving to a refuge or other short-term accommodation. This might be especially so given that teenagers are more likely to have established networks (Malos and Hague 1993a). Our knowledge about domestic violence dynamics suggests, moreover, that violence begins and is prevalent when children are young, thus rendering escape more difficult for the woman. Therefore, by the time children are older, women may have already left, or may have given up hope of leaving and so come into contact with any agencies only infrequently.

However, one recent Swedish study has looked specifically at older children's experiences of, and reactions to, living with domestic violence (Weinehall 1997). The study involved in-depth interviews with 15 young people aged 15 or 16 at the start of the research (10 females and 5 males) and was carried out over a period of 4 years. All the teenagers lived in situations of domestic violence. According to these young people, they had all tended to adopt passive responses to the violence when they were younger, whereas when they were older they were able to react differently, either by staying away or running away from home, or by using drugs and/or alcohol. At other times they had dealt with the violence by denying it, lying about it or by creating another fantasised reality for themselves in which there was no violence. It was not unusual for them to experience difficulties at school, including irregular attendance, truancy and poor performance and concentration. Rather than using violence to solve problems, as anticipated by other research (see, for instance, Straus, Gelles and Steinmetz 1980), at school they were more often subjected to bullying by others. Unlike younger children, none of the young people reported having physical signs of their distress, such as headache or sleep disturbances, but some did appear to have eating disorders and mood swings, and some had made suicide attempts.

Domestic violence can continue to have specific effects on older children even after women have left a violent relationship, especially in relation to re-housing. Malos and Hague (1993a, 1993b) found under the previous housing legislation, where councils had a responsibility to permanently re-house women and their dependent children, that 'dependency' was not clearly defined. In practice, any children over 16 tended to be excluded unless they were aged 16-18 and in full-time education. Thus, older children over 16 and not at school, and those over 18, who had previously lived in the mother's household were not considered for re-housing, and were either forced to stay with the violent partner, or find themselves alternative accommodation. This was particularly difficult at a time when they, in common with younger children, were experiencing uncertainty and emotional upheaval. Similarly, with larger families where there was a shortage of adequately sized council accommodation, older children could sometimes find themselves under pressure to live away from their families. For those older children living with their mothers in refuges, there is evidence to suggest that refuge life can present particular difficulties. These include having little space and privacy, and a lack of facilities to do homework and have activities separate from the

younger children (Hague, Kelly, Malos and Mullender 1996; Mullender, Hague, Kelly and Malos, forthcoming).

3.7 Gender as an influencing factor

Whilst domestic violence can clearly have adverse effects on both boys and girls, it would be wrong to assume that responses can be presumed to follow some 'given' or 'pre-determined' gender pattern. The reality is not as straightforward as this, and is further affected by other variables, especially age. There is no single common response to the way in which boys and girls deal with their experiences of domestic violence. This does not, however, mean that gender is not important, but that there is a need for more sophisticated methods of looking at its impact:

> To say that simple models of gendered responses are unhelpful, however, is not to say that gender is irrelevant. Rather, what we need is a framework which takes gender into account as a critical factor, but which allows for differences within, as well as between, the responses of girls and boys. (Kelly 1994: 49)

The earliest research concerning the impact of gender on children's ways of reacting to and dealing with domestic violence tended to be characterised by an assumption that girls and boys will respond in stereotypically gendered ways. According to this belief in the 'inter-generational transmission of violence', it was presumed that girls will identify with their mothers and boys with their fathers. This implies that boys will copy their father's violent behaviour and adopt externalised responses (such as aggression, disobedience and bullying) whilst girls will become 'victims' and learn internalised responses (such as anxiety and depression). This has also been linked to a view that boys will automatically be more adversely affected by domestic violence than girls – perhaps explaining why some studies have chosen to focus exclusively on the impact on boys (e.g. Rosenbaum and O'Leary 1981; Hershorn and Rosenbaum 1985).

Closer examination of the findings from the earlier research, however, shows that the reality is more complicated and that the stereotypical impact of gender has been over-stated (see Hughes 1992). Some of the earlier studies did find a correlation between gender and the gender role stereotypes defined by society as aggression in males and passivity in females (such as Hilberman and Munson 1977; Porter and O'Leary 1980; Hughes and Barad 1983). Others, however, have not replicated this in such a clear-cut way. The difference between boys and girls which does appear to persist across a number of these studies, is a greater propensity by boys, and as adult men, to condone or accept violence to women.

A number of studies suggest that both boys and girls can react in externalising and/or internalising ways at different times:

■ Christopoulos, Cohn, Shaw, Joyce, Sullivan-Hanson, Kraft and Emery (1987) had expected boys who had lived with domestic violence to show more externalised behaviour problems, but in fact this was true of both girls and boys in comparison to children from a matched group of children who had not been exposed to violence.

- Stagg, Wills and Howell's (1989) study on the effects of witnessing violence amongst younger children (aged 4–6 years), found indications that boys displayed more externalising *and* internalising problems than girls.

- Jouriles, Murphy and O'Leary (1989) did find externalising behaviour amongst the boys they studied, but they also found that both boys and girls expressed internalised problems, such as inadequacy and immaturity.

It can be seen, therefore, that there is a diversity of findings in relation to the idea that boys and girls learn and model 'gender role appropriate' behaviour. This was echoed in the conclusion of a review of the literature on children who witness domestic violence (Kolbo, Blakely and Engleman 1996):

> ...a linear social learning model is not adequate for explaining the relationship between children's witnessing domestic violence and their subsequent development. (p290)

Retrospective studies, which have looked at the perspectives and outcomes of adults who lived with domestic violence as children, indicate a similar lack of clarity in relation to findings on gender:

- Pagelow (1981) (and later replicated by Telch and Lindquist 1984 and O'Leary and Curley 1986) found that living with and witnessing domestic violence was related to men's subsequent violent behaviour in their own relationships, but was not linked to women becoming victims.

- Ulbrich and Huber's (1981) telephone survey of attitudes concerning violence to women found that men, but not women, were more likely to condone violence against women if they had witnessed their father's violence as children.

- Kalmuss (1984) found that there was a correlation between children living with domestic violence and subsequent aggression in adult marital relationships. However, this correlation was not gender specific – both boys and girls could be victims as well as perpetrators.

- Alexander, Moore and Alexander (1991) concluded that witnessing violence had an influence on attitudes rather than directly on behaviour. These attitudes were gender specific in that men had more conservative attitudes to women, whilst women had more liberal attitudes. These attitudes had an impact on behaviour only through the interactions between partners.

- Forsstrom-Cohen and Rosenbaum's (1985) study, focusing on college-age adults, found higher levels of aggression amongst females. The same study also recorded higher anxiety levels for both males and females, although there was more depression noted amongst females.

It has to be noted that there are methodological limitations as well as definitional and reliability issues concerning such retrospective data. These limitations are compounded by the possibility of differences in accounts and interpretations between men and women (see Hearn 1996a).

Thus, gender can be seen to be an influencing factor, but its impact varies considerably. As indicated earlier, the findings from some studies appear to link differences in gender to the *age* of the child, although again findings in this respect are not conclusive and can be contradictory (see Peled and Davis

1995). Davis and Carlson (1987), for instance, found that in both the pre-school and the school-age groups girls responded to their experiences of domestic violence in stereotypically passive ways, but that amongst the school-age group girls were more likely than the boys to exhibit aggressive behaviours. Overall, they concluded that pre-school boys and school-age girls were most affected by living with violence.

Other studies, by contrast, have concluded that boys are most negatively affected by domestic violence (Emery and O'Leary 1982), and that this is particularly true of school-age boys, who have more behavioural problems generally, especially in relation to aggressive responses (see Wolfe, Jaffe, Wilson and Zak 1985; Jaffe, Wolfe, Wilson and Zak 1985 1986a 1986b). The studies by Jaffe and his colleagues, in particular, have also tended to be seen to highlight the 'acting out' responses of boys and the passive or internalised responses of girls (although it is worth noting that the 1986b study focused only on boys). However, in their later overview of the research on domestic violence and children, Jaffe, Wolfe and Wilson (1990) suggest that such conclusions may be over-simplified. Jaffe and his colleagues cite other research (Rosenberg 1984) which found that boys adopted aggressive responses and girls passive responses when they were exposed to low levels of domestic violence, but that higher levels of exposure to domestic violence led to more aggressive responses from girls and more passive response from boys.

Some studies also seem to indicate that differences in the responses of girls and boys may vary in adolescence. Hilberman and Munson (1977) reported that while adolescent boys tended to run away, adolescent girls might develop a distrust of men. Carlson (1990) also found that adolescent boys were more likely to run away from home and that they reported more suicidal thoughts then adolescent girls. Weinehall (1997) reported that the young women in her study felt more threatened by their fathers than did the young men, and that they worried about the possibility of their fathers killing them and the rest of the family.

3.8 Race as an influencing factor

Very little of the research on children and domestic violence has examined the impact that race and racism might have on the reactions and coping mechanisms of Black children. This lack of attention to race/ethnicity in existing studies was pointed out by Fantuzzo and Lindquist (1989), who suggested this could be an important variable, both in terms of how families responded and in how agencies responded to families. Two studies in the US which did attempt to measure this factor (Stagg, Wills and Howell 1989; Westra and Martin 1981) both found that white children had more externalising ('acting out') and internalising (withdrawn and depressed) behavioural difficulties than African-American children.

In the UK, no similar studies have been carried out, although the large cross-institutional study being undertaken by Mullender, Kelly, Hague, Malos and Imam, and is in the process of looking at race factors. There is, however, beginning to be some literature pointing to the particular difficulties and experiences of Black women and children living with domestic violence, especially when set against a racist and hostile society (Mama 1996; Imam 1994; Bowstead, Lall and Rashid 1995). Some of the impacts on children are

likely to be exacerbated by the fact that some children may be subjected to the additional threat of abduction abroad, or by being asked inappropriately to act as interpreters or translators if their mother's first language is not English (Bowstead, Lall and Rashid 1995).

Children acting as interpreters is unsuitable in situations of domestic violence, whether this involves children interpreting between their mothers (or fathers) and professional agencies, or for more informal networks. It might restrict the amount of information women feel able to disclose in the presence of their children, or force women to give details which they believe they have protected their children from knowing. It may also raise difficult issues with regard to confidentiality. It could also prove to be an onerous responsibility for children, thereby increasing any stress they may already be experiencing.

Imam (1994) also points out that for many Black children the family home is considered a refuge from the daily hostility and racism they experience. Thus, any violence inside the home can seriously undermine that sense of safety and can lead to particular feelings of vulnerability and insecurity for children. She also suggests that cultural and religious expectations for Asian girls might lead to them being ostracised by family and community if they try to leave with their mother to go to a refuge or other safe place (this might also apply to a lesser extent to Asian boys, as well as to girls from other cultures). To prevent this ostracism, some mothers may choose to leave their (female) children behind when they escape the violence. This in turn may lead some young Asian women to run away from home (the reverse of some of the studies mentioned earlier where (white) adolescent boys, in particular, were found to be more likely to run away from home).

The impact for children of living with domestic violence is probably influenced by how they make sense of what has happened, and race may again have an impact on this. This will be further influenced by the institutional racism women and children will encounter and by the probable lack of action by professionals to help them. For children from mixed race relationships, trying to understand their experiences might be made more difficult by not knowing with which parent to identify, and this might be further complicated by whether the violent man is black or white, as well as by the age and gender of the child. Workers at a specialist refuge for Black women and children in Hague, Kelly, Malos and Mullender's study (1996) reported one such example where the white father had been telling his children that it was wrong/awful to be Black, with the result that the children were 'absolutely torn apart' (p51) – unable to identify with the father because of what he had done, and unable to identify with their mother as a result of what their father had said.

Black children may also have difficulties with identification within Black families where abusive men might use racism as a further means of control. This might apply in relation to immigration, for instance, or as a reason to encourage women (and children) not to contact the police or have men excluded from the home. (Mama 1996). Clearly, it is important to gain more knowledge about the impact of race and racism on children's reactions to domestic violence, especially as it involves a significant number of children – most refuges, for example, at any given time will contain 'a significant population' of ethnic minority children (Hague, Kelly, Malos and Mullender 1996: 19).

3.9 Socio-economic status as an influencing factor

In their overview of the research on the effects of witnessing domestic violence on children, Fantuzzo and Lindquist (1989) point out that studies are limited by their omission of economic status as a variable in terms of children's responses to domestic violence. There is no consideration, for instance, of how factors relating to poverty and poor housing, or to being more affluent and adequately housed, may have a bearing on how children react to living with domestic violence. Economic status will undoubtedly have some impact on how agencies respond to families, as well as on how women are able to deal with, and find solutions to, the violence they are experiencing. This is especially so given that many research samples, as outlined earlier, are inevitably skewed to more lower income families. This is again an area where there is a much to learn.

3.10 Disability as an influencing factor

Very little attention had been paid to how children's disability might influence the impact of domestic violence on children. This is despite the fact that attacks on women during pregnancy may mean that there is a higher proportion of children with disabilities living in domestic violence situations (see Chapter One). Kelly (1992) has documented how both physical and learning disabilities can be caused by direct and indirect abuse within the context of domestic violence.

Confirmation of this possible link appears in Hague, Kelly, Malos and Mullender's (1996) survey of refuges, which found that over a quarter of the refuge groups had at least one child resident who had a disability. The most commonly reported impairments (though not necessarily linked directly with domestic violence) were asthma and learning disabilities, and there were also children with down's syndrome, cerebral palsy, spina bifida and hydrocephalus. Some refuges were attempting to address the needs of disabled children (and women) by employing specialist workers and improving the accessibility of buildings, but were obviously restricted to some extent by funding limitations. However, it is important that any developments in this area also recognise the fact that disability is a socially constructed concept. Thus, workers and refuge residents need to be aware of and challenge stereotypical attitudes and beliefs about disability if any long-term change, and improvements in service are to occur.

Again, this is an area where there is still much to learn as there has been little consideration of the long-term implications of violence in pregnancy for children's physical and mental health.

3.11 Mother–child relationship as an influencing factor

Some studies have suggested that the impact on children of living with domestic violence might be affected by the relationship between mother and child, especially linked to the amount of stress experienced by the mother. As mentioned earlier (see Chapter One), some women may experience depression as a result of being abused by their partners (Hughes 1992), possibly exacerbated in some cases by other negative life events and by poor housing and poverty (Peled and Davis 1995). This may result in the care of

children being particularly stressful for these women (Holden and Ritchie 1991; Wolfe, Jaffe, Wilson and Zak 1985). Such maternal stress may at times compound the behavioural problems of their children (Wolfe, Zak, Wilson and Jaffe 1986; Wolfe, Jaffe, Wilson and Zak 1988). This is especially the case where the mother's experiences mean that she is emotionally distanced, unavailable or even sometimes abusive to the child, such that the consequent lack of support and attachment may increase the impact of the domestic violence for the child.

Mothers may find it difficult to talk to children about the violence, believing this to be protective and/or because they are unsure how to do this (McGee forthcoming). Many mothers do their utmost to protect children from witnessing the violence (Hoff 1990), although, as outlined earlier, the reality is that most children are aware of its occurrence and can describe episodes they have witnessed without their parents' knowledge (Jaffe, Wolfe and Wilson 1990; Hester and Pearson 1998). Thus, although children generally want to talk about their experiences of domestic violence, they are often unable to do so with their mothers (McGee forthcoming). This may in turn have its own impact on children.

Some children might also have to deal with the confusing situation of their mothers being stricter and less affectionate in the presence of their violent partners. This might be compounded by the fathers' negative and strict involvement with their children (Holden and Ritchie 1991).

3.12 Frequency and form of violence as influencing factors

As outlined in relation to women, domestic violence can take many forms (from verbal/emotional abuse to murder), and yet very little of the existing research has examined whether the amount and forms of violence children witness have any impact on how children are affected. In their review of 29 articles/studies relating to the effects on children of witnessing domestic violence Fantuzzo and Lindquist (1989) discovered that the frequency of violence was not reported in 77.3% of them, and that the form of violence witnessed by the children was not detailed in 65.5% of them. Furthermore, 73.9% of the studies did not reveal how recent the last violent episode had been.

In a study which looked at the impact of different forms of violence, Fantuzzo, DePaola, Lamber, Mariono, Anderson and Sutton (1991) suggested that children who observed both physical and verbal violence displayed more behavioural difficulties than those children whose observations had been limited to verbal violence alone. Hughes (1992) also found that the difficulties experienced by children were greater when they were exposed to more forms of violence. However it is important to remember that for children, as for women, there is no obvious hierarchy of abuse, and the impact on each individual may differ. Pagelow (1982), for instance, observed regression in children as young as one as a result of exposure to 'simply' verbal abuse from one parent to another.

There has been virtually no consideration in any of the studies of the fact that children may also witness or overhear the sexual abuse or rape of their mothers, and of whether the impact of this is different to the impact of other

forms of abuse. There is mention in Weinehall's study (1997) of the fact that the 5 adolescent boys in her project often had to listen to their fathers raping their mothers, and of their sense of powerlessness at not being able to intervene to stop this. In the NCH study (Abrahams 1994) 1 in 10 of the mothers reported that they had been sexually abused or raped by their partners in front of their children. One of the mothers described the difficulties this presented for her children:

> I was raped once, in front of the children, with a knife at my throat. The children tried to pull him off, and it was just awful. (p31)

On the whole, however, the issue of sexual violence and its impact on children remains secret and invisible, as tends to be the case with sexual violence to women generally.

In addition, there may be a correlation between the length and frequency of exposure to violence and an increase in the adversity of children's reactions (Hershorn and Rosenbaum 1985; Christopoulos, Cohn, Shaw, Joyce, Sullivan-Hanson, Kraft and Emery 1987; Jouriles, Barling and O'Leary 1987).

3.13 Children's coping/survival strategies as influencing factors

Whilst living with domestic violence can undoubtedly have adverse effects on children, it is important to recognise that children are not merely passive by-standers to events around them, but will act and make choices in highly individualised ways in order to cope with and improve their situation. Some of the choices made by children, especially older children, have been outlined above. Research evidence suggests that many children will develop complex strategies of survival in order to deal with the stress and adversity they are experiencing (see, for example, Hester and Radford 1996). Obviously, these strategies will depend to a certain extent on each child's behavioural and emotional development (Jaffe, Wolfe and Wilson 1990).

The survival strategies adopted by children living with domestic violence can be diverse and may appear contradictory. For instance, some children become very protective of their mother and/or their siblings, and will choose various reactive and pro-active methods to try and keep their mother safe, including physical intervention, withholding information, or getting help from neighbours or from formal organisations (Dobash and Dobash 1984; Hoff 1990; Jaffe, Wolfe and Wilson 1990; Abrahams 1994; Hester and Pearson 1998). Some children feel so concerned for their mother's safety that they want to protect her all the time. In such cases children might refuse to go to school or feign illness so that they can stay at home with their mother (Jaffe, Wolfe and Wilson 1990; Jaffe, Wolfe, Wilson and Zak 1986c). Some children's coping strategies will change over time. One young woman (aged 17) interviewed in Hague, Kelly, Malos and Mullender's study (1996), who had lived with violence over a 10 year period, explained how her initial protective way of coping had changed to staying away:

> At first I was: I wouldn't leave my mam. Wouldn't leave her anywhere. I was round her all the time. And then, when I was about 14, I used to just stay out all the time .... I used to stay at my real dad's, at my sister's. At my boyfriend's. Anywhere. Anywhere I could just to get out of the house. (p98)

Even young children can show very complex patterns of protective intervention, such as trying to mediate between their parents or acting as a distraction to bring the violence to an end. These protective responses may become more frequent than distressed responses as children get older. (Cummings, Zahn-Waxler and Radke-Yarrow 1984). Many of the children in the NCH survey (Abrahams 1994) were younger children (the average age was 6.7 years), but almost a third (31%) were reported by mothers as being protective towards them, which for 22% of the children also included physically intervening to try and stop the violence:

> .... My mother sounded so desperate downstairs ... crying and screaming....
> so we went downstairs with our tennis racquets and started hitting him
> (Abrahams 1994: 37)

For some children this desire to protect their mothers also included fantasising about killing the violent partner and plans for revenge (Weinehall 1997). For others, these fantasies might be a way of dealing with the guilt, shame and fear they feel concerning their own perceived inability/failure to protect their mothers.

Other children protect their mothers in less direct ways, for example, by learning that their presence in the room will bring the violence to an end (Hester and Radford 1996). Children may also try and protect their mothers by gaining practical help and information for them. Many children contacting Childline about domestic violence, for instance, requested details of women's refuges to pass on to their mothers and said that they encouraged their mothers to leave (Epstein and Keep 1995).

Another way some children protect their mothers is by taking on responsibilities in the home, such as child care for younger siblings and household chores, in the hope that this will help to keep the peace. If this fails then they will provide support for other members of the family after a violent episode and/or they may try to placate their fathers (Jaffe, Wolfe and Wilson 1990). This assumption of adult responsibilities can lead to children becoming 'parental children', which can be burdensome, and may also prevent children from asking their mother for help (Epstein and Keep 1995). After a woman has left a violent partner this sense of responsibility to protect their mother might be expressed by some children wanting to live with their father. Though apparently contradictory, this might appear to the child to be the best strategy to adopt to keep their mother safe from further violence. It may also serve to allow children to act as caretakers for their fathers in those situations where the father has made threats to commit suicide if the mother and/or children leave (Hester and Radford 1996). Other children, especially older children, may adopt strategies aimed at self-protection, including presenting an external front of fearlessness in order to hide the fear and anxiety that lies beneath the surface (Grusznski, Brink and Edleson 1988).

Children are likely to believe that they are somehow responsible for the violence, and indeed are aware that violence can stem from arguments over child-care, children's behaviour or discipline or from resentment about the amount of time women devote to their children (Grusznski, Brink and Edleson 1988; Hilton 1992). This sense that they have in some way 'caused' the violence (Saunders 1995) can lead children to attempt to modify their behaviour (by being quiet or 'perfect' – this latter might include excelling at

school) in the hope that this will prevent an episode of violence, thereby protecting their mother. Even babies are reported to sense that changing their behaviour can have an effect on what happens in their environment. A children's' worker in Hague, Kelly, Malos and Mullender's (1996) refuge survey, for instance, noted how living with domestic violence could lead to babies being withdrawn and 'unnaturally' quiet:

> ...this baby just sits there and stays stumm, because it has learned that is the best coping tactic. (p43)

Similarly, one of the mothers in the same survey reported that her two older children had immediately taken to sleeping all through the night, as though this was a way of ensuring that 'nothing bad would happen' (p43).

Other children decide that their optimum chance of survival might lie in siding with the father, including sometimes joining in with the abuse of the mother (Hilton 1992). This identification with the abuser might also provide some children with a sense of control in a frightening situation (Grusznski, Brink and Edleson 1988), and might include expressions of anger and aggression towards their mother, either for her (perceived) failure to protect them and/or because they mirror the process of the abuser blaming her for causing the violence (Abrahams 1994; Saunders 1995).

3.14 Children's secrecy as a coping strategy

Many children living with domestic violence learn from an early age that the violence must be kept secret at all costs. This may be because of the shame and social stigma attached to it, to protect the abuser, through fear of the mother being blamed or the children being removed (Abrahams 1994; Epstein and Keep 1995). Children may not necessarily understand the reasons for the secrecy, but they learn to use a range of strategies to prevent disclosure and maintain the secret. These might include lying about the violence, inventing stories to conceal the facts, limiting their contact with others and not bringing friends to the home (Grusznski, Brink and Edleson 1988; Abrahams 1994; Saunders 1995). The pressure of secrecy obviously makes disclosure difficult for children, who may go to great lengths to hide the reality of what is happening:

> My teacher tried to find out, but I just didn't let anything slip. I just said, 'No, everything's okay'. You just smile, don't you, and try to cover it like....(Abrahams 1994: 81)

In addition to this, as Goddard and Hiller (1993) have pointed out, the presence of domestic violence, and the dynamics created by this, will serve to silence children about their own or their siblings' physical and/or sexual abuse by the same perpetrator:

> The existence of other forms of violence, and the victimisation of others by violence, will present a major obstacle to the disclosure of abuse. Resistance to disclosure can clearly be created by violence. (p27)

In this way domestic violence can be seen to be a factor in the continuation of abuse to children.

3.15 Children's resilience as an influencing factor

Jaffe, Wolfe and Wilson (1990) suggest that resilience may be a factor in understanding why some children who live with domestic violence do not appear to be as adversely affected as others. In Wolfe, Jaffe, Wilson and Zak's (1985) study, for instance, a significant number of children showed few negative reactions to domestic violence, and some were rated as having above average social skills and social adjustment. Similarly, two of the studies in Fantuzzo and Lindquist's (1989) overview of the impact of witnessing domestic violence found no significant adverse emotional effects of this on the children involved

The fact that children may cope very differently to similar stressful and adverse experiences has, thus, been partly explained by the notion of psychological resilience. Resilience does not necessarily act as a protection against adversity, but somehow works to provide the ability to recover more readily from it, thereby preventing impacts in the longer term. An International Resilience Project, set up to study how different cultures and countries promoted resilience, adopted the following definition of it:

> Resilience is a universal capacity which allows a person, group or community to prevent, minimise or overcome the damaging effects of adversity. (Grotberg 1997: 19)

Relatively little is known or understood about this quality of resilience in children and how it shapes children's experiences of domestic violence both as it occurs and in terms of recovery. As Kolbo, Blakely and Engleman (1996) point out there is a need for:

> ...the examination of factors protecting children from adverse life events. There is much to be learned from the children who are not presenting or not reporting developmental problems (p291)

Resilience as a concept has, in fact, been explored for many years in attempts to develop an understanding of what factors, if any, might contribute to the promotion of resiliency. According to Rutter (1985) these 'protective factors' against adversity might include self-esteem, the timing of incidents, the child's ability to attach meaning to and make sense of events, and the child's relationships with others. Other studies (see, for instance, Thomas, Chess and Birch 1968; Garmezy 1985; Fonagy, Steele, Steele, Higgitt and Mayer 1994 and Smith 1997 for overview) have identified factors potentially leading to resilience in children, although as yet little is known about how these factors interact with each other and how they work in different contexts (Grotberg 1997). These factors include:

■ an even and adaptable temperament

■ a capacity for organised thinking and to problem solve

■ physical attractiveness (in the sense that this enhances self-esteem and positive interactions with others)

■ a sense of humour

■ good social skills and a supportive peer network

■ a sense of autonomy and purpose

- secure attachments to parent(s)

- connections to a wider community (such as religious groups, school or extended family members)

Resilience is often assumed to reside within the individual, yet it is clear that the above factors are also influenced by their interaction with environmental or social contexts. The self-esteem of Black children, children with impairments, or economically disadvantaged children, for instance, may be affected by negative perceptions of them as different or 'other'. Some research indicates that when parents (or other adults) identify and acknowledge the adverse reaction children will probably encounter, then they are better able to cope (this was the case in relation to Black children in Rosenberg and Simmons' (1971) study). Thus, it is possible for adults to deal with children in ways that can actually encourage resilient responses. From her work on the International Resilience project, Grotberg (1997) suggests that adults can do this in various ways, including encouraging children's autonomy and independence, teaching communication and problem solving skills and showing children how to handle negative thoughts and behaviour. In turn children themselves will become active in developing their own resilience.

Clearly, there is a need for more detailed work to be undertaken to identify and understand what these protective or resilient factors for children living with domestic violence might be. This would help adults to promote resilience in such children, thereby reducing the potential for continued harm:

> Not all children are equally vulnerable nor are they all equally resilient. But a combination of a resilient child who is also vulnerable means it is more likely they will find competent and functional ways of dealing with their vulnerability, reducing its potential negative impact. (Smith 1997: 52)

3.16 Witnessing domestic violence and Post Traumatic Stress Disorder

Some clinicians and researchers have linked the trauma of experiencing and witnessing domestic violence with the impact exemplified by post traumatic stress disorder (PTSD). This is seen as a type of enduring anxiety disorder following exposure to a traumatic event. In the context of domestic violence it may be particularly difficult and stressful for children to deal with the fact that the trauma is occurring within the family, undermining the child's notions of safety and protection from harm. The child might react in ways consistent with the symptoms of PTSD. However, the reactions may become apparent much later than the traumatic event and may, therefore, be difficult to link to the original trauma:

> ...the notion of post-traumatic stress implies that children who chronically witness wife abuse in their homes may display emotional symptomatology at some point in time that may be quite far removed from the initial traumatic events. (Jaffe, Wolfe and Wilson 1990: 72).

Silvern and Kaersvang (1989), for instance, proposed that children living with domestic violence perceived each episode of violence as a traumatic event. They concluded that this traumatic impact alone is enough to produce distress for children. Jaffe, Wolfe and Wilson (1990) suggested that some children's coping reactions to witnessing domestic violence can lead to

behaviours which are similar to those of children suffering from PTSD.

In the UK there has been some resistance to the notion of traumatic stress in childhood, as until 1985 some members of the psychiatric profession still considered that children reacted to even their most stressful experiences by displaying only very slight and short-lived emotional and/or behavioural changes (Harris Hendriks, Black and Kaplan 1993: 9). There is now a growing body of research to suggest that children can experience PTSD in similar ways to adults, and may react in such a way to witnessing violence (Pynoos and Eth 1985 in Harris Hendriks, Black and Kaplan 1993) and to parental murder (Harris Hendriks, Black and Kaplan 1993; Malmquist 1986 in Harris Hendriks, Black and Kaplan 1993). However, it is important to treat the concept with caution, and not to apply it as some generalised pathology to all children living with domestic violence. As Finkelhor (1996) points out, it would be wrong to assume that all sexual abuse 'fits' into the PTSD model because a whole range of individual and social factors affect each person's reactions to sexual abuse. The same complexities apply to the impact for children of living with domestic violence.

Harris Hendriks, Black and Kaplan (1993) are in no doubt that in some cases child witnesses to domestic violence can be viewed as experiencing distress equivalent to PTSD:

> ... domestic violence can produce reactions identical to those seen as a result of war or major disaster. (p18)

They suggest that PTSD may affect older children more than younger children because of their greater understanding of what they have witnessed, but that girls of all ages seem more susceptible to it than boys. They summarise some of the main manifestations of PTSD in children as:

- numbness and detachment with withdrawal

- disturbed sleep (possibly with recurrent dreams)

- impaired concentration and memory

- hyper-alertness and 'jumpiness'

- experiencing of 'flashbacks' (p13)

The link between children witnessing violence and PTSD was also echoed by Brandon and Lewis (1996) who found that three children out of the six over 8's in their intensive sample could possibly be identified as suffering from Post Traumatic Stress Disorder. However, they add the rider 'that the relationship between the behaviour and the violence is probable rather than proven' (p40), and acknowledge that their sample is very small.

3.17 Summary

- Domestic violence is likely to have a detrimental impact on children.

- In the context of domestic violence, many children may experience both direct sexual or physical abuse as well as witnessing violence to their mother.

- Children witnessing domestic violence has tended to be minimised by professionals, even though in some cases this might cause the child to

react in ways consistent with the symptoms of Post Traumatic Stress Disorder.

■ Children might experience a wide range of behavioural, physical and psychological effects, which may be short term and/or long term.

■ Children's perceptions and reactions to living with domestic violence will be influenced, both in the short and longer term, by factors such as age, race, economic status, gender, disability, sexuality and children's resilience. Their responses to living with domestic violence vary enormously, with some children being affected far more than others. Children within the same family may be affected differently.

■ Generally, *pre-school children* are more likely to have physical symptoms of their anxiety; *primary school children* present their fears behaviourally and emotionally; *adolescents* may try to gain relief through drugs, early marriage or pregnancy, running away, or through criminal activity.

■ Gender can be an influencing factor in the impact of domestic violence on children, but this varies considerably and there is no single common response to the way in which boys and girls deal with their experiences of domestic violence.

■ There may be particular difficulties for Black children living with domestic violence, especially when set against a racist and hostile society. Some of the impacts on Black children are likely to be exacerbated by additional threats of abduction abroad, and/or by being asked inappropriately to act as interpreters or translators.

■ The impact on children of living with domestic violence might be affected by the relationship between mother and child, especially linked to the amount of stress experienced by the mother, and how this affects the mother's parenting role.

■ Children are not merely passive by-standers to the domestic violence occurring around them, but will act and make choices, and many children will develop a wide range of complex strategies of survival in order to deal with the stress and adversity they are experiencing.

■ Children's resilience may be an influencing factor to explain why some children who live with domestic violence do not appear to be as adversely affected as others.

■ There is a need for more detailed research, looking at a wider range of the population, in order to understand more about the complexities, similarities and differences between children's experiences of, and reactions to, living with domestic violence.

Part Two

The Legal Context

This part of the reader looks at the legislative framework within which women and children experiencing domestic violence can seek protection. While the same provisions apply in England and Wales, there are differences for Scotland and Northern Ireland, both in the legislature itself and in its practical implementation, which fall outside the remit of this Reader.

Improving criminal justice responses to domestic violence and the effectiveness of remedies under civil law has been the focus of government attention for the last decade. There have been some undoubted improvements to the protection afforded by the law, although there has been little systematic monitoring or research into their effectiveness. There have also been a number of contradictory and opposing trends in social policy and legislative change: aspects of the *Children Act 1989*, the *Child Support Act 1993*, the *Housing Act 1996*, and the new divorce arrangements within the *Family Law Act 1996* have all been criticised for the ways in which their construction and implementation can undermine rather than enhance the safety and protection of abused women and children (see for example, Harwin and Barron 1998).

The *Children Act 1989* is the main piece of legislature which specifically focuses on the needs of children. However, concern for the welfare of children is implicit in many aspects of other legislature discussed within this part, and in all aspects of family proceedings, but children themselves are rarely the main actors within it. The adequacy or otherwise of current legal provisions for the protection of abused women has direct implications for the safety and welfare of their children who have witnessed or experienced domestic violence. For abused women themselves, finding their way through the legal system is a complicated and difficult process, crucially dependant on their access to information, and to effective advocacy and representation. This is still too often simply a lottery, depending on where they live and their own financial and personal resources.

This Part will identify key areas of legal provision relating to children and domestic violence, and their limitations, within four main areas:

■ Making safe arrangements for children: public and private law within the *Children Act 1989* and the new arrangements for divorce under the *Family Law Act 1996*

■ Protection from domestic violence under the criminal law, the role of the police, the prosecution process, and the provisions of the *Protection from Harassment Act 1997*

■ Legal remedies for protection from domestic violence under civil law, and part IV of the new *Family Law Act 1996*

■ Help with protection from violence under the *Housing Act 1996*.

CHAPTER FOUR : MAKING SAFE ARRANGEMENTS FOR CHILDREN: PUBLIC AND PRIVATE LAW

The *Children Act 1989* redefined child care law and introduced new measures for working with children and families in both public and private family law. It was the first child care legislation to take into account the child's religious, ethnic, cultural, and linguistic background. It embodied a new approach to working with and for children, underpinned by the principle that the child's welfare is paramount.

4.1 The Children Act 1989 and domestic violence

The *Children Act 1989* does not overtly acknowledge the context of domestic violence in which many children live. Despite the fact that the Act is accompanied by ten volumes of guidance, there is none on the issue of domestic violence, nor any recognition that domestic violence is a key factor in the break up of many relationships. Until very recently, the concept of risk of violence to one parent figure from the other parent figure (or from another family member), and the possible impact of this on the first parent's ability to protect and care for children, was not identified as a factor requiring consideration. In the light of better understanding since the Act's implementation, an amendment to include the risk of domestic violence within the welfare checklist or elsewhere might now be timely.

The need to minimise the risk of violence during family proceedings was highlighted during the passage of the *Family Law Act 1996*, and was recognised as one of the key principles of Parts II and III of that Act (divorce, legal aid and mediation). The recognition by Parliament that this principle was needed was due, in part, to greater awareness following the Home Affairs Select Committee Inquiry Into Domestic Violence in 1992, and to subsequent publicity about the extent and nature of domestic violence. This was accompanied by growing concerns about the unfortunate effects of its absence within the *Children Act 1989* itself, particularly in relation to section 8 orders (private arrangements for children after relationship breakdown).

While Parts I–V of the *Children Act 1989* all contain implications for the welfare of children living with or witnessing domestic violence and their (usually) mothers, there are a number of key sections that have specific relevance for individual and corporate strategies to improve protection and safety. The main features are set out below, and are further discussed in Part Three of the Reader.

4.2 Part I of the Children Act 1989

Under the *Children Act 1989*, proceedings can be heard in any court, concurrent with other proceedings, for example, alongside proceedings for injunctions under the *Family Law Act 1996* (see Chapter Six). Part I of the Act also introduced two new central features: the *welfare checklist*, and the concept of *parental responsibility*.

The welfare checklist [Children Act 1989, s.1(3)]

The court has to take into consideration the following factors in every case involving a child's upbringing where the making, variation or discharge of any

order is opposed by any party, and in every case where the child may be at
risk of harm. This applies both to orders in family proceedings under s.8 and
for applications by local authorities relating to care and supervision under Part
IV.

a. the ascertainable wishes and feelings of the child concerned, (considered
    in the light of his age and understanding)

b. his physical, emotional and educational needs

c. the likely effect on him of any change in his circumstances

d. his age, sex, background and any characteristics of his which the court
    considers relevant

e. any harm which he has suffered or is at risk of suffering

f. how capable his parents, and any other person in relation to whom the
    court considers the question to be relevant, are of meeting his needs

g. the range of proceedings available to the court under this Act in the
    proceedings in question.

From the perspective of those experiencing domestic violence, the
implementation of the welfare checklist can be problematic in practice. For
example, there is no formal requirement on the court to consider the effects
of the decisions made under the *Children Act 1989* on the safety of an adult
(usually the woman) who may be at risk.

Parental responsibility

'Parental responsibility' is defined in the Act as:

> "all the rights, duties, powers, responsibilities and authority which by law a
> parent of a child has in relation to the child and his property." [*Children
> Act 1989*, s.3 (1)]

Parental responsibility is awarded according to birth status and residence
arrangements, as follows:

■   the natural mother automatically has parental responsibility and never
    loses it until the child reaches 16

■   the natural father has parental responsibility, if he was married to the
    mother at the time of the child's birth, or if he marries her subsequently

■   if father and mother make a parental responsibility agreement

■   if the father applies to the court and the court grants permission

■   anyone with a residence order in respect of a particular child has parental
    responsibility, for as long as that residence order lasts, unless they are a
    parent of the child, in which case they keep it even after the order ends

■   the local authority has parental responsibility when a care order is in
    force, but they share this with the natural parents.

Once parental responsibility has been given to a natural father (if he is not
automatically entitled through marriage), he cannot have it removed from him
even if the child does not live with him. The natural father has precedence
over others in relation to guardianship of children after the death of the

natural mother; however, if there is a residence order in force in someone else's name when the mother dies, that person may be granted parental responsibility.

Welfare reports

A welfare report is often of vital importance in the court's decision-making in relation to the welfare of a child. While this is normally prepared by court welfare officers from the probation service, the court can ask a social worker or other officer of the local authority to provide one [*Children Act 1989* s.7 (1)]. National Standards (1994) for probation service family court welfare work state clearly that where there is domestic violence, the preparation of such reports should not require women to attend joint interviews with their abusers. However, these standards are not always enforced (see Hester, Pearson and Radford 1997; Debbonaire 1997). Not requiring women to attend joint interviews with their abusers has been adopted by some local authority social services departments where they have developed domestic violence policies.

4.3 The care and protection of children under the Children Act 1989 Parts IV and V

The Act introduced a number of new measures in relation to local authority (and others') powers and duties under public law:

■ Under **s. 47** of the *Children Act 1989*, local authorities have a duty to enquire into the welfare of any child suffering or likely to suffer 'significant harm', and to decide whether they should take action to safeguard the child's welfare.

■ Under **s.44** local authorities can apply for an *emergency protection order*, lasting up to 8 days.

■ Under **s.31** local authorities (and the NSPCC) may apply to the court for a *care or supervision order*, which may initially be granted on an interim basis. The applicant must be satisfied that the child is suffering or is likely to suffer significant harm because of a lack of reasonable parental care or because he is beyond parental control.

■ Under **s.20** local authorities must provide accommodation for children in need where the child is lost, has no parent, or where parents are prevented (temporarily or permanently) from providing suitable accommodation or care.

■ Under **s.46** the police (through police protection orders) also have powers to remove children at risk of significant harm, or to take steps to ensure that they are not removed from a safe place where they are being accommodated.

4.4 Removing a suspected child abuser from the family home

Under Children Act guidance [Volume 1, paragraph 4.31] social workers are encouraged to remove the abuser rather than the child from the family home, wherever possible. Under **s.52** of, and **Schedule 6** to, the *Family Law Act 1996*, an amendment has been made to **s.38** and **s.44** of the *Children Act*

1989. The courts now have powers to exclude someone from the home who is suspected of abusing a child within the home. Where an *emergency protection order* or *interim care order* has been applied for, or is in place, local authorities can now apply for an order to:

■ remove a suspected abuser from the family home where the child lives

■ prevent the relevant person from entering the property

■ exclude that person from an area around the family home.

Such an order can only be granted alongside an interim care order or emergency protection order in respect of the child if the following conditions are satisfied:

(a) that there is reasonable cause to believe that if a person ("the relevant person") is excluded from a dwelling-house in which the child lives, the child will cease to suffer, or cease to be likely to suffer, significant harm,

and

(b) another person living in the dwelling-house (whether a parent of the child or some other person) –

(i) is able and willing to give the child the care which it would be reasonable to expect a parent to give him, and

(ii) consents to the inclusion of the exclusion requirement.

[Children Act s 38A (2)]

There are several points to note about an exclusion requirement attached to an interim care order or an emergency protection order:

■ it may last for a shorter period than the interim care order or emergency protection order

■ it may be granted *ex parte* (that is, without all parties being present at the hearing or notified in advance)

■ it may have a power of arrest attached (although this can be for a shorter period than the order)

■ it can only be included within an interim order (by the time the court considers making a final care order, a proposed carer, usually the woman, will be expected to have excluded the abuser either by her own legal remedies or through the intervention of criminal justice agencies)

■ it will cease to have effect if the child is subsequently removed from the house by the local authority for a period of more than 24 hours

■ the local authority must notify all relevant parties including the person who is excluded and the carer who consented when an exclusion requirement ceases to have effect.

The court also has the power to accept undertakings (a promise made to the court to do or not do something) instead of making an order if the case is appropriate. (See Chapter Six for a discussion of undertakings).

The Department of Health Circular (September 1997) on Part IV of the *Family Law Act 1966* gives important guidance on the implementation of this

new power to support the protection of children, and its implications for practice in working with women at risk from domestic violence. Firstly, court rules require that:

■ The mother's consent should be informed consent – it should not be elicited for reasons of convenience.

■ The local authority should discuss the understanding of the carer giving consent to the exclusion order, including the purpose and effect of the order, whether or not they are legally represented in the proceedings.

■ If the person consents, the local authority should ensure that this is available in writing for the court, signed and dated.

■ Any application to renew or vary the order should be similarly agreed to by the person consenting to the exclusion requirement.

Secondly, the following points of guidance are also noted:

■ The welfare of the child has to be seen alongside the welfare of the child's carer. Where domestic violence may be an important element in the family, the safety of (usually) the mother is also in the interests of the child's welfare.

■ Local authority staff working in child protection should recognise the possible conflicts of interest in respect of responsibilities for the child, and the need to give objective information and advice before, say, the child's mother agrees to consent to an exclusion requirement.

■ There may be a significant risk to the mother's safety if there has been a history of domestic violence, which an exclusion requirement might exacerbate.

■ Where possible, the local authority should ensure that the mother receives advice and information from a person within the authority other than the caseworker with primary responsibility for the child.

■ The mother could also be referred for specialist help to local Women's Aid services or the Women's Aid National Helpline.

■ The mother may need considerable support throughout the duration of the order if there are threats against her, or attempts to persuade her to agree that the order (and any attached power of arrest) be rescinded.

Under **schedule 2, paragraph 5** of the *Children Act 1989*, social services can also offer financial assistance to enable the abuser to pay for alternative accommodation. This may be helpful in situations where there is domestic violence towards the proposed carer from the excluded abuser, as it may decrease the risk to her.

4.5 Providing support for 'children in need': Section 17 of the Children Act

In recent years, following publication of *Messages from Research* (Department of Health 1995), local authorities and other agencies have been encouraged to place child protection work within the context of wider services for children in need. This was to redress the concern that children were being routed inappropriately within the child protection system as a means of

gaining access to services. The Government is aware that inquiries into suspicions of child abuse can have traumatic effects on children and families. It is, therefore, important that professionals work in partnership with parents and their children, whilst at the same time ensuring the child's welfare is safeguarded. This 'refocusing' by local authorities and others has been characterised by a shift from emphasising Part IV of the *Children Act 1989* (in particular **s.47** investigations or inquiries) toward Part III of the Act (in particular providing services for children in need under **s.17**).

Under **s.17.1(a)** of the Children Act 1989, local authorities have a duty to 'safeguard and promote the welfare of children within their area who are in need'. Local authorities can provide a range of services for children who are 'in need'. Such services are intended to provide support and help to families, including families of children with disabilities and other special needs.

Every local authority is required to undertake an audit of the needs of local children, recognising a range of special needs. Each local authority must also develop a Children's Services Plan to include a strategy for how such needs are going to be met, for example, by funding specific projects, employing staff, or paying for services. Financial assistance under **s.17** exists to promote the welfare of 'children in need', and can be applied to address the needs of children living with or leaving domestic violence, in the following ways:

a) **s.17 (1) (b)** to promote children's upbringing in their own families, provided that this is consistent with the child's welfare

There are a number of ways that social workers can give direct support to abused women to enable them to support their children's welfare, for example, help and support in getting re-housed in safe accommodation.

b) **s.17(5) (a)** to facilitate the provision of services to children through voluntary organisations

Financial support for Women's Aid work with children living in refuges and children's aftercare can be provided under this section. The change in focus since 1995 has given rise to some additional financial support for work in refuges with children who have witnessed or experienced domestic violence, in particular, funding of specialist children's workers in some areas. Such assistance could also include funding for a child's place at a nursery or playgroup, or funding for other services for children with special needs.

c) **s. 17(6)** for giving assistance in kind, and, in exceptional circumstances, cash payments to help children in need

These can be made to help women and their children leave abusive situations or survive within them. Such assistance might include:

■ cash for new clothes for children

■ cash for travel to get away from a violent man

■ assistance with fitting new locks, getting a telephone or alarm system

■ transport to a refuge.

Assistance might also be given to help a family where children are in need because of immigration rules that mean their abused mother has no recourse to other public funds. (These rules are now being reviewed by government in relation to women fleeing domestic violence).

4.6 Private proceedings under Part II of the Children Act 1989: making safe arrangements for children after relationship breakdown

Under **s.8** of the *Children Act 1989* the court may make four types of orders within family proceedings in respect of the child's welfare:

- **contact orders** – an order requiring the person with whom a child lives, or is to live, to allow the child to visit, stay or have contact with the person named in the order

- **residence orders** – an order settling arrangements about with whom the child is to live

- **prohibited steps orders** – prohibiting a person with parental responsibility from taking any steps contained in the order without the consent of the court

- **specific issue orders** – giving direction regarding a specific question in relation to any aspect of parental responsibility for a child.

The court may also, within its powers under **s.10** of the *Children Act 1989*, make an order in any family proceedings where questions arise with respect to the welfare of the child (for example with proceedings under the *Family Law Act 1996* – see below and Chapter Six).

A number of problems have been identified with respect to **s.8** orders under the *Children Act 1989* in cases where there is domestic violence. There is a lack of recognition within the Act in general, and within the welfare checklist in particular, of the risks and practical problems faced by women and children experiencing domestic violence in making safe arrangements after relationship breakdown. This has only recently been acknowledged.

Practitioners interpreting the Act have frequently assumed that, when parents do separate, the children will almost always benefit from continuing to have substantial and frequent contact with the non-resident parent (usually the father). These assumptions are often unrealistic, and, where one parent is violent, (whether or not he has directly abused the children) they can be dangerously mistaken (see Chapter One).

When a woman leaves home because of her partner's violence, she will usually take the children with her, and will probably wish to continue to care for them and make a home for them. Usually, this will also be in the children's own interests. The children and the absent parent may wish to see each other regularly, and sometimes this can be arranged without major problems. In many cases, the mother will be reluctant for her children to see her abusive ex-partner because she is fearful for their safety or her own. These fears may, however, be ignored or minimised by professionals who believe, mistakenly, that, where there is no clear evidence of substantial risk to the *child*, contact with both parents is in his/her best interests (see Barron, Harwin and Singh 1992; Hester and Radford 1996; Hester, Pearson and Radford 1997; Debbonaire 1997).

This failure to recognise the risks of domestic violence to the safety of both the (usually) mother and the child has sometimes been compounded by the apparent lack of hard evidence of previous or present violence to the mother, and/or to the child. This itself results from a number of other problems,

including: a lack of co-ordination of information and evidence across criminal justice and family welfare proceedings; the pre-1996 difficulties of gaining injunctive protection (and therefore proof); the absence, until very recently, within statutory responses of full recognition of the impact of domestic violence on children living with it; court pressure to reach agreement over arrangements for children; inadequate legal representation that leads to the full nature of the abuse being hidden or minimised; as well as the intrinsically 'private' nature of the abusive behaviour itself.

The process of determining where the best interests of the children lie can also be traumatic for many women. Where there is no agreement between the parents on where a child should live, or how much contact (if any) the non-resident parent is to have, a family court welfare officer (FCWO) will usually be appointed to prepare a report on the child's circumstances, and to make recommendations to the court. Under the *Children Act 1989*, decisions about a child's welfare are taken by those with parental responsibility. In the past, many FCWOs have interpreted this to mean that joint meetings of both parents, together with the FCWO, are necessary, and they have sometimes persuaded or pressured women into attending (see Hester, Pearson and Radford 1997). Meeting her abuser again face to face can be a frightening experience for the woman, and in many cases it has led to further threats and abuse against her and/or the children. Such practices are now less common, as a result of improved awareness and the development of practice standards (see earlier).

In summary, therefore, the combination of the *Children Act 1989*'s lack of focus on domestic violence-related issues and insufficient awareness among many involved in operating within its tenets has produced many situations in which children and women have been left at continued risk of violence and abuse. These issues are more fully discussed within Part Three.

In Australia and New Zealand, growing awareness of these issues in recent years, highlighted by some particularly tragic cases, has resulted in changes to the equivalent legislation. In Australia, the *Family Law Reform Act 1995* specifies that, in determining the best interests of the children (when for example residence or contact is disputed) the court must be aware of the need to protect them from physical or psychological harm, and must specifically look at all the issues of family violence.

The New Zealand legislation goes further in stating that when a court is deciding custody or access, and is satisfied that a party to the marriage has used violence against a child or another party in the proceedings, neither custody nor unsupervised access should be granted until the court is satisfied that the children will be safe. A list of criteria for assessing 'safety' is appended to the legislation. That is, rather than the focus being on the mother's 'implacable hostility' to contact (as in this country) the onus is on the abuser to convince the judge that he can be trusted with the children (Kaye 1996).

The implementation of Parts I, II, and III of the *Family Law Act 1989* (see below) may be helpful in improving family proceedings in this area, as more attention has to be given to the risk of violence to any party involved in relationship breakdown. This may result in domestic violence issues being highlighted more fully in considering the welfare of, and arrangements for, children.

4.7 Divorce and the new Family Law Act 1996

The *Family Law Act 1996* is made up of five parts:

Part I: Principles of Parts II and III

Part II: Divorce and Separation

Part III: Legal Aid for Mediation in Family Matters

Part IV: Family Homes and Domestic Violence

Part V: Supplemental

Part IV of the *Family Law Act 1996* was implemented in October 1997 (see later in this section for details of its provisions). Parts II and III of the Act are unlikely to be implemented before 1999, and will be introduced after the completion of research concerning the piloting of mediation and information meetings, which is currently being carried out across England and Wales.

This chapter focuses mainly on Part II and some aspects of Part III of the Act. The general principles in Part I which govern Parts II and III are as follows:

- The institution of marriage should be supported. Where a marriage may have broken down the couple should be encouraged to take all practical steps to save the marriage, whether by marriage counselling or otherwise.

- Where marriages are being brought to an end, this should be done with minimum distress to the couple and children, so as to encourage the best possible relationships between them in the future.

- **Any risk of violence to a party to a marriage or to any other children, on account of the other party should, as far as possible, be removed or diminished.**

The Act introduces new stages which must be undertaken before a divorce or separation order can be granted:

- Information meeting

- Statement of marital breakdown (after three months minimum)

- Period of reflection and consideration (of varying length)

- Arrangements for the future, including financial matters

- The welfare of any child of the family is considered

- Application for divorce or separation order.

Before anyone can begin the process of divorce, they have to have been married for at least 12 months – this is in line with the current legislation.

Information meeting

Anyone wishing to divorce will have to attend an information meeting with a trained professional. Couples may attend together if they wish but this is not compulsory and recognition has been given to the need to safeguard those at risk of domestic violence. Information will include:

- marriage support services

- the importance of the welfare, wishes and feelings of any children

- protection available against violence

- financial matters which might arise following divorce

- legal aid (to pay for legal representation or mediation)

- the divorce process

- the availability and advantages of mediation.

Couples will be encouraged to meet a marriage counsellor – free to those eligible for non-contributory legal aid.

Statement of marital breakdown

After the information meeting, there is a three month minimum period before anyone wishing to proceed with the divorce may make a statement of marriage breakdown. This must state that one or both parties believe the marriage has broken down, confirm that they understand the purpose of the period for reflection and consideration, and wish to make arrangements for the future in respect of finance, property and children. The grounds for divorce will continue to be the irretrievable breakdown of a marriage, but the mixture of fault-based and separation-based facts that applied under previous legislation will be removed.

Period of reflection and consideration

The purpose of this is 'to allow couples time to think through such an important decision, and be fully aware of all its consequences. It allows them an opportunity to examine what has gone wrong in the marriage, and whether there is any hope of reconciliation. If they consider that the breakdown is irretrievable, it gives them the opportunity to make proper arrangements for living apart before a divorce order is granted' (Lord Chancellor's Department 1996).

This period lasts for a minimum of nine months. It will be extended by a further six months if one of the parties requests it, or if there are children under 16 involved. **'It may not be extended if there is evidence of domestic violence or if the court is satisfied that the delay would be detrimental to the welfare of any child of the family'.**

A further 12 months (known as the lapse period) is available to couples to decide arrangements, if required. Couples can also suspend the period for reflection and consideration and the lapse period for a maximum of 18 months in order to attempt reconciliation.

The evidence required to limit the extension of the period of reflection to nine months only is limited to a non-molestation order under Part IV of the Act (see Chapter Six). Other evidence of domestic violence (for example, the existence of an undertaking, or proceedings under the criminal law) will not count as evidence for this purpose.

Mediation

During the period of reflection and consideration, divorcing couples will be encouraged to use mediation, as opposed to legal representation, to resolve disputes. Legal Aid, for those eligible, will be available to cover the cost of mediation, on the same basis as for legal representation. People in receipt of

Legal Aid are required to attend an initial meeting with a mediator. In such cases, legally aided representation will be available to eligible parties. State funding will be available to some people for marriage counselling. A mediation code of practice specifies that the mediator must have arrangements designed to ensure:

- that parties participate in mediation only if willing and not influenced by fear of violence or other harm;

- that cases where either party may be influenced by fear of violence or other harm are identified as soon as possible;

- that the possibility of reconciliation is kept under review throughout mediation; and

- that each party is informed about the availability of independent legal advice.

[*Family Law Act 1996, Part III, s.27*]

Application for a divorce or separation order

After the period of reflection and consideration, a divorce application may be made to the court. It will be granted provided that the court is satisfied that:

- the marriage has broken down irretrievably;

- the marriage cannot be saved;

- arrangements for the future have been made;

- the process outlined above has been followed;

- there is no need to use the hardship bar (see below).

Conduct

The *Family Law Act 1996* has removed the concept of fault in obtaining a divorce. However, conduct will be assessed by the courts in making the final divorce settlement 'where it would be inequitable not to do so', for example, in property settlements in favour of a woman who is looking after children, financial settlements in cases of domestic violence.

The court can prevent a divorce if it is satisfied that 'substantial financial or other hardship would be caused to the applicant or to the children of the family by the dissolution of the marriage' (known as the 'hardship bar').

4.8 Implementing the Family Law Act

The overall aim of the Act is to enable a genuinely 'no fault' divorce, with divorce being allowed on request from either party – subject to an 'information session' and a waiting period of at least a year following the original statement that the marriage has broken down. It is hoped that during that waiting period, the divorcing couple will reach agreement (preferably through mediation rather than legal proceedings) about arrangements for the children, and the division of any property (including the matrimonial home.) The stated objectives of the legislation are:

- to support the institution of marriage

- to minimise bitterness and hostility (and hence enable ongoing co-operation in joint parenthood)

- to minimise costs – both to the parties and to the state.

The latter objective may be particularly problematic: it is not clear to what extent Legal Aid will be provided to those who are unable to negotiate by other means.

Also, realistically, the ideal of an on-going friendly, co-operative relationship between the ex-partners cannot be achieved in the majority of those cases where a relationship breaks down after years of abuse. In such cases, to impose a twelve month waiting period, in the expectation that agreement can be reached largely through mediation, will prolong the woman's distress and may endanger her and her children.

Many abused women will now have to wait at least a year to get a divorce, and up to 18 months if their spouse requests it – all of which is likely to have a knock-on negative effect on their re-housing options, as well as on the welfare of children who have to live in temporary accommodation if returning home is unsafe. If an injunction is in force, the waiting period cannot be extended to 18 months, but this excludes other forms of proof of the violence experienced by so many women currently seeking divorce for unreasonable behaviour. It is an unfortunate example of how intended improvements to social policy may well produce a negative outcome for abused women. Increasingly stringent criteria for granting Legal Aid for injunctions (see Chapter Six) emphasise that police action should be taken first, yet evidence from the police or from criminal justice processes cannot be used to prevent the extension of the divorce process.

The original proposals leading up to the *Family Law Act 1996* contained references to much research on the effects of divorce and separation, but there was no specific mention of domestic violence and its impact, despite the statistics which show 'unreasonable behaviour' (usually including allegations of violence) to be currently the major stated reason for women applying for divorce. Lobbying during the passage of the Bill led to the new principle being laid down in Part 1, that any risk to the safety of the parties should be minimised or reduced by the court or other professionals. Lobbying also led to the following amendments: information about support and protection from domestic violence must now be provided in the divorce information sessions; parties have a right at the court directions stage to have separate meetings to receive information about mediation or other matters; and an acknowledgement that mediation, which is voluntary, is inappropriate where there is fear of violence by either party.

4.9 Summary

- The *Children Act 1989* redefined child care law, and introduced new measures for working with children and families in both public and private family law. It does not contain guidance on the implications for the welfare of children living with or witnessing domestic violence, nor on ensuring the safety of adults who may be at risk.

- Part I of the Act introduced two new central features: the *welfare checklist* and the concept of *parental responsibility*. The lack of recognition within the *Children Act 1989* in general, and within the welfare checklist in particular, of the risks and practical problems faced by women and children experiencing domestic violence in making safe arrangements after relationship breakdown has only recently been acknowledged.

- Welfare reports are often of vital importance in the court's decision-making in relation to the welfare of a child. National Standards (1994) for probation service family court welfare work state clearly that where there is domestic violence, the preparation of such reports should not require women to attend joint interviews with their abusers.

- Under **s.47** of the *Children Act 1989*, local authorities have a duty to inquire into the welfare of any child suffering or likely to suffer 'significant harm', and to decide whether they should take action to safeguard the child's welfare.

- Under an amendment made through the *Family Law Act 1996*, where an emergency protection order or interim care order has been applied for, or is in place, the courts now have powers to exclude from the home a person who is suspected of abusing a child within that home. Guidance has been given by the Department of Health on the implementation of this new power to support the protection of children as well as women at risk from domestic violence.

- Under **s.17.1(a)** of the *Children Act 1989*, local authorities have a duty to 'safeguard and promote the welfare of children within their area who are in need', and can provide a range of services.

- Under **s.8** of the *Children Act 1989* the court may make four types of orders within family proceedings in respect of the child's welfare: contact orders, residence orders, prohibited steps orders, specific issue orders. A number of problems have been identified with respect to s.8 orders under the *Children Act 1989* in cases where there is domestic violence.

- The *Family Law Act 1996*, Parts I, II, and III will be introduced after piloting. The overall aim of the Act is to enable a 'no fault' divorce, with divorce being allowed on request from either party – subject to an 'information meeting', and a waiting period of at least a year. During that waiting period, the divorcing couple will be encouraged to reach agreement (preferably through mediation rather than legal proceedings) about arrangements for the children and the division of any property (including the matrimonial home.)

- Part I of the *Family Law Act 1996* contains a new principle, that any risk to the safety of the parties should be minimised or reduced by the court or other professionals. Other amendments include that information about support and protection from domestic violence must now be provided in the divorce information meetings; that parties have a right at the court directions stage to have separate meetings to receive information about mediation or other matters; and an acknowledgement that mediation, which is voluntary, is inappropriate where there is fear of violence by either party.

- The combination of the *Children Act 1989*'s lack of focus on domestic violence-related issues, and insufficient awareness among many involved in operating within its tenets, has produced many situations in which children and women have been left at continued risk of violence and abuse. Growing awareness of these problems has led to recent changes in policy and practice, and to the introduction of provisions within the new *Family Law Act 1996* that may lead to improved responses.

CHAPTER FIVE: PROTECTION UNDER THE CRIMINAL LAW

5.1 Police responses and the need for change

Until very recently the criminal justice system has paid little attention to the needs of women and children experiencing domestic violence. Up until the mid-1980's, the police response to domestic violence was very variable, depending on the attitudes and approach of the individual officer. A number of studies have documented the dismissive and derogatory way in which police officers tended to handle 'domestic disputes' (for example, Dobash and Dobash 1980; Hanmer and Saunders 1984; Edwards 1989; Bourlet 1990). Domestic violence was frequently defined as 'rubbish work', was seen as a private matter, not 'real' violence, and the sympathies of a predominantly male police force were often with the violent man/husband. Women seeking refuge and help from Women's Aid complained frequently about the lack of protection, effective action or information about other sources of help from the police. Despite the overall approach, there were some individual police officers who did as much as they could to help.

While many women have sought help from the police in an emergency, often unsuccessfully, for others, calling the police is not the first option, and is often only a last resort after repeated attacks (Smith 1989). Much domestic violence goes unreported to the police – one recent London study showed that only 22% of women who had been assaulted by their partners contacted the police for help. The majority first sought help from relatives or friends (Mooney 1994). Similar findings were reported by Dobash and Dobash in their Scottish study (Dobash and Dobash 1980). Many abused women are ambivalent about calling the police: they fear they will not be believed or taken seriously; they may believe that the police can only respond to actual physical assault; they may fear it will provoke further or greater violence by challenging the man; they may not want their partner/ex-partner to be taken to court.

Mama (1996) found that Black women, in particular, are less likely to call the police if they fear racism against themselves or their partner and, consequently, whether the police would act or, indeed, overreact. Racist stereotypes, lack of interest in the needs of Black women, and racist immigration laws mean that Black women are often reluctant to call the police. Research shows that, for some Black women, doing so resulted in more problems, including being assaulted themselves or being threatened with arrest.

From 1986, the need for changes in police practice to both domestic violence and rape was accepted by the Home Office. This led to the first circular in 1986, followed in 1990 by a much more substantial circular to Chief Constables. Now, all 43 police forces have policies on domestic violence and many Domestic Violence Units (or Domestic Violence liaison officers in some areas) have been set up around the country. Since 1990, there has been a significant change in police response to domestic violence, which has led to improvements in policy and practice (Home Affairs Select Committee 1992; Grace 1996).

The 1990 circular clearly signalled that domestic violence is now viewed as a crime, both by practitioners in the criminal justice system and by government itself. Yet, domestic violence cannot, by its nature, be dealt with effectively

under the criminal law alone. Many aspects of domestic violence are difficult to define as crimes, nor do they fit readily into common categories of 'assault' under criminal law. The criminal law and the courts perceive harm in terms of physical abuse. In the absence of independent witnesses they will usually require some evidence of physical injury or harm as proof that a crime has been perpetrated. This 'incident-focused' system, therefore, ignores many aspects of ongoing coercive, abusive and threatening behaviour, and the psychological effects and harm that this can cause, as detailed in Chapter One.

Nevertheless, the criminal justice system has an important role to play in preventing and challenging domestic violence, both symbolically and practically. Within the past decade local and national attention has, therefore, focused on encouraging more women to seek help from the police and the criminal justice system, and on encouraging this system to provide a better response for them and their children when they do.

5.2 Police powers under the law

The police are a key 24 hour agency for women experiencing domestic violence, perhaps the first port of call in an emergency. *Circular 60/90* instructs police that the 'immediate duty is to secure the protection of the "victim" and any children, and then to consider action against the offender' (Home Office 1990). Each police officer has the discretion to use his/her powers to intervene, arrest, caution or charge an abusive man. They do not need a warrant to arrest someone who they suspect is about to commit an arrestable offence, nor do they need to witness an assault.

The police have the same powers to deal with domestic violence under common law, the *Offences Against the Person Act 1861*, or the *Police and Criminal Evidence Act 1984*, as they do in any other criminal assault or offence. Arrestable offences for which the police can take action include:

- assault occasioning actual bodily harm (ABH);

- unlawful wounding or inflicting grievous bodily harm (GBH);

- rape, attempted rape or indecent assault;

- attempted murder;

- threats to kill;

- criminal damage and public order offences.

Arrests can be made to prevent further injury or to protect 'a vulnerable person or child'. The police can also arrest someone who has broken bail conditions or an injunction with associated powers of arrest, or they can arrest for a breach of the peace where there are no powers of arrest. Common assault (for example, slaps, shoves), is not an arrestable offence under the law, but in practice, police will often arrest for ABH if there is evidence under the law (for example, bruising), although this may be downgraded later to common assault in the charging process.

'Actual bodily harm' has also recently been defined by case law to include shock and nervous conditions, suggesting that more recognition is now being

given to the psychological effects of abuse, both directly and indirectly, on the survivor/victim. These changes are echoed in the widening of definitions of harm for protection orders under the civil law (see the discussion below on the *Family Law Act 1996*).

The police have strictly limited powers as to the length of time they can keep a suspected criminal at the police station (usually 24 hours), and they cannot impose conditions when forced to release him on police bail. If a man is arrested and admits his offence, the police can decide to issue a formal caution against him instead of referring the case to the Crown Prosecution Service. This then goes on his criminal record.

5.3 The Protection from Harassment Act 1997

In 1997, new 'stalking' legislation was introduced which may provide more effective protection for abused women than has been previously available. This will particularly apply to those women who no longer live with their abuser. Much of the media publicity in the run-up to the legislation focused on obsessive stalking of strangers and celebrities. In fact, a survey of worst cases carried out by ACPO (Association of Chief Police Officers), found that nearly 40% of these cases involving harassment were where the (usually) woman was the ex-partner, or where there had been a close relationship – in other words, post-separation domestic violence (Wallis 1996).

The *Protection from Harassment Act 1997* introduces new measures for protection under both the criminal and civil law, and also provides a new link between criminal and civil law. The provisions include two new criminal offences: the offence of *criminal harassment* (under **s.2**, a summary offence, tried in the magistrates court), and a more serious *offence involving fear of violence* (under **s.4**, triable either as a summary offence, or as an indictable offence in the crown court). If convicted of either of these offences, there is an additional measure for protection: a *restraining order* can also be granted by the court, prohibiting the offender from further similar conduct. Under the civil law there is also a new injunction for prevention of harassment for those who are not eligible under the *Family Law Act 1996* (see Chapter Six for further discussion of the usefulness of this).

Under **s.2** (the offence of criminal harassment), a person must not pursue a course of conduct which amounts to harassment of another, and which he knows, or ought to know, amounts to harassment of the other, that is, if any 'reasonable person' in possession of the same information would regard such conduct as harassment. The term 'reasonable person' may be problematic in practice but the aim of the legislation is to shift the emphasis from the subjective harmful intent of the alleged offender, which is often difficult to prove, to what actually happens and its effect on the victim.

Under **s.4** (the offence involving fear of violence), anyone whose course of conduct causes another to fear, on at least two occasions, that violence will be used against her, is guilty of an offence 'if he knows, or ought to know, that his course of conduct will cause the other so to fear on each of those occasions'. Although there are already powers under existing criminal law to deal with fear of physical violence, this new offence may be useful, as it will allow the courts to deal with serious stalking without having to wait until psychological or bodily harm is caused.

The police can arrest without warrant anyone whom they suspect of committing either of these offences, and the separate incidents do not have to be the same kind each time. For example, shouting obscenities outside a woman's house on a Saturday, followed by a broken window the next Friday could constitute a related 'course of conduct', even though the conduct is different each time. Both could be prosecuted under existing legislation (for example, as public order, or criminal damage offences) but would also constitute an offence under **s.2** of the *Protection from Harassment Act 1997*. The police and the Crown Prosecution Service (CPS) would have to decide whether to take forward one offence or two. The advantage of going for the single offence of harassment is that it allows the court to hear the entire catalogue of incidents, the evidence for which may be weak individually, but strong collectively.

A number of potential advantages of this new law have been identified (Harwin 1997a). Firstly, the options for police protection and use of the criminal law against men who continue to threaten, pester and harass women after the relationship has ended, will be strengthened. Secondly, women without children who do not live with their abusers, and who cannot apply for injunctions under Part IV of the *Family Law Act 1996*, will now be able to gain protection under the *Protection From Harassment Act 1997*. In particular, criminal proceedings resulting in a conviction will mean that a restraining order can be attached. Restraining orders can provide the same protection as injunctions under the civil law, and may be more effective as they carry stronger penalties. Lastly, action under the criminal law, coupled with restraining orders, may avoid the problem of the costs of legal aid for civil remedies. This would apply in those cases where women do not need to apply for injunctions to exclude their abuser from the property (see Chapter Six for further discussion of civil law remedies).

5.4 Improving the police response

Circular 60/90 urged the police to develop explicit policies on domestic violence, and to establish dedicated units with specially trained officers to deal with it 'where practicable and cost effective'. It also specified the following central features that should be included in any force policy statements:

- the overriding duty to protect victims and any children from further abuse;

- the need to treat domestic violence at least as seriously as other forms of violence;

- the use and value of powers of arrest;

- the dangers of conciliation between victim and offender;

- the need to establish effective recording and monitoring systems.

The circular reminded officers that the primary duty was to protect the victim and any children and then consider what action should be taken against the offender. Immediate protection could include referring or taking the woman to a refuge, as well as liaison with statutory and voluntary agencies for long term support. Chief Constables were also urged to liaise on the development and implementation of these policies with a wide range of

agencies. Particular consideration was given to the need for good liaison with the CPS, including the discussion of evidential and other matters to ensure consistency of aims and approach in the prosecution of domestic violence.

Detailed description is also given of how to respond to an incident, including the need to check previous records, action at the scene of the incident, the value of having women officers present, the need for separate interviews, and the importance for abused women's safety of not asking questions about her willingness to give evidence, prosecution or other matters in front of the assailant. Clear guidance is also given on the options for arrest and detention of the abuser, both as a deterrent and as a signal to the woman that she is entitled to society's protection and support. There is also guidance on other matters relating to the prosecution of the assailant and keeping the victim informed.

5.5 *The prosecution process: key issues for women survivors of domestic violence*

Once a man has been arrested and charged, the file passes to the CPS. When considering whether to proceed with the charge or whether to discontinue, the CPS may consult with the police, or ask them to clarify or obtain more evidence. Decisions about whether to proceed are informed by two key criteria:

- whether there is sufficient evidence to continue

- whether it is in the public interest to do so (see CPS Statement on Domestic Violence, April 1993).

In cases of domestic violence, the likelihood of there being 'sufficient evidence' will be depend on there being independent evidence of the crime (other witnesses, forensic evidence) or on whether the complainant is herself willing to be a witness for the CPS.

If the woman decides to withdraw the complaint for whatever reason, the police will interview the woman and establish what the reason for this is. She will have to make a written statement under **s.9** of the *Criminal Justice Act 1967*. Under **s.80** of the *Police and Criminal Evidence Act (PACE) 1984* the courts have been empowered to compel a witness to give evidence against her or his spouse. Research by Cretney and Davis (1996), however, has found that these provisions were almost never used. A woman who refuses to give evidence in these circumstances will be in contempt of court. In extreme instances, she could be sent to prison, while all charges against her assailant are necessarily dropped. While there may be a few instances in which compelling a woman to give evidence against an abusive partner or ex-partner may ultimately operate in her interests (or those of her children), an abused woman may be inappropriately compelled to support a prosecution which damages or endangers her life. It should be noted that the court can also use **Section 23** of the *Criminal Justice Act 1988*, whereby a woman's evidence can be given in a sworn statement rather than in person, if she is frightened, or is being 'kept out of the way'. However, many judges are unwilling to use **s.23** unless there is extreme physical violence, as the defendant's counsel should have the right to cross-examine the witness.

The immediate arrest and removal of the abuser by police will often be helpful in providing many women and children with much needed 'breathing space' and time to consider what they should do. Proceeding with prosecution may not, however, always be in their best interests. The difficulties include the following:

■ women may be extremely reluctant to give evidence against someone whom they love or have loved, and with whom they share or have shared a home, and who may be the father of their children

■ women may feel under pressure to protect the family reputation

■ Black and ethnic minority women may be unwilling to risk community ostracism, and fear allegations of disloyalty or collusion with police racism

■ women are often at risk of further violence – waiting times in criminal proceedings are too long, and women will frequently be left without adequate legal protection while waiting for the case to come to court

■ going to court is an ordeal, where women may have to 'run the gauntlet' of their abuser's friends and supporters and hostile defence advocates

■ when assaults are prosecuted outcomes at court are not necessarily helpful – usually either a fine (which women often end up having to pay on behalf of their abusive partner), or a suspended sentence, whereupon the man goes home, free to harass again. Imprisonment is rare and often provides only temporary relief as confinement is short

■ effective action under the criminal law may be undermined by civil proceedings, which can force women to have contact with violent men via the children, and by an uncoordinated approach across the criminal and civil courts.

In fact, under the present system, for many abused women there may be few or no individual benefits in being a witness in terms of increased protection or safety. On the contrary, there is greater chance or increased danger of reprisals from a vengeful partner or ex-partner.

For this and other reasons, therefore, many women's support organisations hold ambivalent attitudes towards prosecution, and towards the predominant focus on this area by government until very recently (see written and oral evidence to the Home Affairs Select Committee Inquiry on Domestic Violence 1992). As part of their advocacy role, local refuge workers will inform a woman about all the options and support her in whatever she wants to do. They recognise, however, that prosecution may, in reality, be of limited use in promoting or ensuring the safety of the majority of women who come to them for advice or accommodation. Nevertheless, many believe that recourse to the criminal law, and the protection of the police and courts *could* be developed in order to provide more effective protection and redress than is the case at present.

Improving court procedures and outcomes

The Government has recently recognised the need to improve provision for vulnerable witnesses within criminal proceedings. It is currently carrying out a welcome review under the auspices of a Home Office Working Party, which is examining recommendations from statutory and voluntary bodies for improved protection and safety throughout the prosecution process.

Another major deterrent to effective prosecution in the UK has been the time it takes to get to court. In some groundbreaking US jurisdictions, for example, Duluth and San Diego, offenders are taken back to court within 24 hours and the case dealt with immediately. The case has to be prepared in the intervening period, and survivor and offender made aware of options and choices. At court, the judge offers the offender the choice of custody or attendance at a specific perpetrators' re-education programme (subject to suitability), and ancillary orders are made. The court will grant protection orders which may include both non-molestation and occupation orders. It will also grant interim child contact orders, which may either suspend a child's contact with the violent man for a limited period, subject to review, or order contact to be made through specialised child contact centres. These initiatives and improvements to the criminal justice response are further developed in Part Three on intervention and practice.

5.6 Summary

- Until very recently, the criminal justice system has paid little attention to the needs of women and children experiencing domestic violence. Many women have sought help from the police in an emergency (often unsuccessfully). For other women, calling the police is not the first option, and is often only a last resort after repeated attacks.

- Many abused women are ambivalent about calling the police, fearing they will not be believed or taken seriously. Black women, in particular, are less likely to call the police if they fear racism against themselves or their partner.

- The recognition of the need for changes in police responses to both domestic violence and rape led to the first Home Office Circular in 1986, followed in 1990 by *Circular 60/90*. Now, all 43 police forces have explicit policies on domestic violence, and many Domestic Violence Units (or Domestic Violence liaison officers in some areas) have been set up around the country.

- *Circular 60/90* reminded officers that the primary duty was to protect the victim and any children and then consider what action should be taken against the offender. Immediate protection could include referring or taking the woman to a refuge, as well as liaison with statutory and voluntary agencies for long term support.

- The *Protection from Harassment Act 1997* introduces new measures for protection under both the criminal and civil law, and also provides a new link between criminal and civil law. The provisions include two new criminal offences: the offence of *criminal harassment*, and a more serious *offence involving fear of violence*. If convicted of either of these offences, there is an additional measure for protection: a *restraining order* can also be granted by the court, prohibiting the offender from further similar conduct.

- The immediate arrest and removal of the abuser by police will often be helpful in providing many women and children with much needed 'breathing space' and time to consider what they should do. Proceeding with prosecution may not always be in their best interests. There are a number of practical and emotional difficulties, and prosecution does not

guarantee protection or safety in the long-term, as there may be increased danger of reprisals from a vengeful partner or ex-partner.

■ Effective action under the criminal law may also be undermined by civil proceedings which can force women to have contact with violent men via the children, and by an uncoordinated approach across the criminal and civil courts.

■ Recourse to the criminal law and the protection of the police and courts *could* be developed in order to provide more effective protection and redress than is the case at present. Examples from the US and elsewhere may herald new initiatives in the UK.

CHAPTER SIX: PROTECTION FROM VIOLENCE UNDER THE CIVIL LAW

6.1 Background to recent changes in legislation

Over the last 20 years, the need for better protection from domestic violence under the civil law has been highlighted through a number of reports and enquiries. Since 1976, injunctions could be obtained under three different statutes:

- the *Domestic Violence and Matrimonial Proceedings Act 1976*

- the *Domestic Proceedings and Magistrates' Courts Act 1978*

- the *Matrimonial Homes Act 1983*.

Courts also had powers to grant orders ancillary to other matters, such as, linked to divorce, or to an action for assault and trespass. In practice, which legislation was used depended on a number of factors: in particular, marital status, whether the woman lived with her abuser, whether the action was taken in the county or magistrates' court, and the preferences of local solicitors. Some orders had a power of arrest attached, and this made them somewhat more effective. However, research has shown that injunctions and protection orders were more often breached than not, and that enforcement was virtually impossible (Barron 1990; unpublished WAFE refuge surveys 1992 and 1994.)

Abused women face a number of problems within the legal process. For example, under the above legislation, gaining access to legal representation was often stressful and confusing. Lack of specialist services or interpreters meant that Black and ethnic minority women were denied effective access to the law (including those women whose immigration status made them ineligible for help with Legal Aid). The process of going to court was itself traumatic and frightening, partly due to the lack of separate waiting areas. Equally, Women's Aid research in the late 1980s highlighted the inadequacy of any legislation without effective implementation and training for court staff on the impact of domestic violence on women and children (Barron 1990). The courts, like many other agencies, have often failed to understand the whole range of emotional, psychological and practical reasons why many women stay with or return to a violent partner. This can, and still does, have the effect of the women not being taken seriously.

Growing awareness of these problems led to the recommendations made in the Law Commission's report *Domestic Violence and the Occupation of the Family Home* published in May 1992. The report took account of evidence from lawyers and lay advocates, including Barron's (1990) findings about the ineffectiveness of injunctions. The National Inter-agency Working Party Report in 1992, and evidence from a wide range of statutory and voluntary agencies to the 1992 Home Affairs Select Committee Inquiry into Domestic Violence, confirmed the inadequacy of protective remedies for abused women under the civil law. The reforms to civil remedies for protection from violence in the home, introduced by the *Family Law Act 1996* (sections 30–63) were, therefore, long overdue.

Despite the widespread recognition of the need for change, lack of real political interest meant that the Family Homes and Domestic Violence Bill was not introduced into Parliament until three years later. After nearly completing its passage, parliamentary and political pressures led to the original Bill being abandoned in 1995. Following pressure from women's organisations and others, it was re-introduced in a modified form in 1996 as Part IV (Family Homes and Domestic Violence) of the *Family Law Act 1996* (which also contained new proposals for the regulation of divorce).

6.2 New remedies under the Family Law Act 1996 Part IV

The *Family Law Act 1996* incorporates both the new divorce legislation and, in Part IV, the revised provisions of the Family Homes and Domestic Violence Bill. Part IV, in force since October 1997, rationalises and consolidates the previous mishmash of legislation governing injunctions and protection orders. It is a comprehensive piece of legislation, which is intended both to remove anomalies and to make civil protection against domestic violence more effective. The existing legislation in this area – the *Domestic Violence and Matrimonial Proceedings Act 1976* (DVMPA), the *Matrimonial Homes Act 1983*, and relevant parts of the *Domestic Proceedings and Magistrates Courts Act 1978* (DPMCA) – are all repealed and replaced by the new provisions.

Part IV of the *Family Law Act 1966* provides a single set of domestic violence remedies available in all family courts, including the High Court, County Court, and Family Proceedings (Magistrates) Court. It extends eligibility to a wider range of people in family or similar relationships, although it gives weaker rights to protection from violence to some cohabitants. There are two main types of orders under the Act:

■ *occupation orders*, which regulate the occupation of the family home; and

■ *non-molestation orders*, for protection from all forms of violence and abuse.

These orders are 'free-standing' injunctions, that is, they can be applied for directly, and do not have to be made ancillary to any other proceedings, such as divorce. Provisions for enforcement, through the attachment of powers of arrest, have been strengthened. There are also a number of related new provisions under the Act, one of which is directly related to the risk of harm to a child (see Chapter Four):

■ the court, when making an emergency protection order or interim care order for a child under the *Children Act 1989*, can exclude a person who poses a risk to the child;

■ the Act makes provision for the transfer of tenancies between spouses and cohabitants;

■ it allows a number of other connected provisions.

The related provisions for excluding suspected child abusers and for transfer of tenancies are discussed in the sections on the *Children Act 1989* (see Chapter Four) and the *Housing Act 1996* (see Chapter Seven) respectively.

6.3 Who can use this law?

Eligibility for orders under the *Family Law Act 1996* Part IV depends on the type of order, and the relationship between the applicant and the other party (the respondent). The Act considerably extends the categories of people who may seek protection. It introduces the new concept of *associated persons* – to apply for a *non-molestation order* or an *occupation order* the applicant must be 'associated' with the person against whom they wish to take out an order.

S.62(3) defines *associated persons* as people who:

- are or have been **married** to each other

- are or have been **cohabitants** (defined as a man and a woman, not married to each other but living together as husband and wife)

- have lived in **same household** (other than one of them being the other's tenant, lodger, boarder or employee). This does, therefore, include those in lesbian and gay relationships and those sharing a house

- are **relatives** (this is defined to include most immediate relatives)

- have **agreed to marry** (evidenced by a written agreement, the exchange of a ring, or a witnessed ceremony)

- in relation to a child (they are both **parents**, or have or have had **parental responsibility** for a child) (see Chapter Four for definition of parental responsibility)

- are **parties to the same family proceedings** (other than under Part IV, but excluding the local authority).

And where a child has been adopted, two people are associated if they are:

- natural parent/grandparent and adopted child

- natural parent/grandparent and adoptive parent.

One of the limitations of the definition of associated persons is that it does not include people in a close relationship who have *not* lived together, where there is *no child* for whom they both are either a parent or have had parental responsibility. In such cases, therefore, protection from violence or harassment will still need to be sought through common law actions 'in tort' – that is, as ancillary to other legal actions, for example, actions suing for assault, trespass, or under the injunction provisions of the *Protection from Harassment Act 1997* (see Chapter Five). This exclusion will, therefore, continue to leave many women vulnerable to violence, threats and harassment from men with whom they have never lived. Moreover, powers of arrest cannot be attached to these orders to assist enforcement (see Harwin 1997b).

Within the Act, an order may be sought to protect from molestation, or regulate occupation rights for the applicant and any 'relevant child'. A relevant child is defined under **s.62(2)** as :

- any child who might be expected to live with either of the parties involved;

- any child who is the subject of adoption or Children Act proceedings;

- any other child whose interests the court considers relevant.

This extends the scope of previous remedies that were available, which were previously limited to any 'children of the family'.

6.4 Non-molestation orders

Under **s.42**, non-molestation orders reproduce and extend the previous powers of the courts to make orders prohibiting a person (the respondent) from molesting another person associated with him or any relevant child. The term molestation is perhaps unfortunate as it tends to denote sexual molestation, and can be confusing to potential applicants or respondents. However, as under previous legislation, an order prohibiting molestation can include both general or particular acts of molestation, none of which need be overtly 'violent'. Thus, it can be used to order a person to stop using or threatening violence against (usually) a woman or relevant child, or to stop a person intimidating, harassing, or pestering them. It can also have very specific instructions in it to suit a particular case – for example, it could order an ex-partner to stop telephoning or pestering the applicant at work.

The court can make an order either if the applicant is an 'associated person', or, by its own motion, within any family proceedings to which the respondent is party, if the court considers it of benefit to any other party or relevant child. Children under 16 may apply for non-molestation orders with leave of the court [**s.43(1)**] if the court decides the child has sufficient understanding.

In deciding the outcome of any application, courts *must* have regard to the health, safety and well-being of the applicant or any relevant child. 'Health' is defined broadly in **s.63(1)** to include both physical and mental health.

An order may be made for a specified period (usually six months), for an open-ended period, or until a different order is made if further provisions are needed. However, if the court decides of its own volition that an order should be made in the course of other family proceedings (for example, under the *Children Act 1989*), then the order will cease to have effect if those proceedings are withdrawn or terminated.

6.5 Occupation orders

An occupation order regulates the parties' occupation of their present, former, or intended home and replaces all previous legislation (see above) and terminology. Previously, similar orders were known as ouster orders, and exclusion orders.

An occupation order may take a number of forms, including:

(a) enforcing the applicant's right to remain in the house;

(b) requiring the other party (respondent) to allow the applicant to enter and occupy the home;

(c) prohibiting, suspending, or restricting the respondent's right to occupy the house;

(d) excluding the respondent from the house itself and/or from a defined area in which the house is situated.

These orders do not, however, alter either party's financial interests in the home.

Occupation orders may be granted under five different sections of the Act, depending on the nature of the relationship between the parties, and whether the applicant has an existing right to occupy the home. The parties must first be *associated* (see 6.2 above).

The Act introduces a new concept of *entitlement*:

■ An *entitled* person is someone who has some legal right to occupy the property, for example, s/he is the freehold owner, tenant, contractual licensee or someone with a beneficial interest; or s/he has matrimonial home rights. The term 'matrimonial home rights' in the new legislation replaces the term 'rights of occupation' contained in the *Matrimonial Homes Act 1983*. Spouses of entitled persons automatically have matrimonial home rights under the Act. These rights are also sometimes obtained through the divorce process.

■ A *non-entitled person* has neither the legal right to occupy the property, nor matrimonial home rights.

The main differences between the five different categories of order are:

■ the range of people who can apply;

■ the criteria the court must use in assessing whether to grant an order;

■ the length of time the orders may last.

An application may be made:

(a) Under **s.33**, by a person who is *entitled* to occupy the home because she is either a legal owner or tenant, or has matrimonial home rights in · relation to it *against* another person with whom she is *associated*, whether or not that person is also entitled to occupy the home. This provision will apply to most married couples and cohabitants, and to others who are sole or joint owners, or tenants of their home. An order can be made for a specified period, or until further order.

(b) Under **s.35**, by a former spouse who is *not entitled* to occupy the home or who has matrimonial home rights in relation to it *against* his or her former spouse who is so *entitled*. An order under this section can only be made for an initial period of six months, but can be extended for periods of up to six months on one or more occasions.

(c) Under **s.36**, *by* a (heterosexual) cohabitant or former cohabitant who is *not entitled* to occupy the home *against* the other cohabitant or former cohabitant who is so *entitled*. An order under this section can be made for six months, and can be extended for one further period of up to six months.

In the case of non-entitled former cohabitants, this is an extension of the previous law, as previously exclusion of a former partner was not possible. However, restriction to a maximum of one year discriminates against those women who have cohabited for several years with a partner, and may well have made a substantial personal and economic contribution to the family home (see Harwin 1997b). The definition of cohabitants as heterosexual will also leave lesbians and gay men unable to apply for occupation orders for protection from violence if they live with violent partners but have no legal right to occupy the home.

(d) Under **s.37**, *by* one spouse or former spouse *against* the other spouse of former spouse where *neither of them is entitled* to occupy the home. This situation could include a couple lodging in a relative's or friend's house, or squatting. An order can be made for up to six months, and extended on one or more occasions, for further periods of up to six months.

(e) Under **s.38**, *by* one (heterosexual) cohabitant or former cohabitant *against* the other cohabitant or former cohabitant, where *neither of them is entitled* to occupy the home. An order can be made for up to six months, but can be extended for a further period of six months.

6.6 Grounds for making an occupation order

Sections 33, 35, 36, 37, 38 each contain details of the matters which the court should consider in deciding whether to make an occupation order. The criteria differ somewhat between the sections but in general courts must have regard to all the circumstances of the case including:

■ the respective housing needs and resources

■ the respective financial resources

■ the likely effect of the order on the health and safety, and well-being of the parties or any relevant child

■ the conduct of the parties in relation to each other and otherwise.

Where the application is under **s.35** (non-entitled former spouse), the court must also take account of the length of time since the parties ceased to live together, and since the marriage ended, and whether there are other proceedings taking place.

In an application under **s.36** (non-entitled cohabitant) the court should also consider

■ the length of the cohabitation

■ the length of time since separation

■ whether or not there are any children

■ the existence of any pending proceedings.

In addition, the court is to have regard to the nature of the relationship including the fact that they have not 'given each other the commitment involved in marriage'. This latter criterion was inserted as a result of pressure from government back-benchers during the passage of the Act.

Balance of Harm Test

Additionally, the Act introduces the 'balance of harm' test, which in some cases will oblige the court to make an order. In applications by spouses, former spouses, and applicants entitled under **s.33**, it is mandatory for the court to apply the test, the results of which override other criteria.

> If it appears to the court that the applicant or any relevant child is likely to suffer significant harm attributable to conduct of the respondent if an order... is not made, the court *shall make the order* unless it appears to it that:

a) the respondent or any relevant child is likely to suffer significant harm... if the order is made; and

b) the harm likely to be suffered by the respondent or child in that event is as great as, or greater than, the harm attributable to conduct of the respondent which is likely to be suffered by the applicant or child if the order is not made.' [s 33 (7)]

'Harm' is defined under **s.63** as 'impairment of health' (including both physical and mental health) or 'ill treatment'. In relation to a child, 'harm' means ill-treatment or the impairment of health or development.

In applications by cohabitants or former cohabitants under **sections 36** and **38**, the court is required to have regard for the balance of harm test but it does not override other criteria. The implications for implementation of the balance of harm test are further discussed below.

6.7 Further provisions

Ancillary orders

The court can also make ancillary orders to occupation orders, imposing obligations on either party in relation to repairs and maintenance, discharge of rent or mortgage, or other payments, as well as use or care of possessions or furniture. These must be made, however, with regard to the financial needs and resources, or the financial obligations, of the parties.

Ex parte (emergency) orders

A court may make ex parte non-molestation or occupation orders (without the normal period of notice to the respondent of the proceedings), if it considers it just and convenient to do so. The court must have regard to all the circumstances including whether

- there is 'a risk of significant harm' to the applicant or child

- the applicant is likely to be 'deterred or prevented' from making any application, if the order is not made immediately

- the respondent is evading service of notice of an inter-partes hearing

In all cases, a full hearing should follow as swiftly as possible to enable the respondent to have the opportunity to make representation.

Undertakings

An undertaking is a promise made to the court to refrain from certain behaviour, and in the past has been used by the courts as an alternative to granting an order. An amendment was added at the Report stage of the Bill in the Lords to make specific reference to the fact that undertakings could be accepted instead of granting an order. These are likely to be less easy to enforce in practice, as no power of arrest can be attached, although the respondent can be committed for breach. Research has shown how unsatisfactory such promises may be in affording protection from violence (Barron 1990). However, under **s.17** the court cannot accept an undertaking if a power of arrest would (normally) be attached, that is, where (physical) violence has been used or threatened. This may, therefore, be less problematic in the future than it has been in the past.

Powers of arrest

These *shall* be attached to one or more provisions of a non-molestation or occupation order, where the respondent has used or threatened (physical) violence against an applicant or any relevant child, unless the applicant or child is adequately protected without a power of arrest. This duty does not apply to ex *parte* orders but the court *may* still attach a power of arrest where

(a) violence is used or threatened; and

(b) there is a risk of significant harm, if a power of arrest is not attached immediately.

New provisions and amendments to other legislation

The Act makes a number of other new provisions, including changes to police powers in relation to breaches and enforcement of orders, and other provision with direct reference to the protection of children:

■ An important amendment to the *Children Act 1989* under **s.52**, and **Schedule 6** enables the court, when making an emergency protection or interim care order, to make an order to exclude the suspected abuser from the house, removing him instead of the child. This was discussed earlier in Chapter Four.

■ Within the general provisions of the *Family Law Act 1996*, children under 16 may also apply for orders if given leave of court to do so, for which the court must judge that they have sufficient understanding.

■ The Act brings in new powers under **s.53**, and **Schedule 7** to transfer joint tenancies into one party's name (see also Chapter Seven). This remedy was not previously available for (heterosexual) cohabitants. This may enable abused women, who are afraid to stay in their former home area, to exchange their existing tenancy for one in another area. This may result in women and children having to spend less time in refuges or other temporary accommodation. However, these powers do not apply in the magistrates' court.

6.8 How much will Part IV of the Family Law Act help abused women and children?

The strengths of Part IV are that it will enable a much larger group of applicants who have been abused, threatened or assaulted by someone with whom they are living or have (or have had) a family-type relationship, to gain access to a uniform package of protective remedies in both magistrates and county courts. The legislation is also now more accessible for users, as well as advisers and legal professionals. Unfortunately, as noted above, there are still loopholes in eligibility, as the legislation does not extend to those who have never lived with their abusers, except where there has been a formal promise of future marriage, or if there is a child for whom both are parents or have parental responsibility. While other injunctive remedies are available under common law for women who are in this situation (as well as a new civil remedy against harassment introduced within the *Protection from Harassment Act 1997* alongside the new criminal offences – see earlier), these orders are not likely to be as effective, as powers of arrest cannot be attached. Similarly,

a homosexual partner can only apply for occupation orders if s/he has existing rights to occupy the home (that is, is a tenant or owner).

Nevertheless, Part IV is a significant improvement in many respects. For instance, powers of arrest will be attached as a matter of course to all orders made 'on notice', whenever physical violence has been used or threatened, except where clear argument can be made as to why this is unnecessary. This should make more of these orders readily enforceable, as those with powers of arrest are lodged at police stations. Many advocates still feel, however, that the new law does not go far enough, and that powers of arrest should also be mandatory in ex parte applications where violence has been used or threatened. Monitoring is needed to see if powers of arrest will be attached with more regularity than heretofore.

Some potentially retrogressive amendments were also introduced during the passage of the Act, the impact of which will not be clear until tested under case law. In particular, in relation to occupation orders, the conduct of the parties (that is, past behaviour) was re-introduced as a criterion. In relation to cases of domestic violence, this means that conduct not related to matters of safety and protection from violence may be a factor when considering whether or not to make an order. Research since 1978 has consistently confirmed how violent men frequently cite the conduct of the non-violent partner (in relation to domestic services, mothering, or sexual fidelity) as 'provoking' or 'causing' the abuse (Barron 1990). Such justifications have also been accepted by courts as reasons not to grant occupation orders, or in more extreme cases within criminal law, as defences for killing wives or ex-wives on grounds of 'provocation'.

On the other hand, consideration of conduct (that is, violent or abusive behaviour) could be helpful in certain contexts. There has always been concern that, in cases where women who are at risk of violence from their partners or ex-partners apply for orders after many years of abuse, the effects of that abuse on their mental or physical well-being may be used against them. For instance, the respondent might argue that his partner is mentally unstable and unfit to have care of children, which is itself often a determining factor in who is permitted to occupy the property. In such cases, the removal of all considerations of past behaviour could lead to a 'snapshot' picture at the time of application, without sufficient consideration of its causes, of harm in the past, and the potential for harm in the future. In practice, whether consideration of conduct proves to be positive or negative for abused women, will be related to the applicant's access to effective legal representation.

The 'balance of harm' test (to be used when assessing the need for occupation orders) is intended to be more effective in not only addressing physical violence and abuse, but also mental and emotional cruelty. In principle, it removes the concept of hardship present in previous legislation, which in practice, frequently led to the failure of ouster applications because 'hardship' to the respondent (the abuser) was given greater weight than the need for protection from violence. The balance of harm test also gives greater attention to the needs of children. It was the intention of the Law Commission to remove any considerations of behaviour, in line with the trend of reducing the need for recrimination in matrimonial law, and instead to

focus on the question of 'harm'. However, during its passage through Parliament, a number of worrying changes were made which dilute the 'balance of harm' notion.

A second reference to conduct has been introduced into the 'balance of harm test' itself. Any 'significant harm' suffered by the applicant and any relevant child has to be 'attributable to the conduct of the respondent', whereas this is weighted against (any) harm likely to be suffered by the respondent or any relevant child. The effect of this appears to change 'the balance of harm test' to favour the respondent (violent partner), as all forms of potential harm (defined as impairment of health or ill-treatment) may be considered on his part, whereas only harm attributable to his behaviour may be considered in relation to the applicant. It has been pointed out that the fairness of the balance of harm test is now open to question, as this amendment could give unfair weight to an abuser's rights to occupation of the home over a survivor/victim's rights to protection from violence through a temporary order (Harwin 1997b). However, interpretation of this test remains to be challenged in court practice or by case law, both of which could consider the widest definition of harm suffered by the applicant attributable to the respondent's conduct. For example, if a woman is forced to leave her home, the harm she suffers as a result of becoming homeless could be considered to be due to the respondent's conduct.

Legal Aid

Those women who wish to obtain remedies under this Act may find that they are unable to do so because of the increasing difficulty in getting Legal Aid. Recently, there has been increasing concern about the difficulties of accessing Legal Aid to pursue applications for injunctions. This follows the introduction of revised criteria in 1997 for applications for injunctive protection – these include the requirement that a warning letter should have already been sent to the home, a measure that women might refuse for safety reasons. The new criteria also appear to be partly connected to an assumption that civil protection is only required if criminal law measures are not in place. However, in some cases, lay advocates have reported that Legal Aid was refused both in cases where the police had been called and in cases where they were not involved, often by the same regional Legal Aid Board (Harwin 1997b).

New opportunities

Finally, Part IV may allow new opportunities for a more holistic response to domestic violence, through the more effective linking of action under the criminal law and protection for the future under the civil law. **Section 60** offers the opportunity to pilot new powers by third parties to take out injunctions on behalf of abused women; for example, for police to take out orders on behalf of women at the same time as going before magistrates for criminal proceedings. Such measures have been used very successfully in Australia and the United States (with the woman's consent), and carry a number of advantages, including, their speed, and the removal of problems associated with legal aid (see Humphreys, Kaye and Harwin 1997; Humphreys and Kaye 1997).

6.9 Summary

- Over the last 20 years, the need for better protection from domestic violence under the civil law has been highlighted through a number of reports and enquiries. Research has shown that injunctions and protection orders were often breached, and that enforcement was virtually impossible.

- Abused women face a number of problems within the legal process, including access to legal representation, lack of specialist services or interpreters for Black and ethnic minority women, the trauma of the court process, the lack of training for court staff on the impact of domestic violence on women and children, and lack of awareness as to the reasons why many women stay with or return to a violent partner.

- A review of the law by the Law Commission led to recommendations for change, supported by many statutory and voluntary bodies, and eventually the introduction of the *Family Law Act 1996*, Part IV, in October 1997.

- Part IV of the *Family Law Act 1996* provides a single set of remedies available in all family courts including the High Court, County Court, and Family Proceedings (Magistrates') Court. There are two main types of orders under the Act: *occupation orders*, which regulate the occupation of the family home, and *non-molestation orders*, to provide protection from all forms of violence and abuse.

- Eligibility for orders under the *Family Law Act 1996* Part IV depends on the type of order, and the relationship between the applicant and the other party (the respondent). The Act considerably extends the categories of people who may seek protection. It introduces the new concept of *associated persons*.

- Non-molestation orders reproduce and extend the previous powers of the courts to make orders prohibiting a person (the respondent) from molesting another person associated with him, or any relevant child.

- An occupation order regulates the parties' occupation of their present, former or intended home, and replaces all previous legislation. An occupation order may take a number of forms, including, for example, enforcing the applicant's right to remain in the house or restricting the respondent's right to occupy the house. Occupation orders may be granted under five different sections of the Act, depending on the nature of the relationship between the parties, and whether the applicant has an existing right to occupy the home.

- The court must consider a number of different criteria in deciding whether to make an occupation order, including the respective housing needs and resources, the respective financial resources, the likely effect of the order on the health, safety and well-being of the parties or any relevant child and the conduct of the parties in relation to each other and otherwise.

- The Act introduces the 'balance of harm' test, which in some cases will oblige the court to make an order. In applications by those entitled by legal right to occupy the home, it is mandatory for the court to apply the test, the results of which override other criteria.

■ The court can also make ancillary orders to occupation orders, imposing obligations on either party with regard to repairs and maintenance, discharge of rent or mortgage, or other payments, as well as use or care of possessions or furniture.

■ A court may make ex parte non-molestation or occupation orders (without the normal period of notice to the respondent of the proceedings), if it considers it just and convenient to do so.

■ A court may accept an undertaking unless a power of arrest would (normally) be attached, that is, where (physical) violence has been used or threatened.

■ Powers of arrest must be attached to one or more provisions of a non-molestation or occupation order where the respondent has used or threatened (physical) violence against an applicant or any relevant child, unless the applicant or child is adequately protected without a power of arrest.

■ The Act makes a number of other new provisions. There is a specific amendment to the *Children Act 1989* which enables the court, when making an emergency protection or interim care order, to make an order to exclude the suspected abuser from the house. There is also provision for children under 16 to apply for orders if given leave of the court to do so, and new powers to transfer joint tenancies into one party's name, a remedy not previously available for (heterosexual) cohabitants.

■ Part IV will enable a much larger group of applicants who have been abused, threatened or assaulted by a person with whom they are living or have (or have had) a family-type relationship to gain access to a uniform package of protective remedies in both magistrates and county courts. Measures for enforcement have also been strengthened. The legislation is also now more accessible for users, as well as advisers and legal professionals.

■ Part IV has loopholes in eligibility in that the legislation does not extend to those who have never lived with their abusers, except where there has been a formal promise of future marriage, or if there is a child for whom both are parents or have parental responsibility. Homosexual partners can only apply for occupation orders if s/he has existing rights to occupy the home (that is, is a tenant or owner).

■ The impact of certain amendments to the new law will not be clear until tested under case law. The re-introduction of the conduct of the parties as a criterion may mean conduct not related to matters of safety and protection from violence may be a factor when considering whether or not to make an order. The fairness of the 'balance of harm test' will also depend on interpretation.

■ Improved legal protection from violence may depend crucially both on access to Legal Aid and on its effective enforcement by the police and the courts.

Advantages and disadvantages of using civil and/or criminal law for abused women

Criminal Law	Criminal Law
Advantages	*Disadvantages*
■ State takes action: not left to women	■ Woman is 'passive' witness – the situation is out of her control
■ Woman can feel that the violence is taken more seriously	■ Proceedings are held in open court
■ Abuser can be arrested immediately and easily and he can be held in custody for short periods	■ Intended to punish the man, not protect the woman
■ Abuser can be punished/removed from circulation for a certain period	■ The prosecution process can take a very long time
■ There is a clear indication of who is at fault	■ Woman might not want the man prosecuted for a number of reasons (see above)
■ Bail conditions can be more powerful than an injunction (but have limited duration)	■ Court personnel attitudes: lack of understanding of nature and dynamics of domestic violence
■ Proceedings have a symbolic value – domestic violence is not acceptable	■ There is a risk of increasing the threat and danger to the woman and any children
■ No problems with costs, or access to legal aid	■ Cannot deal with many 'non-physical' aspects of domestic violence

Civil Law	Civil Law
Advantages	*Disadvantages*
■ Woman makes choice of what protection is sought	■ Costs and/or limited access to legal aid
■ Can deal with a wide range of harmful behaviours	■ Some women are not eligible or do not have the same rights to protection
■ Court hearing is in closed court	■ Court personnel attitudes: lack of understanding of nature and dynamics of domestic violence
■ Legal Aid may be available	■ Pressure on court time and other factors means women often pressed to accept undertakings instead
■ Woman can get immediate protection (in theory)	■ Reluctance to grant *ex-parte* occupation orders and *ex-parte* powers of arrest
■ It is intended to protect the woman and her children and not punish the man	■ Penalties are non-custodial unless there is a severe and recurrent breach
■ Can offer protection for the future and a route to safe housing	■ There is a risk of increasing the threat and danger to the woman and any children

CHAPTER SEVEN: PROTECTION UNDER HOUSING LAW

As discussed in Chapters Six and Seven, the options for protection available under the civil and criminal law have a number of limitations to their effectiveness. Therefore, it is likely that many women will continue to rely on provision under homeless legislation for safe housing, and longer term protection from violence for themselves and their children. However, housing provision and resources have been greatly reduced in many areas of the country in the last decade. The *Housing Act 1996*, while widening the definition of those eligible for emergency and temporary accommodation, has set new limitations on local authorities' duties to help secure longer term safe accommodation for women and children who are homeless through domestic violence.

7.1 The provisions of the 1996 Housing Act

The *Housing Act 1996* became law in January 1997 and has made a number of major changes to public and private rented accommodation. The legislation is split into eight parts, each dealing with different areas of housing policy. Parts VI and VII of the Act affect decisions about who is housed in the social rented sector, and are of particular relevance for women and children experiencing abuse.

The legislation has removed any automatic link that existed between being homeless under the law, and being given permanent housing. Under previous legislation, people who were unintentionally homeless, and in priority need, were offered permanent accommodation. Now Part VII gives local authorities a *temporary*, but *renewable* two year duty to house certain applicants. The duty to provide permanent accommodation has been removed. To obtain permanent accommodation, the applicant must apply through the council's waiting list (housing register) under Part VI of the Act.

Local authority duty to provide temporary housing

Temporary housing is provided in three stages:

1. *Interim accommodation*

   If the local authority believes an applicant:

   ■ may be homeless or is threatened with homelessness; and

   ■ is eligible for assistance; and

   ■ is in priority need

the local authority must secure interim accommodation, for example, in a refuge or hostel, while it investigates whether it has a duty to provide accommodation.

   ■ The interim duty to accommodate arises whether or not there is a possibility of referring the application to another local authority.

   ■ The interim duty ceases when the local authority conveys its decision to the applicant.

   ■ If the applicant seeks a review of the decision, the local authority has a *power* but not a *duty* to continue the interim accommodation pending the review.

If the local authority's decision is in the applicant's favour, the interim duty is likely to be superseded by a temporary, two year duty.

2. *Temporary accommodation*

The local authority has a duty to ensure the provision of temporary accommodation for a period of *two years* to people who are:

- homeless or threatened with homelessness;

- eligible for assistance;

- in priority need;

- not intentionally homeless;

- unable to access other 'suitable accommodation';

- and who have a local connection with the area.

The duty ends before the two years are up if the person housed under this section:

i) having been informed of the consequences unreasonably refuses an offer of housing under Part VI, or of other suitable accommodation;

ii) ceases to be eligible for assistance;

iii) ceases to use as his or her only or principal home the accommodation provided under this section; or

iv) accepts an offer of housing under Part VI.

3. *Extended accommodation*

At the end of this period the local authority can continue to, but is not obliged to, secure accommodation for the person. It can only extend the accommodation if it has reviewed the circumstances, which means checking that they are still in priority need and that no other suitable accommodation is available.

7.2 Homelessness and threatened homelessness (Part VII)

- A person is homeless if s/he has no accommodation available for occupation in the UK or elsewhere.

- A person is threatened with homelessness if this situation is likely to arise within 28 days.

- Accommodation is available for a person's occupation if s/he has a legal right to it, such as freehold or leasehold ownership, a tenancy including a statutory tenancy, or an express or implied licence, and only if it is suitable for that person together with anyone who normally resides, or might reasonably be expected to reside, with her or him as a family member. It is not available if the person cannot secure entry to it, or if it is a movable home (and there is nowhere to place it and live in it legally), or if it *would not be reasonable* for her/him to continue to occupy it.

- Accommodation would not be reasonable to continue to occupy if the applicant's continued occupation of it *would be likely to lead to domestic*

violence directed against the applicant or someone who lives, or might reasonably be expected to live, with the applicant. Domestic violence means actual or threatened violence by someone *associated* with the victim, such as a current or former partner, or another family member.

The Act has broadened the definition of homelessness for women experiencing domestic violence. Part III of the *Housing Act 1985* only accepted violence or threats of violence from people *living in the home.* In the *Housing Act 1996,* domestic violence is defined as violence or threats of violence from a person who is *associated with the person under threat.* An *associated person* is defined in the Code of Guidance to the Act (and the definition is the same as under Part IV of the *Family Law Act 1996* – see Chapter Six), and, therefore, also includes people who are or have been married, engaged or living together in the same household; relatives; or people who are parents of a child under 18 or have shared parental responsibility for such a child.

Priority need for accommodation

Homeless people are in 'priority need' if they are in one of the following circumstances:

1. A pregnant woman or a person with whom she resides or might reasonably be expected to reside.

2. A person with whom dependent children reside or might reasonably be expected to reside.

3. A person who is vulnerable as a result of old age, mental illness, or handicap or physical disability, or other special reason, or with whom such a person resides, or might reasonably be expected to reside.

4. A person who is homeless or threatened with homelessness as a result of an emergency such as flood, fire, or other disaster.

The above categories are taken almost verbatim from the preceding legislation (Section 59 of the *Housing Act 1985*).

The local authority's only duty to those who are not in priority need is to provide advice, and such assistance as it thinks reasonable.

Intentional homelessness

Once the local authority has established that the applicant is homeless, and in priority need, it must then decide if s/he is homeless intentionally. 'A person becomes homeless intentionally if she/he deliberately does or fails to do anything in consequence of which she/he ceases to occupy accommodation which is available for his/her accommodation and which it would have been reasonable for him/her to continue to occupy'.

In making their decision, the local authority is likely to consider the following:

- whether the loss of 'suitable' accommodation happened because of the applicant's deliberate act, or failure to act;

- was it reasonable for the person to have continued to occupy the accommodation;

- was the person aware of all the facts;

- has the person colluded to bring the accommodation to an end (this could apply to an applicant who has been asked to leave by a friend or relative or by a landlord);

- has the person been given advice and assistance in order to get accommodation, but failed to secure it.

Where an authority is satisfied that other suitable accommodation is available in their district for occupation by the applicant, but s/he unreasonably fails to secure such accommodation, s/he shall be treated as having become intentionally homeless. However, the Code of Guidance (see below) states that such a finding on this ground would not be justified unless the authority was satisfied that alternative ·accommodation was both suitable for, and available to, the applicant (particularly with regard to affordability), and there was no good reason why s/he did not obtain it.

A local authority must give advice and assistance to those who are found to be intentionally homeless and must ensure that they have accommodation for 28 days while they find somewhere else to live.

Local connection

Local connection is established by current or previous voluntary residence, current employment, family association, or other special circumstance. If no one in the applicant's household has any connection with the local authority to which the application was made, the authority may refer the household to another local authority, with which at least one member of the household has a connection, *provided that no one in the household runs a risk of domestic violence in the other area.* An applicant can ask for a review if s/he objects to the referral. S/he must be given accommodation by the first authority pending the outcome of the review.

7.3 *The provision of temporary accommodation*

A local authority can satisfy a duty under Part VII to secure accommodation by:

- providing the accommodation itself;

- obtaining an offer of accommodation from some other body, such as a Registered Social Landlord (any organisation which is allowed to receive transfers of local authority housing and to administer it, for example, housing associations, building societies or non-profit making private companies); or

- providing the applicant with sufficient advice and assistance to enable her/him to obtain accommodation.

Irrespective of how many applications a person may make for assistance under Part VII, the authority may not provide her or him with housing in its own stock for more than two years out of any three, except in a hostel or in housing that the local authority has leased specifically for temporary accommodation. This prohibition of the use of local authorities' permanent self contained housing for more than two years out of any three makes it less likely that stock intended for permanent lets will be used for temporary accommodation under Part VII.

It is, therefore, likely that women and children experiencing domestic violence, who are re-housed by a local authority under the homeless legislation, may be placed in the worst housing on run down estates. It is advisable for homeless families seeking re-housing because of domestic violence to apply, through Part VI of the Housing Act, to be put on the housing register to access permanent accommodation either through nomination to a housing association, or from a local authority's housing stock.

Other 'suitable' temporary accommodation

A local authority can fulfil its duties to homeless applicants by temporarily housing them in its own accommodation or by giving advice and assistance to help applicants secure access to private rented accommodation, if it is satisfied that suitable accommodation is available in its area.

The local authority may assist an applicant to secure the accommodation with rent guarantees, or help with deposits whilst providing interim housing. 'Suitable' accommodation must be available for at least a two year period, and preferably longer, to avoid recurring homelessness. It must be adequate to accommodate the needs of the family, and should take into account medical or social needs. People on low incomes are not expected to take on a rent above the housing benefit level. The local authority must take into account the characteristics and circumstances of the applicant and the state of the local housing market. For example, a woman and children who are escaping domestic violence may not be in a position to take on private accommodation.

Review of local authority decisions

Within 21 days of being notified of the decision (or longer if the local authority agrees) the applicant can request a review of any decision by a local authority concerning:

■ whether s/he is eligible for assistance under Part VII

■ whether a duty is owed, and if so which duty

■ whether the case should be referred to another authority.

If requested under section 202 the authority must review its decision and notify the applicant of the result, giving reasons if it is not in the applicant's favour. Notification must be in writing, must inform the applicant of the right to appeal under section 204, and must be sent to the applicant, or left for a reasonable time for collection at the authority's office.

If the applicant is dissatisfied with the outcome of a review, or has not been notified of the result within time limits, s/he has 21 days to appeal to the county court on a point of law. The court may uphold, vary, or quash the local authority's decision.

Protection of property

Where a local authority is under a duty to an applicant under the legislation, it must (if the applicant is unable to do so) take such reasonable steps as it considers necessary to prevent any loss of or damage to property belonging to the applicant's household. The local authority may make a reasonable charge, and failure to pay such a charge may lead to its disposal.

This means that the local authority must store the property of women and children who leave their homes because of violence, either within their own storage facility, or elsewhere. There is a small charge made for this which can be claimed by the woman from the Benefits Agency. The family pet can be defined as property, and can therefore be 'kennelled'. This has been successfully achieved by some groups on behalf of women and children in their refuges.

7.4 Help with permanent housing

Part VI of the Act determines who will get access to permanent accommodation in the social rented sector. It requires local authorities to decide who does and who does not qualify for re-housing. People who must qualify are unintentionally homeless people in priority need. Asylum seekers and people from abroad who are subject to immigration control will not qualify.

Only those who *qualify* can be included on the housing register, and only those on the register can receive an offer of re-housing. The local authority must have an allocations scheme for deciding who gets priority when it allocates its own tenancies and its nominations to Registered Social Landlords. The scheme must give 'reasonable preference' to the following groups:

1. people occupying insanitary or overcrowded housing or otherwise living in unsatisfactory housing conditions

2. people occupying housing accommodation which is temporary or occupied on insecure terms

3. families with dependant children

4. households consisting of or including someone who is expecting a child

5. households consisting of, or including someone, with a particular need for settled accommodation on medical or welfare grounds

6. households whose social or economic circumstances are such that they have difficulty in securing settled accommodation

7. people who are unintentionally homeless (or threatened with homelessness) and in priority need.

Allocation schemes will differ between authorities, but each must be accompanied by a policy explaining how the allocation scheme works. Local authorities are being encouraged to give priority to married couples with children, and to vulnerable individuals who are living in unsuitable housing. A copy of the scheme must be available for public scrutiny. People on the register are entitled to information about their place on the register, so that they can work out how long it will take for them to be re-housed.

The Act encourages local authorities to:

■ provide translations of forms for applicants whose first language is not English;

■ provide audio tapes or Braille copies for people with a visual impairment;

■ provide help with filling in the application form where required;

■ adopt an equal opportunities policy relating to all aspects of the allocation process.

The Act requires that people are removed from the housing register if they:

■ are no longer a qualifying person

■ have become homeless intentionally.

7.5 Implementing the Housing Act 1996: the Code of Guidance

The Code of Guidance suggests how local authorities should implement the Housing Act 1996. It does not have force of law, but local authorities should have regard to it in exercising their functions relating to homelessness and the prevention of homelessness. It makes a number of specific references to the needs of women and children experiencing domestic violence. In relation to domestic violence, under the heading 'Domestic Disputes', the Code of Guidance has this to say:

> In some cases, threatened homelessness will arise because of a domestic dispute. Housing authorities should be ready to take action where household members are at risk from violence or abuse. Where young people under 18 are involved because of a breakdown in the relationship with their parents, or where there is a risk of abuse, the housing authority should alert the social services authority to the case. In other cases, depending on the severity of the dispute, the housing authority may still wish to ask the social services authority for help. In this respect housing authorities should be aware of the duties of social services and certain other specified authorities under S20 and S 27 of the *Children Act 1989.* An approach to the social services authority might be directed at relieving tension within the household to enable members to continue to live together. Social services may be able to offer counselling and support or to advise on other local services and agencies which might provide specialist help. [s.9.39]

> In assessing homelessness, authorities should also consider whether it is reasonable for a person to continue to occupy accommodation if s/he (or a person who normally resides with him/her) will thereby be subject to domestic violence, or the threats of violence (S177). This may also impact on the authority's assessment of whether a person's homelessness or threatened homelessness is intentional. [s9.40]

Making enquiries

During the period when the local authority is providing interim accommodation, for example, within its own Homeless Persons Unit or by referral to a Women's Aid refuge, the local authority carries out enquiries to establish whether a woman fleeing violence is eligible for assistance. The Code of Guidance states that the authority may make enquiries to discover:

■ whether the applicant is eligible for assistance;

■ if any duty is owed to the applicant and, if so, what duty [**s.184 (1)**];

■ whether a local connection exists with the area of another authority in England Wales or Scotland (**s.184**). (See above, on local connection.)

The Code of Guidance also states:

- The obligation to make enquires rests with the authority. It is not for the applicant to prove her case.

- Authorities will wish to ensure that their enquiries are always undertaken quickly, sympathetically and, as far as possible, in confidence.

- The authority may request another relevant body to assist in discharging the enquiry duty under **s.213** (co-operation between relevant housing authorities and bodies). If they do, the other body will be under a duty to co-operate in rendering such assistance in the discharge of the function to which the request relates, as is reasonable in the circumstances.

- Enquires should not be over-elaborate or over-long.

- Women fleeing violence (because they are often under stress) can be accompanied during interviews.

- Authorities should ensure access to competent interpreters for community languages of the area, and have access to intermediaries for people with hearing or speech disabilities.

- In cases of domestic violence, wherever possible an officer of the same sex as the applicant should conduct the interview.

- If the applicant reports violence or threats of violence, the authority should not normally seek proof directly from the alleged perpetrator, since doing so may delay the assessment and may generate further violence.

Injunctions

The Code informs local authorities that they 'may inform applicants of the option to take out an injunction, but should make it clear that there is no obligation to do so if she feels it would be ineffective'.

Referrals to another area

An authority cannot seek to refer to another authority if by doing so any member of the applicant's household would be at risk of domestic violence from a person with whom she is associated, or is at risk of threats of violence which are likely to be carried out.

Women's refuges

Authorities are recommended to develop close links with local women's refuges. They should not delay securing suitable accommodation elsewhere, in the hope that she might return to her partner. The Code stresses that places in refuges must be available to others in need (that is, that they do not silt up because of lack of move on). If a refuge terminates a licence to occupy because the household no longer needs to be in the refuge, the authority has a duty to secure alternative accommodation straight away.

Vulnerability as a result of violence or abuse or sexual and/or racial harassment

The Code states that local authorities should consider whether *women without children* are *vulnerable*, as a result of having suffered violence from

persons with whom they are associated, or whether they are at risk of further violence or abuse if they return to those persons. They should also consider whether those who have suffered or are under threat of harassment or violence on account of their gender, race, colour, ethnic or national origin, or religion are *vulnerable and therefore in priority need as a result.*

7.6 Transfers and exchanges

The *Housing Act 1985* gave local authority tenants the right to apply to live in another *empty* property belonging to the local authority within the same area. Applications are considered on the basis of need and priority. To get on the priority list either medical or other evidence is usually required. Individual authorities have different ways of interpreting need, and each will have a policy outlining how they prioritise people for transfer.

For women with joint tenancies, however, until the introduction of Part IV of the *Family Law Act 1996*, transfers could only be completed on divorce, as the tenancy has to be in the woman's name only. It is now possible to apply under Part IV for the tenancy to be transferred to the woman's sole name, and this then can, if she wishes, enable her to use her existing tenancy to access alternative safe accommodation either through a transfer or through an exchange (see below). It is also possible to arrange reciprocal transfers between local authorities, that is, where two authorities each agree to house a woman from the other area in one of their empty properties.

Transferring from a joint to single tenancy

County courts have the power to transfer certain tenancies from one party to another under the new *Family Law Act 1996* Part IV legislation. This is contained in **s.53**, which provides that **Schedule 7** to the Act shall have effect. Previously, this power had only existed in respect of spouses and former spouses, but the new Act has extended the provision to cohabitants and former cohabitants.

Tenancies which can be transferred are:

- protected or statutory tenancies;

- secure tenancies;

- assured tenancies.

Assured shorthold tenancies (duration six months only) are not included.

Spouses or former spouses can apply for a transfer of tenancy order under Schedule 7 if they are entitled, or jointly entitled, to occupy the home, and are applying for a divorce or are divorced. They cannot apply if they have remarried. A transfer of tenancy order cannot take effect before decree absolute.

Similarly, cohabitants or former cohabitants can apply for a transfer of tenancy order if they are entitled, or jointly entitled to occupy the home. However, there are no restrictions on the time within which an application may be made, and they do not lose their right to apply if they marry someone else.

Criteria for making an order

In all cases when deciding whether to make an order, the court must have regard to a number of factors, including:

- how the tenancy came into being and to whom it was granted;

- the respective housing needs of the parties and any relevant child;

- the respective financial resources of the parties;

- the effect of an order (or not) on the health, safety or well-being of the parties and any relevant child;

- the suitability of the parties as tenants (this allows the court to take account of the landlord's interests).

For cohabitants and former cohabitants, where only one of the parties is a tenant, the court must also have regard to:

- the nature of the relationship;

- the duration of the cohabitation;

- whether there are children for whom they are responsible;

- the length of time since they ceased to live together.

Payment

The court can also order that one party makes a payment to the other party in the event of a transfer of tenancy. In deciding whether to exercise this power, the court must take into account all the financial affairs of each party and consider the case carefully.

Exchanges

There are also a number of exchange mechanisms, by which women experiencing domestic violence may be able to access new safe accommodation.

- The *Housing Act 1985* gave local authority and housing association tenants the right to mutually exchange houses anywhere in England and Wales, provided that each tenant obtained the written consent of their respective landlord.

- Through HOMES (Housing Organisation Mobility and Exchange Services), a government funded organisation set up to work with local authorities and housing associations to help people move home. It operates two schemes: 'Homeswap', which is a national mutual exchange scheme, and the 'Homes Mobility' scheme, through which people are 'nominated' by one landlord to another.

- Exchanges may also be arranged informally by advertising in local newspapers and shops of both areas or at local offices of councils and housing associations in home area and new areas. After an exchange partner has been identified, it is important to then go through the proper channels with both housing bodies in order to ensure that security of tenure is safeguarded.

The tenancy status of individuals wishing to transfer or exchange was affected by the *Housing Act 1988*. It is important to check before making a transfer or exchange, whether security of tenure or other housing rights will be affected. Exchanges, transfers and mobility schemes all take time. They are not overnight solutions to immediate housing difficulties.

7.7 *Implementation of housing law: limitations and problems for women and children experiencing domestic violence*

Research has documented the continuing need of women (and children) experiencing domestic violence for safe permanent housing, as well as safe emergency accommodation. It has particularly shown the continuing importance of access to local authority and social rented housing (Malos and Hague 1993a). Similarly, a study commissioned by the Department of the Environment demonstrated the significant part played by local authority housing entitlement for women experiencing violent relationship breakdown (Bull 1993).

However, for many years homelessness legislation (under Part III of the *Housing Act 1985*, and before that the *Housing [Homeless Persons] Act 1977*), has been interpreted inconsistently throughout the country. Some local authorities have recognised the serious nature of domestic violence and consequent homelessness, and have developed good practice guidelines and domestic violence policies to govern their practice. Others take a much harsher view of the law, such that many women are left in insecure and dangerous situations (Malos and Hague 1993a; Hague and Malos 1994).

Malos and Hague's research confirmed the existing evidence that local authority responses vary widely from one area to another, in terms of the use of their discretion under the homelessness legislation to accept, or attempt to limit, their acceptance of homeless people (Thomas and Niner 1989; Evans and Duncan 1988; Evans 1991). Women who become homeless because of domestic violence are no exception to this pattern.

In Malos and Hague's (1993a) study, some authorities interpreted their duties very narrowly. This included adopting a stance of 'minimum compliance' with the law, and attempting to deter women from pursuing their applications by pointing them in the direction of legal remedies which have been ineffective. Some authorities demanded a high degree of 'proof' and conducted stringent and detailed investigations into the violence women had experienced (which can often be very distressing for women in these situations because of the very private and intimate nature of the abuse experienced). Some authorities would not consider re-housing women escaping violence if they did not have dependent children with them, or interpreted the 'local connection' clause of the homelessness law more narrowly than the law prescribes in situations involving domestic violence. This might involve the authority attempting to refer women on to another authority, even if they might be in danger there, or keeping them in uncertainty for very long periods of time about whether they would be accepted for re-housing

As noted earlier, local authorities may now only offer permanent housing to those on their housing register. Homeless families, including women and children made homeless by domestic violence, will be placed in temporary accommodation. The definitions of 'homelessness' and 'priority need' remain the same as under the 1985 Act, and Government has now added 'homelessness' to the list of categories (identified under s.167 of the Act) to which local authorities are required to give 'reasonable preference' when offering accommodation to those on the register. It is essential, therefore, that women escaping violence, and those staying in refuges, ensure that they are included on the housing register. Failure to do so could mean their repeatedly

being moved on from one temporary home to another. There is some evidence from refuges that, where local authorities are operating what Hague and Malos (1993) called 'minimal compliance', women are returning home rather than live in short-term, inadequate private sector accommodation.

The legislation also allows local authorities to refuse accommodation to those whom they believe to have suitable available accommodation elsewhere. This provision particularly affects some women from minority ethnic groups who might be deemed to have access to accommodation in another country. As before, women who have no permanent right of residence in Britain, perhaps because they have stayed with their abusing partners for less than 12 months, have 'no recourse to public funds', and hence no assistance under the law. Current attention by Government to this issue may result in improvements in the near future.

There is also a concern that these legislative changes may cause a crisis in the provision of temporary safe refuge for abused women and children in an emergency. This will particularly be the case if existing refuge residents are unable to move on to safe permanent accommodation within a reasonable period of time. It is, at the time of writing, still too early to know what the effects of these changes will be.

Concern is already being expressed by practitioners from a number of agencies about the impact of the *Family Law Act 1996* on local authority housing policy and practice. There is some anecdotal evidence that, since the introduction of Part IV, pressure on abused women by local housing departments to return home with injunctions has increased, which may put their lives, and their children's, at risk. Where Part IV is used to exclude an abusive partner, or to transfer the tenancy to the woman's sole name, concerns have also been expressed that this must be quickly followed up with transfers to other accommodation by local authorities. This is essential if those experiencing domestic violence are to be effectively protected from abuse.

Abused women may also feel under pressure to apply for occupation orders, as a means of avoiding the risk of losing their children in contested residence applications. If they cannot access refuge or safe temporary accommodation while this is happening, or gain housing benefit to cover both rents, then they may have to return home with an injunction, even if they do not feel safe to do so. They must then wait for an exchange or transfer, because this might seem the only option to keep both a secure home and their children.

7.8 Summary

■ The options for protection available under the civil and criminal law have a number of limitations to their effectiveness. It is likely that many women will continue to rely on provision under homeless legislation for safe housing, and longer term protection from violence for themselves and their children.

■ The *Housing Act 1996* has made a number of major changes to the provision of public and private rented accommodation. Parts VI and VII of the Act affect decisions about who is housed in the social rented sector, and are of particular relevance for women and children experiencing abuse.

■ The legislation has removed any automatic link that existed between being homeless under the law, and being given permanent housing. Under previous legislation, people who were unintentionally homeless and in priority need were offered permanent accommodation. Now Part VII gives local authorities a number of temporary duties.

■ The local authority has a duty to secure interim accommodation, for example, in a refuge or hostel, while it investigates whether it has a further duty, if it believes an applicant may be homeless or is threatened with homelessness and is eligible for assistance and is in priority need.

■ The local authority has a *temporary*, but *renewable*, two year duty to house certain applicants who fit all the following criteria: homeless or threatened with homelessness, eligible for assistance, in priority need, not intentionally homeless, unable to access other 'suitable accommodation' and who have a local connection with the area.

■ The duty to provide *permanent* accommodation has been removed. To obtain permanent accommodation, the applicant must apply through the council's waiting list (housing register) under Part VI of the Act.

■ The Act has broadened the definition of homelessness for women experiencing domestic violence. Previously, domestic violence was defined as violence from a person living in the home. In the *Housing Act 1996*, domestic violence is defined as violence or threats of violence from a person who is *associated with the person under threat*. An 'associated person' is defined in the Code of Guidance to the Act (and the definition is the same as under Part IV of the *Family Law Act 1996*).

■ Homeless people are in 'priority need' for accommodation if they are pregnant, have dependent children, are vulnerable, or are threatened with homelessness as a result of an emergency.

■ Once the local authority has established that the applicant is homeless and in priority need, it must then decide if s/he is homeless intentionally, and if she has a local connection. They may refer to another local authority with which at least one member of the household has a connection, *provided that no one in the household runs a risk of domestic violence in the other area.*

■ A local authority can fulfil its duties to homeless applicants by temporarily housing them in its own accommodation, or by giving advice and assistance to help applicants secure access to private rented accommodation, if it is satisfied that suitable accommodation is available in its area.

■ The prohibition of the use of local authorities' permanent self-contained housing for more than two years out of any three makes it more likely that those re-housed by a local authority under the homeless legislation may be placed in the worst housing on run down estates. Women and children seeking re-housing because of domestic violence should apply through Part VI of the *Housing Act* to be put on the housing register to access permanent accommodation either through nomination to a housing association or from a local authority's housing stock.

■ Part VI of the Act determines who will get access to permanent accommodation in the social rented sector through the housing register. It requires local authorities to decide who does and who does not qualify for re-housing. People who must qualify are unintentionally homeless people in priority need. Asylum seekers and people from abroad who are subject to immigration control will not qualify. The local authority allocations scheme must give 'reasonable preference' to a number of groups, including people who are unintentionally homeless (or threatened with homelessness) and in priority need.

■ The Code of Guidance suggests how local authorities should implement the *Housing Act 1996*. It does not have force of law, but local authorities should have regard to it in exercising their functions relating to homelessness and the prevention of homelessness. It makes a number of specific references to the needs of women and children experiencing domestic violence. These include good practice recommendations on making enquiries, injunctions, local connection, referrals to another area and to women's refuges and the vulnerability of women without children who are at risk of violence.

■ For a woman with a joint tenancy, it is now possible to apply under Part IV for the tenancy to be transferred to the woman's sole name. If she wishes, this can then enable her to use her existing tenancy to access alternative safe accommodation, either through a transfer or through an exchange. It is also possible to arrange reciprocal transfers between local authorities, that is, where two authorities each agree to house a woman from the other area in one of their empty properties.

■ There are also a number of exchange mechanisms by which women experiencing domestic violence may be able to access new safe accommodation.

■ Research has documented the continuing need of women (and children) experiencing domestic violence for safe permanent housing as well as safe emergency accommodation, and in particular the continuing importance of access to local authority and social rented housing. Inconsistent interpretation throughout the country has meant that some local authorities have recognised the serious nature of domestic violence and consequent homelessness, and have developed good practice guidelines and domestic violence policies to govern their practice. Others have taken a much harsher view of the law, leaving many women in insecure and dangerous situations.

Part Three

Practice Interventions

■ Domestic violence is an important indicator that a child may be at risk of abuse.

■ Child abuse is an indicator that mothers may also be being abused by their male partners.

■ The effects on children of living with domestic violence – both direct abuse and witnessing such violence – may be deemed to constitute 'significant harm'.

■ All children living in circumstances of domestic violence may be deemed to be 'in need'. Many are also at risk of physical and/or sexual abuse.

An awareness of these issues clearly has practice implications for different professional agencies, including doctors, health visitors, solicitors, social workers, foster/adoptive carers, teachers, youth workers and mental health practitioners. There is now beginning to emerge a growing body of literature on practice interventions and guidelines on children and domestic violence, which will be examined in detail in the following chapters.

This Part of the Reader provides overviews and ideas about practice interventions in circumstances of domestic violence with children, with women and with men. The final chapter examines useful multi-agency approaches to children and domestic violence.

CHAPTER EIGHT: SOCIAL SERVICES RESPONSES TO DOMESTIC VIOLENCE AND ABUSE OF CHILDREN

Practice in relation to domestic violence varies between child care professionals, and there are examples of positive as well as negative practice. Practice continues to change over time. This chapter provides an insight into the development of positive social work and related practice with regard to domestic violence. The provision of support to non-abusive carers (usually mothers) can be a particularly effective child protection strategy, and this is detailed below.

Mullender (1997), in her overview of the social work response to domestic violence, identifies the directions that social work practice has taken during the past couple of decades.

- In the 1980s the expectation that women should stay with the violent man 'for the sake of the children' was particularly prevalent.

- During the 1990s the onus on women to protect their children has increasingly been translated into demands that women leave violent men or have their children accommodated due to a perceived 'failure to protect'.

Both of these responses by child protection professionals, while seemingly very different, actually arise from the same perspectives and developments within child protection practice. In relation to child abuse the prevalent social work view has been to see the family, and in particular 'dysfunctional' families, as central to the problem. This has led to 'whole family' approaches where all members of the family must take responsibility for its dysfunctional manifestation. As Parton (1990) explains, 'this includes the mother, who is seen as colluding with the man's behaviour and failing to protect her children'. (p 15). This has been combined with an increasing emphasis in policy on abuse 'prevention', that is, the identification of 'high risk' cases and prevention of an abusive event before it takes place. Consequently the role of the child welfare professional 'is to try and identify and manage the "high-risk" individual or family' (Parton 1990: 20).

The earlier emphasis in social work practice on keeping families together also reflected both a psychological perspective that children might be better served by having two parents and a shift in the policy emphasis away from children remaining in care (see Parker 1995).[1] With an increasing focus in social work on child protection and abuse prevention, practice moved away from keeping children with both parents to an emphasis on removing children from situations where there was risk of significant harm.

---

[1] Both issues may in fact be detrimental to children's well-being. Research generally indicates that where there is 'conflict' between parents it is not necessarily in the best interests for children to be in contact with both parents post-separation (see Amato and Keith 1991; Hooper 1994). It should be noted that this view still provides the rationale underlying the general presumption in relation to divorce and separation of parents that children should have contact with the non-residential parent (see Hester and Radford 1996, Hester and Pearson 1997). With regard to children in care, Parker (1995) points out that the policy against long-term care for children in the 1970s with rapid return to the family may have increased the extent of abuse to the children concerned.

8.1 'Keeping the family together'

The 1980s approach of keeping families together 'for the sake of the children' made it especially difficult for women to leave violent men and thus created difficulties with regard to safety for both women and children. Maynard

(1985), in her study of social work case files and responses to domestic violence provides numerous examples of social workers using such a '1980s approach'. For instance, 7 out of the 34 women in the cases she examined were actively discouraged by social workers from leaving their violent male partners. As one of the social workers commented about her client:

> She was thinking of leaving her husband again. Pointed out that she had Christopher [*son*] to consider in this and her husband's feelings for the baby and herself. Reminded her that she had married and had to accept the consequences. (social worker, in Maynard 1985: 130)

Dobash, Dobash and Cavanagh found similar responses to women attempting to leave violent men in the late 1970s:

> I went to the welfare to get somewhere to stay but they couldn't help me. Mrs Jones [*social worker*] told me I would have to stay and I said, 'I just can't', and they said, 'You'll just have to stay for the sake of the wee ones'. (woman interviewed, in Dobash, Dobash and Cavanagh 1985: 161)

8.2 'Failure to protect'

Moving from an expectation that women and children should stay with violent men to a recognition that women and their children may be better off by leaving such men has clearly been a positive step forward in local authority practice, and has developed alongside a greater public awareness of domestic violence. However, many women have experienced this '1990s approach' as especially punitive.

The problem is that all the responsibility for protecting children has been placed on mothers rather than tackling those responsible for the violence, male abusers. Moreover, the dynamics involved in domestic violence and the impacts on and needs of the women living in violent relationships (as detailed in Chapter One) have often not been understood by professionals. This has led to frustration about why women 'don't just leave'. Professionals, whose prime focus is on protecting children, have tended to respond by threatening accommodation of the children – perhaps seeing this as a means of 'pushing' women to leave violent relationships. Or they may have decided that the woman is no longer able to parent effectively for her children in the context of the violent relationship, and have therefore removed the children into care. These may appear sensible courses of action, but have in reality been counterproductive because they have largely ignored the (primarily male) abuser and have created fear for women that their children will be taken away if they disclose domestic violence.

A number of recent studies provide evidence of child protection professionals using this '1990s approach' (see Farmer and Owen 1995; Humphreys 1997; Hester and Radford 1996; Forman 1995). For instance:

■ In Humphreys' study (1997) the local authority appeared to expect women, in over half the cases involving domestic violence, to protect their children

by not associating with the abusive male partner. Moreover, a quarter were threatened with removal of their children if the abusive man returned.

- Forman (1995) found similarly, in her study of twenty mothers of sexually abused children, that, all the women and children had been through the child protection system. Despite all the women having separated the child from the abuser, social work departments placed the children on the child protection register, or took them into care (in five cases), or referred to children's panels, or did all of these things. Forman suggests that these interventions were linked to the notion that the woman would not be able to keep the abuser away from the house and from the child.

- In Hester and Radford's study (1996), two mothers were told by social services that they must ensure no contact between the children and their father post-separation, and that in the event of a reconciliation the children would be placed into care. However, no support was provided to ensure that contact between the children and the abusive fathers was formally stopped via a *Children Act* section 8 order.

8.3 'Implacable hostility'

The research referred to, concerning 'failure to protect', provides examples of the problems women and children face after they have left violent men. However, the difficulties are made even more complex where both (public law) child protection and (private law) arrangements for children post-separation of the parents intersect (see also Chapter Six). As Humphreys (1997b) points out, mothers have to be seen by social services to be actively, indeed 'aggressively', protecting their children. Yet in relation to divorce and separation, the message is very different. Mothers may not be perceived to attempt to 'aggressively protect' their children from the direct or indirect abuse of a violent father (Hester and Pearson 1997). Within divorce proceedings, mothers who bring up problems related to domestic violence or child abuse issues within that context, are often construed as 'implacably hostile' and seen to be acting against the children's best interests of contact with the father (for instance Re O; and Re F). Jolly points out:

> It is notable that many of the 'implacable hostility' cases also involve harassment or violence from the non-custodial parent towards the custodial parent (who is almost invariably the mother). (Jolly 1995: 228)

As a result, contradictory outcomes may be established where there may, on the one hand, be an expectation that mothers should protect their children, but, on the other hand, formally constituted arrangements for contact that do not adequately take into account that in some instances mothers and/or children may experience further abuse (see Hester and Radford 1996; Hester and Pearson 1997). This is an area where inter-agency working around domestic violence needs to be developed in order to encourage positive and safety-oriented practice.

The social work role with regard to the civil law also needs to be developed. The *Family Law Act 1996* provides a legal framework where civil remedies will require partnership between women, children and statutory agencies to ensure that women and children are protected and remain at home in safety (see Chapter Four for details of the law).

8.4 Focusing on mothers and avoiding violent men

Research in the UK looking at social work practice indicates that social workers tend to be uncomfortable about working with domestic violence, and often have no policies or guidelines on domestic violence to which they can refer (O'Hagan and Dillenburger 1995; Mullender 1997). Consequently, they tend to ignore the domestic violence and the (male) perpetrators. Instead they focus on the women and children – who are more accessible, with whom they are more familiar and more confident, and who are possibly more open to social work influence. Some professionals also assume that women are able to influence or prevent the men's violence against them (see James 1994; Armstrong 1994).

In Farmer and Owen's (1995) study on child protection practice they note that not only was there was a striking shift in focus *'away from an abusing father figure onto the mother'* in relation to physical and emotional child abuse, but that this *'shift of focus from men to women often also allowed men's violence to their wives or partners to disappear from sight'* (p 223, emphasis in original). This appeared to be based on an assumption about parenting by social workers that mothers, but not fathers, were responsible for the children's well-being (p 223). Similar findings have been highlighted in other studies:

- In her study of social work case-files, Maynard (1985) found that in cases involving domestic violence, social workers redefined the issue as one of child welfare and so concentrated their interventions on the mothers.

- In their study of support services available for women experiencing domestic violence, McGibbon, Cooper and Kelly (1989) found that social workers tended to place the onus of change on the woman, focusing their assessment on the impact of the abuse on the mother's parenting abilities, and that frequently they had no contact at all with the man.

- In an Australian study, Goddard and Carew (1988) noted what was termed the 'hostage effect' in some social workers, who failed to openly acknowledge and address the high level of violence within a family. According to Stanley and Goddard (1993) this meant that the social workers unconsciously adopted the viewpoint of the abuser in order to protect themselves and therefore did not protect the children (nor presumably the woman).

- In relation to child protection conferences, Humphreys (1997) found that where fathers who had been violent to the mothers attended conferences, in nine out of eleven cases the domestic violence was either not mentioned in the case plan or conference, or was minimised. Moreover, in the two cases where the domestic violence *was* discussed, the 'recommendations made in the case plan would have put the woman at risk of further abuse' (Humphreys 1997: iv).

- James's (1994) study of *Children Act* section 8 reviews, highlighted that the work being carried out in child protection focused on women and asked 'where were the invisible men' (and see Armstrong 1994).

Milner (1996) points out that even violence from men to their partners which is acknowledged tends to be excused as unintentional, as a one-off act or with women used as a scapegoat. Moreover, unlike women on the

receiving end of the violence, the violent men themselves are not challenged by being told that their behaviour might lead to them risking losing their children. Because of their own intimidation and fear of violence, social workers also avoid any challenging interactions with these men, and often time their initial visits to ensure that the man is not present (see Mullender 1997).

Clearly, child care professionals avoid violent men or minimise their behaviour for a number of reasons that include their assumptions about parenting as well as concerns regarding their own safety. It could be argued that without adequate resourcing and safety precautions social workers are partly justified in their reticence in dealing with violent men. As Milner (1996) points out:

> Confrontation is an entirely acceptable strategy when used by high-status men in a safe environment .... In the home or at case conference, confrontation is a dangerous and ineffective strategy. (Milner 1996: 123)

8.5 Working with and supporting mothers as a positive response

Increasingly, supporting non-abusive mothers to be safe is being considered as the most positive approach in child protection where domestic violence is an issue (see Stark and Flitcraft 1988; London Borough of Hackney 1993; Mullender and Morley 1994). The recent Department of Health Circular on Part IV of the Family Law Act suggests that '[w]here domestic violence may be an important element in the family, the safety of (usually) the mother is also in the child's welfare' (Department of Health 1997: 12; and see Ball 1995).

Such an approach also fits with the new emphasis in child protection where child care staff have been encouraged to place child protection work within the context of wider services for children in need. As indicated in Chapter Four, this was to redress the concern that children were being routed inappropriately within the child protection system as a means of gaining access to services (Department of Health 1995). An emphasis on children 'in need' allows local authorities to provide a range of support to children and their non-abusive carers. This can assist women and their children after the abuser has been removed, or to support women and children to leave violent men and to establish a new life without the abuser (see Chapter Four for the legal details).

With appropriate protection and support many mothers who are being abused by their male partners can be enabled to protect their children. As the Social Service Inspectorate report on *Domestic Violence and Social Care* points out, 'Protection and empowerment of non-abusing women is effective child-protection' (Ball 1995, and see details below). Thus:

> ...those who are concerned about child abuse would do well to look towards advocacy and protection of battered mothers as the best means to prevent current child abuse as well as child abuse in the future. (Stark and Flitcraft 1985: 147)

A number of social work and other child care agencies have begun to adopt approaches that involve the protection and support of mothers in child protection. Humphreys (1997) found instances of change towards such practice in her study of child protection practice in Coventry. Where this practice had been introduced it was having a positive effect. For instance, in

one case the work originally carried out ignored the man's behaviour towards his partner and 'the father was seen as the cornerstone of the family' while his ongoing domestic violence, constituting 'mental abuse, isolation, multiple pregnancies and undermining of the woman', was ignored (p 7). Another worker (a student on placement) changed the orientation of the work to include an emphasis on domestic violence:

> Through careful and sensitive support work with the woman, the domestic violence was named, and the woman supported in finding alternative housing. She then separated from her husband and she and the children are progressing well. (Humphreys 1997: 6)

The NSPCC team in Hester and Pearson's study (1998), who were doing recovery work with abused children, had also decided to move towards work to support both mothers and their children in domestic violence cases. This was considered especially positive for all concerned as it placed the support and protection – and therefore recovery – of the child within a context where the key carer (the mother) was also supported. As one team member explained:

> ... if a child has been abused, it's what happens next in terms of the help, of an acceptance from particular key carers... that will determine the outcome in terms of the child's recovery ....So, therefore, if we can work with women as well as children, carers as well as children, taking account of domestic violence ... of the power dynamics around, and the frequency with which men abuse women we know about just in a factual way, then I think that we can start to create with those carers safer environments for them and their children. (Child protection officer, in Hester and Pearson 1998)

Working with mothers to protect children will often need the involvement of a number of agencies working in unison. The team in Hester and Pearson's study (1998) had concerns, however, that social services might not use the same 'woman-supportive' approach as the other agencies involved, thus making a co-ordinated response to child protection and recovery difficult:

> That's what worries me actually – working together with social services to enable protection of the children to be looked at properly, whilst ensuring that the children and the mother are safe at the same time. (Child protection officer, in Hester and Pearson 1998)

One instance, in particular, showed up the resulting dilemmas and difficulties that may arise for child care professionals when attempting to work supportively with mothers across agencies. In this case the mother, who had previously stayed in a refuge, had returned to the violent partner. (It has to be recognised that women who are under extreme threat of further violence from their ex-partners may return as a part of their 'safety strategy' – see Chapter One). The team were wanting to support both mother and child so that the mother would be enabled to protect and support the child, and so that the mother and child could stay together. This needed to be carried out in a way that recognised the increased danger of abuse for the woman if she was seen to be in direct contact with any agency. They felt, however, that social services were more likely to focus on protection of the child without supporting the mother, as the former was not as difficult:

She's not going to go back into the refuge. So, short of people telling her that she must go into a refuge, which people obviously have, it's about how you're going to match the two together. And all of a sudden it becomes too difficult which is probably why she hasn't had any help ... You've either got to do one – protect the children at the cost of herself, which she knows and feels very guilty about, or try and work with both, and you need an awful lot of time and resources don't you, plus the fact that you've got to find a way of getting to her because she can't come here. (Child care worker, in Hester and Pearson 1998).

How should social services departments respond when women suffer violence from known abusers?

- **Develop and implement policy:** Violence against women is a crime. Women from all backgrounds experience violence. Men from all backgrounds are perpetrators of violence. Protection and empowerment of non-abusing women is effective child-protection.

- **Develop and implement good practice guidelines.**

- **Monitor use of services by women experiencing domestic violence.**

- **Include the issue in basic practice:** On referral forms, Community Care Assessments, Community Care Plans, Child Protection investigations, Child Protection conferences and in supervision.

- **Ensure awareness of domestic violence is integrated** into existing provision of services.

- **Develop in-house practical services and options for women and children** – women's and children's drop-ins and groups; women's groups in day centres and residential establishments; crisis centres, counselling/play with children; use of mental health hostels as safe houses; provision of counselling services to women in hospital.

- **Ensure awareness of domestic violence is integrated** into provision of non-statutory services – for example, enabling discussion about domestic violence in mother and toddler groups, in craft and cookery groups.

- **Finance non-statutory services and options for women and children** – Women's Aid work with children; counselling services.

- **Use current legislation** by displacing the man as the nearest relative, (Section 29, *Mental Health Act*); by recommending that courts attach injunctions or prohibited steps orders to Section 8 orders; by using the *Children Act* (Schedule 1, Para. 5) with regard to removal of perpetrator; by using the *Children Act*, Section 17, for finance to enhance safety – eg new locks, travel refuge, telephone installation.

- **Multi-agency liaison** to provide up-to-date information on delivering services and referral and to clarify the role of each agency.

- **Multi-agency liaison** to provide up-to-date information on delivering services and referral and to clarify the role of each agency.

> ■ **Publish and provide information for the public and staff** – posters, leaflets, help cards, directories of services.
>
> ■ **Training** – professional training, both induction and specialised.
>
> ■ **Personnel policy** to cover both the safety of workers and staff experiencing violence from abusers.
>
> *adapted from Ball (1995)*

Hague, Kelly, Malos and Mullender (1996) give a more positive example of how work carried out with women in refuges and across agencies can be fruitful with regard to child protection.

> [*The refuge*] worked with other agencies with an 'off the wall' family; the mother was abused as a child – sexually, physically – and had seven children. The whole family were known to have been victims of abuse. In-depth work resulted in mother eventually living in the community with her children. It involved learning to be an adult and a mother, learning to protect her children and living as a single parent. With care the family have moved forward. They returned recently to the refuge to say thank you. (1996: 27)

Many local authorities have produced, or are in the process of producing, guides to identifying and prioritising 'children in need'. It is important that they do not continue the counter-productive approach of blaming mothers, who are themselves being abused by their partners, for the failure to protect their children. An emphasis on supporting non-abusive carers should be built into to any assessments or assessment mechanisms. Clearly, in child protection cases, working with and supporting mothers who have experienced domestic violence can be hard work, but is likely to have more positive outcomes in the longer term than more traditional 'mother blaming' approaches.

8.6 Working with and supporting mothers as a positive response – the case of abusive mothers

Women may also be abusive to children. Mothers may abuse children physically or emotionally, and perhaps sexually. Such abusive behaviour may require statutory intervention (Mullender 1996; Violence Against Children Study Group 1990; Farmer and Owen 1995; Saradjian 1997).

Domestic violence can be an important part of the equation where women are being abusive to children, and should therefore always be seen as a possibility. For instance, a mother's parenting capacity may be so severely affected by her experience of domestic violence that she may for a time be unable to meet a child's essential needs, including the need for protection (see Chapter One for discussion of the impact of domestic violence on parenting). In some instances women may be particularly punitive in their behaviour towards children in the presence of a man who is carrying out domestic violence towards them. Where domestic violence *is* an issue, the woman's abuse of the children might therefore stop once the man is no longer there, or may stop in the longer term. As Mullender points out:

> Where women have actually abused or neglected their children, it is always important to ask how much of this has been coerced by the male abuser, or has in other ways directly resulted from his behaviour, since, where this is the case, it may immediately, or with help, stop in his absence. (Mullender 1996a: 105)

Supporting a woman so that she and the children become safe from the male abuser and helping her create a new life can in such circumstances prove to be positive. Clearly, the feasibility and type of support needed will require careful assessment. The support, such as counselling, may need to take into account that 'one or more of the children is identified in her mind with the abuse' (Mullender 1996a: 105). For instance, the child might have been forced to take part in the mother's abuse, might have been conceived through marital rape, or have ended up looking or behaving like the abuser.

8.7 Assessing levels of risk and need

Chapter Four outlined child protection and children in need issues, related to the *Children Act 1989*.

Domestic violence is an important indicator that a child is 'in need' and may be likely to suffer significant harm. Also, it is important for child care professionals to know if a child who is being abused is living in a context where their carer is also experiencing violence and abuse, as this has direct implications for practice. The problem is that *there are no specific indicators of the impact of domestic violence on children*:

- the effects of domestic violence on children's development, behaviour and well-being can be similar to the effects resulting from child abuse without a context of domestic violence

- children who are living with domestic violence, but are not being physically or sexually abused, may exhibit similar difficulties as children who are being so abused

- some children may not be exhibiting difficulties and may have developed coping strategies that involve being high achievers. Such children may still be in need of support and/or protection with regard to domestic violence.

It is therefore crucial to ascertain from the adults and/ or children concerned whether domestic violence is an issue. As Debbonaire explains:

> the clearest indicator of domestic violence is still a woman or child saying that it is happening. The professional role in this is to create the conditions and trust that make it possible for a woman or child to say this, and help to make this process positive and useful, rather than using a checklist of behaviours. (Debbonaire 1998).

Chapter Nine provides details concerning disclosure of domestic violence and safety planning with regard to children. Here the focus is on enabling disclosure of domestic violence from adults, and women in particular.

8.8 Disclosing domestic violence and abuse of children

Routinely asking women about domestic violence

There is evidence to suggest that good practice consists of asking *all* women routinely about domestic violence in *every* case. The very fact of asking about domestic violence conveys an important message to women and children that practitioners are aware of its existence and relevance, thus possibly facilitating disclosure.

> Our acknowledgment of the possibility of violence conveys to a mother that this experience is important to discuss and has a detrimental impact on her children as well as on her. (Hughes 1992: 10)

In communicating with the woman, it is important to relay to her that:

■ it is not her fault

■ you are concerned about her and her child(ren)

■ you are willing to help by giving her information and resources

■ witnessing abuse is having an impact on her child(ren)

■ she may feel that the children are unaware of violence and that has protected them, but children tend to be aware of what is happening

■ there are places to go, and people who can help.

adapted from Children's Subcommittee of the London Co-ordinating Committee to End Woman Abuse, London, Ontario – in Mullender 1994: 235

The process of disclosure might be partly facilitated by ensuring that offices and agency waiting rooms display posters about domestic violence, including information about where women and children can obtain practical help and refuge accommodation if required. This in itself conveys a message to women that domestic violence is not condoned or viewed as 'normal' behavior, which they are simply expected to tolerate.

The fact that domestic violence can be overlooked unless specifically asked about has been demonstrated in a recently completed project with the NSPCC (Hester and Pearson 1998). A major feature of this project was the establishment of a monitoring scheme for domestic violence as one means of incorporating the possibility of domestic violence into all aspects of the team's work with children. In the scheme staff were expected to ask about possible violent and abusive behaviour in the relationship of the parents (or equivalent carers). A monitoring form was devised so that staff could routinely ask about domestic violence every time they met with clients and/or referrers. In practice the monitoring process was used most frequently with the adults. It was found that the incidence of domestic violence in those cases accepted for service rose from one third to nearly two thirds as a result of routinely asking about domestic violence in every case. This is not to say that the research resulted in more referrals involving domestic violence, but that domestic violence became more acknowledged and recognised where it had previously been hidden.

How to ask

It has to be remembered that many women will minimize their experiences and/ or may not define them as domestic violence. For instance if there is no physical violence – which is perceived as the stereotypical domestic violence experience – women may be reluctant to see their experience of abuse in this way. Therefore, it is not helpful to simply ask women if there is/has been any domestic violence, as this might provide a negative (and possibly false) response. Instead, a range of areas of questioning might need to be pursued in order to gain a more complete picture. Some agencies are beginning to develop such domestic violence 'screening' approaches (see, for instance, the National Family Mediation guidelines in Hester, Pearson and Radford 1997; Department of Health Local Authority Circular 1997). Suggestions for questions to open up the issue of domestic violence include some of the following:

- How are things at home?

- How are arguments settled?

- How are decisions reached?

- What happens when you argue/disagree?

- Do you feel/have you ever felt frightened of your partner?

- Do you feel/have you ever felt threatened/intimidated by your partner?

- What happens when your partner gets angry?

- Does your partner shout at you, call you names, put you down?

- Has your partner ever physically hurt you? How, what happened?

- Has your partner ever thrown things?

- Has your partner ever destroyed things you care about?

- Has your partner ever forced you to have sex or engage in any sexual activities against your will?

- What do the children do when (any of the above) is happening?

- How do the children feel when (any of the above) is happening?

(adapted from Department of Health 1997: 20)

Despite being given the opportunity to reveal domestic violence in this way, some women will be very wary of the response and may test out the practitioners' reaction in order to ensure that they will be believed and that they will be safe (Mullender 1996a). Some women only feel able to disclose their experiences over a period of time. Thus, it is important to continue sensitively asking about domestic violence even when it does not emerge immediately. In Hester and Pearson's study (1998) of NSPCC practice, they found, with regard to the use of domestic violence monitoring, that in one case the experience of domestic violence was only disclosed at the fourth session. The first monitoring form indicated that domestic violence was 'suspected'. The third form indicated 'don't know yet', and the fourth form itemised seven forms of domestic violence experienced by the woman concerned – physical, sexual, psychological, emotional, verbal, threats to kill and isolation. This raises concerns about those situations, such as duty social

work, where women will usually only be seen once, and where any domestic violence issues may remain hidden.

Where to ask – separate interviews

It is essential that any such asking about domestic violence be carried out with care and sensitivity, and in a way that does not further endanger women and children. Disclosure is not very likely to occur when the woman is in the presence of her abusive partner, as her fear of the possible repercussions would prevent her from revealing any violence. Therefore, joint interviews or joint meetings should be avoided, especially for initial sessions. This has been recognised in the National Standards for family court welfare work (Home Office 1994), and in the code for mediators arising from the *Family Law Act 1996* (see Hester, Pearson and Radford 1997). Mary McKay (1994) has pointed out that this is also a practice issue for child protection workers, who need to know about the existence of domestic violence if they are to make accurate risk assessments in relation to children, and she recommends use of separate interviews:

> The prevailing method of interviewing both parents together to assess the risk to the child appears to be a detriment to determining if domestic violence is present ....Given the seemingly strong link between spouse abuse and child abuse, interviewing each parent separately seems always indicated. (p 34)

Where there is a history of domestic violence, the survivor should be centrally involved in deciding whether any further interviews or sessions should be joint and how safety might be ensured where joint sessions do go ahead.

Some professionals may be wary of seeing women separately in order to raise the issue of domestic violence, partly fearing that this will be time consuming or might 'invite' malicious allegations (see, for instance, Hester, Pearson and Radford 1997). However, it is vital that the possibility of separate meetings is explored to ensure effective and safe interventions for women and children.

Where to ask – sessions with both women and children

In recovery work with children who have experienced abuse, the professionals involved may use sessions where all the family or a variety of family members are expected to be present. Hester and Pearson (1998) found in their study of NSPCC practice that there were occasions when workers felt it was especially inappropriate or unsafe to ask about domestic violence. This included instances where the family was seen together and the male partner, in particular, was present:

> Sometimes when I have a family in and there's been no reference to domestic violence at all within the referral, I find it difficult to talk about. .... Where I've been working though with just mothers, or mothers and children, or just children, or families where domestic violence has been part of the referral, it's been a lot easier ... I suppose it's because the man is there – that's what makes it difficult. (child protection officer in Hester and Pearson 1998)

On the other hand, asking and talking about domestic violence when both mothers (who have experienced violence from their male partners) and their children (who have also lived with the experience) are present is more likely to be positive, and can help facilitate recovery.

8.9 Fear of what professionals will do

It is essential that:

■ questions about the existence of domestic violence are asked and framed in a non-blaming and sympathetic manner

■ professionals are clear about wanting to know about domestic violence in order to provide support rather than punishment.

Many women and children living with domestic violence have learnt to keep the violence a secret and will go to great lengths to conceal it, especially in relation to authority figures who are perceived as being powerful (Farmer and Owen 1995; Mullender 1996a; and see Chapter Nine in this Reader). Mullender (1997) has suggested that domestic violence is rarely given by women as the reason for requesting a social work service, and that information about the violence is usually hidden behind other presenting concerns, such as child care or mental health issues. Farmer and Owen (1995) found in their interviews with families involved in the child protection process, that women kept incidents of violence concealed from social workers. In half the cases involving domestic violence the domestic violence had not been known to the initial child protection case conference.

> In some cases they revealed [the extent of violence from partners] in interview with us, but withheld the information from their social worker. (1995: 240)

In the NCH study (Abrahams 1994) mothers also talked of the difficulty of telling professionals 'about the problems their children were having because of violence at home'. Three quarters were afraid that their children would be taken away, and four-fifths said it 'was because they felt guilty' (NCH 1994: 4).

There is an over-representation of Black, and in particular African-Caribbean, children in public care, and Black women have a justifiable fear of a heavy-handed response from social services (Bernard in McGee 1996). Lesbian mothers may also have well-founded fears of prejudicial interventions (Harne 1997).

8.10 Fear of what the abuser will do

As discussed in Chapter One, domestic violence can have an impact on mothers' ability to discover, recognise and report child abuse (Forman 1995; Hooper 1992; Tyler Johnson 1992; Hester and Radford 1996). Forman (1995), for instance, found that while the women in her study did act in various ways to protect their children, they did not necessarily report the abuse to the authorities for fear of what the abuser would do.

The domestic violence experienced by the mothers can also reduce their awareness of what else is happening around them. In her small in-depth study of mothers of daughters who had been abused by their fathers, Tyler Johnson concludes that the mothers were rendered unaware or incapable of

discovering the abuse to their children, partly as a result of the violence they were experiencing from their partners:

> The mothers... were all physically or psychologically absent or incapacitated around the time the incest began... However, this absence or incapacity cannot be viewed simply as an active abandonment or a turning away from the family or the needs of their daughters. It was related much more to a number of reality factors... [*including*] all of the mothers' responses to physical and psychological abuse [*from their partners*]. (Tyler Johnson 1992: 107)

Hooper (1995) similarly described women as being so preoccupied with their own daily survival that this restricted their awareness of what was happening to the children. That the children were living with domestic violence also provided an alternative explanation for any difficulties the children appeared to be experiencing. However, once suspicions of sexual abuse had arisen, the woman's own experiences of abuse from the same man helped to facilitate the children's process of disclosure and belief.

Some men will also exploit women's fears that the children will be removed in order to stop the women reporting child abuse. For example, in McWilliams and McKiernan's study (1993) one of the women interviewed explained that:

> I came home with Bob when he was a few days old, I'd been indoors half an hour when there was a row... he threatened to call social services to say that I was an unfit mother. In fact he picked up the phone and pretended to dial the number, pretending he was speaking to somebody and was saying I was an unfit mother. (in McGee 1996: 6).

8.11 Monitoring/recording of domestic violence

Domestic violence should be included as a specific category in all social work referral and assessment forms and in duty records.

Routinely monitoring and recording domestic violence as a specific intake category can:

- help to establish a more accurate picture regarding the scale of the problem

- ensure that existing resources are targeted effectively.

Some agencies are already beginning to develop monitoring and recording of domestic violence, including the family court welfare service and mediators (see Hester, Pearson and Radford 1997).

8.12 Summary

- Practice in relation to domestic violence varies between child care professionals, and there are examples of positive as well as negative practice.

- Research in the UK indicates that social workers tend to be uncomfortable about working with domestic violence, and often have no policies or guidelines on domestic violence to which they can refer.

■ There is often an expectation in child protection work that women should leave violent partners in order to protect children. Not only does this place undue responsibility on mothers for men's violence and abuse, it also ignores the reality that the violence may not cease despite the separation of the spouses or partners.

■ Contradictory outcomes for children may result where there is an expectation that mothers should protect their children, but where formal arrangements for contact do not adequately take into account that mothers and/or children may experience further abuse in such circumstances. This is an area where inter-agency working around domestic violence needs to be developed in order to encourage positive and safety-oriented practice.

■ Child care professionals often avoid violent men or minimise their behaviour for a number of reasons that include assumptions about parenting as well as concerns regarding their own safety.

■ Increasingly, supporting non-abusive mothers to be safe is being considered as the most positive approach in child protection where domestic violence is an issue. Such an approach also fits with the new emphasis in child protection where child care staff have been encouraged to place child protection work within the context of wider services for children in need.

■ Women may also be abusive to children. Domestic violence may be an important part of the equation in such circumstances and should always be seen as a possibility. Where domestic violence *is* an issue, the woman's abuse of the children might stop once the man is no longer there, or may stop in the longer term.

■ There are no specific indicators of the impact of domestic violence on children. The effects of domestic violence on children's development, behaviour and well-being can be similar to the effects resulting from child abuse without a context of domestic violence

■ Good practice consists of *asking* all women routinely about domestic violence in *every* case. A range of areas of questioning might need to be pursued in order to gain a more complete picture.

■ Disclosure is not very likely to occur when the woman is in the presence of her abusive partner, as her fear of the possible repercussions would prevent her from revealing any violence. Therefore joint interviews or joint meetings should be avoided, especially for initial sessions. The survivor should be centrally involved in deciding whether any further interviews or sessions should be joint and how safety might be ensured where joint sessions do go ahead.

■ Many women and children living with domestic violence have learnt to keep the violence a secret and will go to great lengths to conceal it, especially in relation to authority figures who are perceived as being powerful. Black women have an especially justifiable fear of a heavy-handed response from social services.

■ Domestic violence should be included as a specific category in all social work referral and assessment forms and in duty records.

CHAPTER NINE: PRACTICE AND INTERVENTION WITH CHILDREN IN CIRCUMSTANCES OF DOMESTIC VIOLENCE

Chapters Two and Three outlined how children are likely to be at risk of direct physical, sexual and/or emotional abuse in the context of domestic violence, and that the effect of witnessing domestic abuse to their mothers or other carer may in itself lead to emotional harm to the children concerned. This chapter provides an overview of practice issues regarding children who live or have lived with domestic violence. The chapter covers the following areas of work:

1. disclosure

2. safety planning

3. using reframing to incorporate domestic violence

4. behavioural difficulties

5. individual work

6. groupwork

7. work in refuges

8. preventative work in schools.

Adults in a variety of settings will encounter children who are living with/have lived with domestic violence. This will include doctors, health visitors, solicitors, social workers, family centre workers, foster/adoptive carers, teachers, youth workers and mental health practitioners. The practice issues described below will be of relevance to all of these professionals and individuals. Anyone with an understanding of the dynamics of domestic violence may feel able to apply the practice ideas regarding *disclosure* and *safety planning*. The discussion about *re-framing* similarly provides ideas for incorporating domestic violence as an issue in child care work. The sections on *behavioural difficulties*, *individual work* and *groupwork* with children will be of specific interest to those who already have some knowledge and skills in these areas, but are also of relevance to anyone who works with children. The final sections in this chapter, concerning *work with children in refuges* and *preventative work in schools* will be of direct relevance to refuge workers and teachers respectively, but also to others working with children.

We have separated out individual work and groupwork with children into separate sections for the sake of clarity. That is not intended to suggest that children should be offered *either* individual *or* groupwork. In reality children may benefit from both. Moreover, work with children may also incorporate adults, and in particular, mothers. For individual children a combination of individual work, groupwork with other children and/or sessions involving them and their mothers may be the most appropriate. In reality, what children are offered (if anything) will depend on resources and what is available in their locality. The aim here is to provide child care and other professionals who work with children with ideas for extending and enhancing their practice, by incorporating the issue of domestic violence.

Despite the increasingly strong evidence linking the existence of domestic violence with various forms of harm to children, there have been

comparatively few developments in the UK concerning specific intervention strategies for these children. Over the past 20 years the main providers of services in this country for children living with domestic violence have been Women's Aid and other refuges. They have managed to provide much innovative work for children and have built up a body of knowledge and expertise without sufficient funding or recognition from the statutory authorities.

Elsewhere, especially in the USA and Canada, a variety of co-ordinated services for children has begun to develop to address the needs of children who have experienced domestic violence, and to break the silence surrounding the issue. These have included treatment programmes with individual children, support groups for children, and educational groupwork in schools. The initiatives have been accompanied by the expansion and development of services for children in shelters (refuges), often with financial support from government. These interventions and their appropriateness for different situations and age groups will be discussed below.

9.1 Children's disclosure of domestic violence: general issues

Whenever children's behaviour raises anxiety of any kind, or when there is social work involvement because of child protection concerns, the issue of domestic violence may be an important (and key) aspect of the picture. It is therefore important to:

- always bear in mind the possibility that children may be living with domestic violence

- ask children about domestic violence whenever this is possible/appropriate

- do not assume that disclosure will be immediate – it may be necessary to find out or ask over a period of time

It is important to remember that the impact on children of living with domestic violence can manifest itself in a variety of ways (as outlined in Chapter Three), and that there is no specific set of indicators. Many of the children do not necessarily give overt cause for concern, and may have learned their own ways of dealing with the violence. At school, children may be truanting and displaying disruptive behavior or they may be overly compliant, eager to please and anxious to achieve.

9.2 Hiding domestic violence

Some children may have difficulty in disclosing domestic violence to others and may go to great lengths to hide it:

- because children are protective of their mothers

- because children are protective of their abusing parent/parent figure

- because they are extremely fearful of the consequences of sharing the family 'secret' with anyone – this may include fears that it will cause further violence to their mother and/or themselves.

One 11-year-old girl who was receiving therapeutic work from the NSPCC in connection with physical abuse from her father, when asked about the context

of domestic violence (gross physical, sexual and emotional abuse of the mother) within which she had lived, wrote that she found it both upsetting and frightening to talk about because of the potential dangers of disclosure:

> I thought if I tell someone then they go and tell someone and they will come and hurt me. (in Hester and Pearson 1998)

However, being enabled to talk about the domestic violence in a safe context, which included a safe location away from the violent man for her mother and herself, proved positive.

9.3 Routinely asking children about domestic violence

There may be some resistance from adults to the notion of asking children directly about domestic violence issues. This might be linked to concerns that addressing issues with children will evoke painful memories and 'make matters worse' (Catchpole 1997: 151). It may be thought that given time children will simply forget their painful/difficult experiences and therefore recover from them. Adults themselves may find disclosure from children too painful to hear (Silvern and Kaersvang 1989: 427). Evidence suggests, however, that children's recovery and well-being can be aided by greater openness about their experiences (see Harris Hendriks, Black and Kaplan 1993).

It is important that domestic violence issues are discussed and acknowledged if children are to make sense of their experiences and gain the appropriate support. According to Jaffe, Wolfe and Wilson (1990) and McGee (1996 and forthcoming), many children *do* want to be heard and believed. The practitioners need to ask the 'right' questions, to show a sympathetic attitude and to be patient if the child is to feel able to disclose any information. This might include reassuring the child that they are not alone in witnessing/experiencing violence and allowing the child to reveal information at their own pace, which may necessitate the development of trust over several interviews.

Silvern, Karyl and Landis (1995), in their individual psychotherapy work with traumatised children of abused women, have found that a direct approach to asking about domestic violence can be beneficial. They found that children often display feelings of avoidance and numbness, and need to be given the opportunity to disclose the violence to their mothers which they have witnessed. They suggest that this is best achieved by a process of *straight talk*, which is described in the following terms:

> It is necessary to ask specific questions and to draw explicit conclusions about the traumatic event. Directness is necessary to provide cognitive structure, to interrupt avoidance about the details of the trauma ... and to explore and reframe beliefs about guilt, helplessness .... (Silvern, Karyl and Landis 1995: 55)

In their experience, children usually respond well to the need for 'a little straight talk' rather than to indirect or polite questions about the violence. They acknowledge that this might appear overly directive, but argue that without such explicit invitations to disclose the violence, children will continue to see the issue as taboo and assume that adults do not want to hear about it. This will result in isolation for the child and an inability to resolve their trauma.

Similar conclusions have been drawn by Hurley and Jaffe (1990) in relation to their work at children's mental health centres. They found that issues of domestic violence for children could remain hidden unless specifically asked about, and conclude that for mental health professionals (although applicable to others as well):

> .... questions about violence need to be asked as routinely as questions about developmental milestones and temperament. (Hurley and Jaffe 1990: 475)

Depending on the *ages* and *development* of children, disclosure may be facilitated by sensitive questioning or through play and artwork. The Children's Subcommittee of the London (Ontario) Co-ordinating Committee to End Woman Abuse (1994) has drawn up a list of question areas which may be useful to consider when children in any setting are suspected of witnessing violence against their mothers. An adaptation of this list can be found below. The very fact of raising such issues is crucial in showing children that practitioners are aware of the existence of domestic violence and gives children permission to disclose it in the knowledge that they will be believed.

Suggested questions to ask when you suspect a child is experiencing domestic violence

1. What happens when your mum and dad (mum and stepdad, dad and stepmum) disagree?

2. What does your dad do when he gets angry?

3. Did you ever hear or see your dad hurting your mum? What did you do?

4. Who do you talk to about things that make you unhappy?

5. What kind of things make you scared or angry?

6. Do you worry about mum and dad?

adapted from The Children's Subcommittee of the London (Ontario) Co-ordinating Committee to End Woman Abuse (in Mullender and Morley 1994:233)

9.4 Disclosure of child abuse in circumstances of domestic violence

The dynamics of disclosure are particularly complex when children are also being physically or sexually abused by the domestic violence perpetrator. They may have been threatened (either directly or implicitly) that any disclosure of their abuse will lead to more violence to their mother and/or siblings and/or to themselves (see Peake and Fletcher 1997; and Chapters Two and Three). For this reason, children do not necessarily tell their mothers or anyone else that they are being abused, especially as they may be fully aware of the violence of which their fathers are capable. In Forman's (1995) study there were several examples of children believing that their mothers would be killed by their fathers if they revealed the fact that they were being sexually abused by the fathers. Both Forman (1995) and Kelly (1988) have also pointed out that children will deliberately not disclose their own sexual abuse so as not to add to their mother's distress. This means that often disclosures about the child's abuse occur after the partners have separated when children

perceive there may be more safety and when the mother is no longer having to deal so directly with her own abuse. This was acknowledged by one of the mothers in Forman's study:

> .... the disclosures came after we separated.... They protect the mother, they protect the mother's feelings, because she's going to be upset. (Forman 1995: 24; and see Hester and Radford 1996)

Hooper (1987) has suggested that because of the complexity of such situations, disclosure will not necessarily follow a straightforward linear pattern but might ebb and flow over a time span of up to several years.

9.5 Taking domestic violence seriously

Linked to the idea of safety for children living with domestic violence is the importance of consulting with children about what they have seen or experienced, and of taking this seriously. This is particularly vital in relation to child protection work where previous child death inquiries have shown the repercussions of the failure to do this (see Chapters Two and Eight for more details of such inquiries). O'Hara (1994) has pointed out how the inquiries in relation to the deaths of Sukina Hammond and Toni Dales found that neither child was specifically asked about her experiences of witnessing attacks on their mothers. Both had also expressed fears about their fathers to social workers and to hospital and nursery staff and yet these fears were ignored rather than explored. In Sukina's case, where she had also experienced physical violence from her father, Harris Hendriks, Black and Kaplan (1993) suggest that particular care and skills would have been needed to pick up the indicators of what was happening and how this was affecting Sukina:

> ...children like Sukina may be particularly at risk because they become so compliant, silent and eager to please that they give no clues, or only negative ones, about what they are experiencing and so become even more vulnerable. (p 32)

9.6 Handling disclosures by children – emphasis on safety

In whatever setting a child discloses that he or she is witnessing/experiencing domestic violence the primary focus must be on safety and protection from abuse. Any aims to provide therapeutic support or to achieve changes in behaviour at this stage will not succeed if the child does not feel safe at home (Jaffe, Wolfe and Wilson 1990). Because domestic violence can take many forms and children's experiences of it and reactions to it can be very varied, it is important that any disclosure is handled in such a way as to elicit as much information from the child as possible. The Children's Subcommittee of the London (Ontario) Co-ordinating Committee to End Woman Abuse (in Mullender and Morley 1994: 224-231) has produced some useful suggestions on how to deal sensitively with domestic violence disclosures from different age groups of children.

9.7 Assessing safety and risk

An important aspect of handling any disclosure is the need to make a thorough assessment of children's immediate safety needs. If the disclosure is

made in the context of social work involvement of any kind, the social services department have a statutory responsibility to carry out such a safety assessment. Disclosure may give rise to some difficult issues regarding confidentiality, especially if the child discloses information indicating that the child could be exposed to a potentially dangerous situation. In such circumstances, professionals would have a duty (moral rather than mandatory in the case of those professionals not linked to social services departments) under the *Children Act 1989* to report any concerns about risks of significant harm to a child. If possible, it would be preferable if this could be made clear to the child from the beginning.

Again, assessing safety with the child will probably require some careful questioning in order to acquire the necessary information, and some suggestions are given below (adapted from The Children's Subcommittee of the London (Ontario) Co-ordinating Committee to End Woman Abuse):

Assessing the Child's Safety

1. When was the most recent incidence of violence/abuse?

2. Ask the child to give details about this incident.

3. Were any weapons used or threatened to be used? Have any weapons been used or threatened to be used in the past?

4. Was the mother locked in a room or prevented from leaving the house? Have either of these things happened before?

5. Was there any substance abuse involved?

6. How often do violent incidents/abuse occur?

7. Have the police ever come to your house? What happened?

8. What does the child do when there is violence? Does the child try and intervene? What happens?

9. Where were the child's siblings during the violence?

Adapted from The Children's Subcommittee of the London (Ontario) Co-ordinating Committee to End Woman Abuse (in Mullender and Morley 1994:234)

Once such information has been obtained it is then possible to develop a personal safety plan with the child, which can reflect their age and understanding. This should be a straight forward and practical strategy which aims to help the child stay safe, especially when their mother is being physically attacked in some way. This might include:

■ asking children to identify a safe place to go to if there is further violence

■ asking children to identify a person they can go to if necessary

■ ensuring that children know how to contact emergency services

■ making sure children understand that it is neither safe nor their responsibility to intervene to try to protect their mothers.

9.8 Practice interventions with children

> it appears children can recover ..... provided that violence is eliminated and proper supports and opportunities for recovery are provided (Wolfe, Zak, Wilson and Jaffe 1986: 102)

> A ... possibility for improved practice is for positive and healing work with children who are survivors of living with abuse. Once they are safe, children can be helped to come to terms with the past and with the continuing confusions of the present. (Mullender 1996b: 13)

The needs of children who have lived with domestic violence are as many and varied as the children themselves, and may be affected by factors such as age, race and disability. Some children may have lived with violence or the threat of violence for most, if not all, their years of childhood. All will have been affected in some way by living with violence. Some children may need interventions which are both challenging and supportive, especially when they have learnt to excuse their father and blame their mother for the violence (Kelly 1994). Peled (1997) suggests that all children will require support to deal with the aftermath of their experiences:

> The cessation of violence is not sufficient for healing from its effects. Child witnesses of violence need emotional support both during and after witnessing the violence. (p 288)

It is essential that whatever form the support of children takes that it is provided by professionals who have an understanding of domestic violence dynamics and the effects of these on children (see Chapter Three). This will apply even in those situations where the domestic violence is compounded by other difficulties the children (and the mother) may be experiencing. The continuum of support needed will range from low key interventions consisting of validation and affirmation of children's experiences through to long-term therapy, and may include:

- empowering (rather than punitive) work with the mother

- interventions which serve to validate and acknowledge children's difficult experiences, and which reassure them that they are not alone and not to blame

- more long-term 'therapeutic' interventions in order to help children make sense of their experiences and understand the impact it has on them

- support which takes account of children's cultural/ethnic needs.

Given the prevalence of domestic violence and the large numbers of children affected by it, it is clear that many children at present do not receive any support in recovery at all.

9.9 Child abuse interventions and practice – reframing to take domestic violence into account

In Hester and Pearson's (1998) study of NSPCC practice, the team were making a concerted effort to incorporate domestic violence into their recovery work with abused children. The team felt that asking about and incorporating domestic violence as part of the picture had enhanced their

overall practice. For instance, thinking about both child abuse and domestic violence enabled them to reflect more thoroughly on their use of particular approaches, largely because many of the underlying issues were the same or overlapped because both domestic violence and child abuse involve one person exerting power and control over another.

Having a practice framework that included an understanding of domestic violence was also seen to enhance practice and partnership work with parents because it allowed a better understanding of what was going on in many of the cases:

> this framework of domestic violence explains a lot to us – it explains a lot of people's actions, or could help to explain them... I think it can only help us work in partnership much better. (child protection officer, in Hester and Pearson 1998)

As part of their attempt to introduce a 'domestic violence focus' in their work with children the NSPCC team re-examined and reframed some previously finished cases where domestic violence had not been disclosed or apparent, but where it might have been a possibility. This involved the exploration of the effect that taking domestic violence into account might have.

For instance, in one particular case the team had investigated an allegation that the key worker of a 16-year-old girl in residential care was involved with her in a sexual relationship. This was an allegation made by the girl herself, and was subsequently retracted. The man involved was consequently suspended for abusing his position of authority. The team had identified the case as involving child sexual abuse, even though the young woman concerned considered herself in some ways to be in a relationship with this man. As the investigation by the team progressed, they learnt more details about the young woman's relationship with this man, including instances where he had put his hands around her throat in a very threatening way. On at least two occasions she reported that when he was displeased with her 'he was rough and angry ....he pushed her, but did not hit her'. In another instance, 'he frightened her by shaking her violently'. There were also suggestions by her that he was being sexually coercive in that she described how 'he wouldn't leave her alone'.

Reframing did not alter the impropriety or nature of the man's behaviour. Reframing did, however, provide an *additional* way in which the team could have carried out recovery work with the young woman, and would have allowed them to work in a child/person-centred way that incorporated her own apparent perspective. Incorporating domestic violence into the picture would also have allowed information regarding refuges and other support for women experiencing domestic violence to be imparted with regard to safety planning with the young woman.

This use of 're-framing' to incorporate domestic violence proved a very useful mechanism for the integration of work around both child abuse and domestic violence. As one team member explained, it was these re-examinations of cases which had in particular clarified for her how the 'domestic violence lens' could enhance her own practice in relation to children:

> the thing that brought it home to me was that session we had when we looked at some cases, we traced the domestic violence, we traced the

problems back ... and it sort of really brought it home to me that there we all were, all the different agencies, running round in circles basically trying to help families, not actually considering the issue of the domestic violence and how problems that had either arisen from that or been exacerbated by that, and that in fact we probably had to go back and deal with that domestic violence issue to make any headway at all and to get people in a stable sort of settled environment, to be able to benefit from some therapy and get their lives back on course. (child care worker, in Hester and Pearson 1998)

Thus, incorporating domestic violence as a possible feature in the lives of the children concerned provided a much wider view and context for understanding their presenting behaviour. It also resulted in more effective work.

9.10 Children and behavioural difficulties

Children may be referred to social work or other practitioners as a result of behavioural difficulties. Alongside other abusive experiences, this may be an indication that the child is or has been living in a context of domestic violence (see Chapter Three). Jaffe, Hurley and Wolfe (1990) noted that domestic violence may be in the backgrounds of many children with emotional or behavioral difficulties, who are referred to children's mental health centres, and yet this is seldom the presenting problem:

> .... the presence of violence in the family is often overlooked. At times, 'the family secret' is kept from mental health professionals or more commonly, the issue is never raised or actively pursued. (p 468)

Several case examples are given where the domestic violence which children witnessed was not raised or addressed in the clinical assessment of the children (Hurley and Jaffe 1990). As a result, the focus of interventions remained on the behavioral or emotional difficulties of the children without addressing the possibility that domestic violence might be an underlying feature. As Hurley and Jaffe (1990) point out, such interventions fail to meet the needs of children and serve to 'silently condone' violence against women and children.

The London Borough of Hackney's (1993) good practice guidelines for responding to domestic violence include the recommendation that whenever children with behavioural and emotional difficulties are referred to social services social workers need to be aware that such difficulties may be a result of the child's experiences of domestic violence.

Hester and Pearson (1998) also found that, in cases involving children with behavioural difficulties, NSPCC workers' awareness of domestic violence could help to provide a more complete understanding and thereby achieve effective change. In one example, a child whose behavioural difficulties were initially assumed to be symptomatic of sexual abuse, began to be understood more fully in the therapeutic sessions when the child enacted scenes of domestic violence. In another example, a child's angry behaviour was resolved positively in therapy by incorporating the domestic violence both the child and the mother had experienced. By bringing the issue of domestic violence into the sessions the child was able to understand the effect on the mother

of the domestic violence, and that the effect continued despite them having left the violent man:

> [*Mother*] was having difficulties with her little girl's behaviour ... she's very angry because her father wouldn't let her have any of her belongings ever. He's still got all her toys – everything. And mum kept saying things like, but I'm sure you're too big for them. And she started kicking and biting and scratching her mum again. And I said, well maybe she sees you as the strong person now and forgets what it was like – so she doesn't see why you can't go and get them, so just talk to her about what it [*the experience of the domestic violence*] was like .... So just explore that anger with her and tell her, you know, mummy is angry too, mummy can't have any of her things. So that's what she did the next time she got angry and, yes, it worked, and the little girl kind of had a long conversation with her mother about [*it*]. (child protection officer, in Hester and Pearson 1998)

Thus, having a framework that included an understanding of domestic violence enhanced practice by providing insights into children's behaviour.

Even where domestic violence is known to be a factor in the backgrounds of children referred for therapeutic work, the therapist or practitioner may need to be very patient before the impact of this emerges. Silvern and Kaersvang (1989) give one example of an eight-year-old boy (Jon) who was referred for psychotherapy because of his occasional uncontrollable outbursts of aggression against other children, including attempts to choke them. After seven months in therapy, Jon finally described how he had once woken to see his father choking his mother, and how he had felt powerless to intervene. His mother was unaware of this and Jon did not want to upset or embarrass her by telling her about it. This sense of powerlessness had led to a strong sense of self-loathing and Jon's rages could be understood as his way of re-living the traumatic event, but with him in charge. Without an understanding of the impact of domestic violence, the focus of the work being carried out with Jon would have remained on his behaviour, which in turn would have remained incomprehensible and difficult to modify. Instead, one year after completion of therapy there had been no repetition of Jon's violent outbursts. Silvern and Kaersvang conclude that:

> ... current understanding of the inexorable impact of unresolved trauma suggests that it is dangerous to leave children unsupported in their efforts to master the experience of witnessing spousal abuse. (Silvern and Kaersvang 1989: 433)

9.11 Individual work with children

As in the case of Jon, described above, many children would benefit from the opportunity to express (either verbally or through play or art) what living with domestic violence has meant for them. As yet, however, there is very little literature specifically on this issue, especially in a UK context, although many of the general practice accounts of work with abused children are, of course, relevant.

Individual work with children can be carried out in a variety of both formal and informal ways, and can be undertaken by a number of different practitioners, such as social workers, teachers and youth workers. In many

cases, this work will consist of giving children the time and space to reflect on their experiences and to express any feelings of anger, hurt, fear and confusion that they might have. This will help to relieve children of the burden of the secret they have been holding and enable them to understand that they are not alone nor at fault. The basic requirements would be to validate children's experiences, to believe what they say and to take their situation seriously without needing to provide solutions. This is identical to the needs of children who are referred for clinical assessments:

> The children we have interviewed are almost universal in their need to be listened to, believed and supported. They usually are not looking for solutions but an opportunity to share their fears. (Jaffe, Wolfe and Wilson 1990: 83)

There are occasions where the impact of the domestic violence on the child necessitates therapeutic work. This might include situations where the child's behaviour is such that there is concern for the safety of the child or of others, or where concern for the child has persisted over time. This distinction between the thresholds of children whose needs can be met by 'talking with' someone and those who require therapy is an issue that will need careful assessment by the professionals/adults concerned and are similar to the thresholds used in other child abuse contexts.

Any individual or therapeutic work must have a focus on some of the specific effects on the child of witnessing domestic violence. This might include some of the same elements as outlined in the 'disclosure' and 'safety planning' sections above. That is, consideration of basic safety needs, an exploration of some of the confusion and ambivalent feelings the violence has evoked, and ensuring that children learn to understand that they are not responsible for the violence. This must be accompanied by messages that violence is never an appropriate way to resolve conflict and that children are not inevitably going to model such behaviour. Children need help in understanding that it is acceptable to be angry, but unacceptable to express this by means of violence. Jaffe, Hurley and Wolfe (1990) point out that 'children are often frightened by their own anger and feel that the cycle of violence is inevitable' (p 468), and it is important to explain that there is *no* inevitability about them becoming violent adults

Children who need individual work because they are particularly traumatised by witnessing or living with domestic violence will need the opportunity to describe and explore their experiences in some detail. Harris Hendriks, Black and Kaplan (1993) suggest a process of achieving this over time, using a semi-structured interview format for both the initial meeting and for the subsequent assessment work.

9.12 Individual work with children who have been physically, sexually or emotionally abused in the context of domestic violence

Children living with domestic violence who have been physically, sexually or emotionally abused may benefit from a range of levels of therapeutic interventions. Catchpole (1997), talking about therapeutic work with abused children generally, has pointed out that such work is in its infancy, and that some parents and professionals have reservations about its effectiveness.

Obviously, forcing children against their will to talk about difficult experiences will be counter-productive. However, for some children re-telling their story can in itself be of therapeutic value. For some younger children, therapy may be indicated even though they themselves may not recognise the need for it. Farmer and Owen (1995) found in their child protection study that the offer of some direct work was helpful to children who had been sexually abused. Social workers who could offer even a few sessions were reported to have made a difference. In refuges, such individual work with children has also been developed, as will be discussed later in this chapter.

Catchpole demonstrates that intervention can range from quite low level support to more intensive work and can include any of the following:

- therapeutic play

- the use of toys and books to help a child express feelings

- the use of puppets so that children can distance themselves from the conversations enacted through it

- the use of videoed sessions.

Whatever the approach adopted, it is vital that the work is undertaken at the child's pace, otherwise there is a danger of reinforcing the child's lack of control and/or of the child being overly compliant, as is often the case with children who have been (sexually) abused. In individual therapeutic work with children it is also important, as Silvern, Karyl and Landis (1995) have pointed, out, that the diversity of such children is acknowledged and addressed. They argue that race, ethnicity, economic status, family structure and the sexual orientation of the child's carer should all be given consideration if the child is to perceive the service provided as safe and accessible.

9.13 Groupwork with child witnesses of domestic violence

In the USA and Canada there has been the establishment of groups specifically for children who have witnessed the abuse of their mothers. Even though such services are more developed there than elsewhere, such services remain under-developed in comparison with services for abused women and for male perpetrators of domestic violence. The UK has seen the emergence of some similar groupwork programmes for children who have lived with domestic violence, and these will be discussed later in this chapter.

There are several reasons why groupwork is perceived as a valuable method of working with children who have experienced domestic violence. Amongst these is the fact that children themselves welcome the use of such groups. Recent research in this country, for instance, has suggested that the majority of children who have lived with domestic violence would prefer to talk to other children with similar experiences (McGee 1996). This is partly because adults are seen to talk and think differently to children, as one 12-year-old girl explained to McGee:

> I think because adults think differently to children so it's easier for children to talk to people like friends or maybe cousins or brothers and sisters, but hard to talk to adults because their minds are different in a way. (1996: 8)

Peake and Fletcher (1997) outline some of the advantages of groupwork for children who have been sexually abused, many of which are equally applicable to child witnesses of domestic violence. These include the following:

■ children are given the opportunity to talk about their experiences

■ children learn that they are not alone in their experiences

■ sharing experiences with others helps children to understand they are not responsible

■ children may have been isolated and therefore lacking in inter-personal skills – groupwork can offer a safe space to practice these skills

■ individual work can appear to replicate the abusive situation for the child in that the child is having to deal with a powerful adult

■ therapy/treatment that involves videos and one way screens etc. can also appear to the child to replicate the secrecy and lies of the abusive situation

■ in groupwork children outnumber adults and can gain a sense of empowerment and control from this

■ children can learn from each other ways of keeping safe in the future.

9.14 The early Canadian model of groupwork and beyond

Mullender (1994a: 239-254 and 1996a: 160-161) has charted the development of groupwork with children in Canada and the US. This approach first developed in Ontario, mainly as a result of the research by Jaffe and his colleagues (see Chapter Three). Building on earlier work by Alessi and Hearn (1984), a groupwork intervention model for children was devised by Wilson, Cameron, Jaffe and Wolfe (1986 and 1989) to be used in any appropriate setting (such as schools, child care and family agencies). However, it was not originally envisaged that the programme would be used for children currently in crisis, including children in refuges. The programme was aimed at up to 10 children aged 8 to 13 and ran for 10 weeks, covering primarily issues of prevention and education. Part of the value of the groups was seen to be the breaking of the secrecy surrounding domestic violence as well as looking at related issues, such as:

■ expressing and understanding feelings

■ dealing with anger and conflict resolution

■ developing self-esteem and social skills

■ exploring safety skills

■ understanding violence, including myths and stereotypes about this

■ understanding that the responsibility for violence lies with men

■ encouraging children's empowerment and self-protection.

The intention was that this groupwork intervention would form part of a wider response to the child and the non-abusing parent, though it was not made clear how this would work in practice.

children and domestic violence

Such groups (and adaptations of them) have since been offered by other children's services and there is now a co-ordinated system for referrals, intake and the co-running of groups, under the umbrella of the 'Community Group Treatment Program for Child Witnesses of Woman Abuse', based at the London (Ontario) Children's Aid Society. This has been accompanied by the extension of the lower age range from 8 years to 5 years and of the upper age limit from 13 to include up to 15-year-olds. This has also led to the possibility of sub-dividing groups to offer activities and approaches which are age/developmentally appropriate for each child. Siblings are split into different groups in order to prevent rivalry and to counter any fears about confidentiality. Unlike the original model from Wilson and colleagues there are attempts within the newer groups to address issues relating to the gendered nature of power and to address other forms of discrimination and oppression.

An important part of the groupwork process is attendance at the pre-admission interview, where the treatment essentially starts. This interview provides an opportunity to carry out a developmental assessment and to determine if other current events in the child's life might render the group's recovery focus inappropriate or impossible for the child. The mother is also expected to attend this interview in order immediately to begin the process of breaking down the secrecy about the violence. Mothers are also involved in some of the groups with the children as well as in their own separate groups so that they are kept informed and prepared for some potential 'acting out' behaviour from their children when they have to confront difficult issues in the group.

9.15 The 'Domestic Abuse Program' model of groupwork

Another innovative programme, specifically for child witnesses of domestic violence, is situated within the larger Domestic Abuse Program (DAP) in Minneapolis, Minnesota. DAP was established in 1979 to offer a range of co-ordinated services to abused women and their children and work with abusive men. This includes self-help groups, support and education groups as well as individual, couple and family work (when the violence has ended). The groups for child witnesses were first detailed by Grusznski, Brink and Edleson (1988), and since their inception in 1981 until 1993 almost a thousand children had been served by the children's programme (Mullender 1994a). Since then Peled and Edleson (1992) have carried out an evaluation of the programme, the findings from which have been incorporated into a practitioners' manual on groupwork for children who have lived with domestic violence (Peled and Davis 1995). This manual outlines the major issues which are addressed in the children's groups, and which they summarise with a flow chart of process and outcome goals (Peled and Davis 1995:16). These issues are as follows:

- breaking the secret

- defining violence and assigning responsibility

- learning to express feelings

- sharing experiences and breaking the sense of 'aloneness'

- learning self protection

- assertive conflict resolution

- protection planning

- strengthening self-esteem

- having a positive experience within the group.

As with the Ontario programme there is a careful intake assessment interview to ensure that the group is the most appropriate method of intervention for each child at that time. There is also a stipulation that the mother of any child joining the programme must be in a programme herself, and in addition to this there are optional parenting groups running alongside the children's programme. However, Mullender (1994a) points out that the DAP involves parents far less in the direct work with children than does the Community Group Treatment Programme. This can result in mothers being unexpectedly left to deal with supporting children through the difficult issues raised by the groupwork. She suggests that this is an important issue for consideration when establishing such groupwork programmes. Jaffe, Wolfe and Wilson (1990) also recommend that contact and involvement with mothers is essential if they are to be able to deal with the issues the group might raise for the children.

9.16 Evaluation of groupwork for children

There is relatively little recorded information on the effectiveness of the groups for children who have lived with domestic violence, although there are some promising indications from the few evaluations that have been carried out. These have led Peled (1997) to recommend that with regard to witnessing domestic violence:

> ... specialised treatment programs can benefit child witnesses of violence and, thus, are to be offered in every community. (p 288)

A small pilot study (Jaffe, Wilson and Wolfe 1986) suggested that group programmes created some improvements in children's self-esteem, attitudes about violence and safety skills. In a later study, 64 children (aged 7 to 13) were assessed by means of interviews pre- and post-attendance at the group sessions, and by completion of standardised measures. This was supplemented by obtaining similar information from the children's mothers (Jaffe, Wolfe and Wilson 1990: 89). This showed that children enjoyed the group and that it led to improvements for them in terms of safety skills and in their perceptions of each parent, but there were no apparent changes in behavioural or emotional difficulties. According to 88% of the mothers, the children enjoyed the group and they also perceived positive adjustment changes. The group programme also resulted in improved inter-agency liaison and a more integrated community response.

Jaffe and his colleagues conclude that the group programme is best suited to children 'with mild-to-moderate behaviour problems' (1990: 89), and that other children (especially those who have been exposed to long term repeated acts of violence) may require more extensive individual counselling. This confirms the view of the authors of the original intervention model (Wilson, Cameron, Jaffe and Wolfe 1989), who suggested that attitudes and behaviour could not realistically be changed in the course of a 10 week programme. They suggested that some children would require further group sessions.

A more recent evaluation of the same group treatment model, using a control group, has been carried out by Wagar and Rodway (1995). This found significant differences between the children pre and post group attendance, especially in relation to attitudes about and responses to anger, and in an understanding of where the responsibility for the violence should lie.

In the USA, Peled and Edleson (1992) have carried out a more formal qualitative evaluation of the children's group programmes run by the Domestic Abuse Project (DAP). They found that all the children interviewed and observed in groups had to some extent succeeded in the aim of breaking the secret of the abuse they had lived with. The group programme had also mostly achieved the other stated aims of developing children's protection and safety skills, increasing self-esteem, understanding violence and responsibility, encouraging the expression of feelings and experiencing the group as a safe and fun environment. They also found some unintended outcomes. Some children, for instance, respected the confidentiality of the group to the extent that they would not talk about the group with their mothers, thus frustrating the mothers' hopes that the issues would begin to be more openly discussed. For other children, the emotions stirred up by the reliving of painful events led to tensions and stress between the children and other family members. The role of mothers, therefore, is crucial in understanding and supporting the children through their groupwork experience.

Obviously, there are differences with each individual child as to how effective the group process can be, and this will be affected by factors such as personality and family background, as well as by each child's personal experiences of direct and indirect abuse. In their evaluation, Peled and Edleson (1992) reported the difficulties one girl experienced in the group because of her perception of being different because she had also been physically abused by her father. Care needs to be taken in the planning of the group composition in order to reflect the diversity of background and experience of the children involved. Particular attention would need to be paid in this respect to issues of children's race and disability to ensure that children are not isolated and marginalised within groups.

Whatever the success of the groupwork programmes for children, Peled and Edleson (1992) argue that more resources are needed to provide the necessary level of such provision. In addition, other related services for children need to be established, such as preventative work in schools and community organisations for children and young people, advocacy and therapy services for children as well as joint groups for children and mothers. This should all be situated within a co-ordinated response to women, children and abusing men.

9.17 Groupwork with children: the UK context

Until recently, in the UK, recognition of the effects and consequent needs of children living with domestic violence has been very largely confined to the refuge movement. As a result, groupwork for children who have lived with domestic violence developed initially within refuges. Outside refuges, such groupwork for children is in its infancy, and Mullender (1996b) indicates that groups for children are beginning to be established by the voluntary sector in Britain. Indeed, several of the children's charities (such as the NSPCC,

Barnardo's and The Children's Society) have developed, and are in the process of developing, projects to provide such a service.

There have also been more recent developments in groupwork for children which have grown out of inter-agency initiatives (Hague, Malos and Dear 1996). Examples of these include an innovative support group for child witnesses called AWAKENS, which has been created by Keighley Domestic Violence Forum. In Cleveland similar group programmes were developed by the local inter-agency forum and run jointly by the NSPCC and the social services department. These are positive developments, but there remains much to be achieved at a national level.

9.18 Work with children in refuges

A recent research study by Hague, Kelly Malos and Mullender (1996) was the first to detail the history of children's work in refuges in the UK and to examine at a national level the age-specific needs of the children living there. The study also highlighted the innovative and creative work being carried out by children's workers in refuges, and suggested that this work is often restricted by a chronic lack of resources and insecure and/or inadequate funding.

Since the inception of the refuge movement in the early 1970s, refuges have always provided protection for both women and children. However, early studies showed that many refuges were under-resourced and had few facilities specifically for children (Binney, Harkell and Nixon 1988: reprinted from 1981 text). This gradually began to change over the years with the development of policies relating to work with children, and with the employment of specific children's workers during the early 1980s. By 1986 Women's Aid Federation England (WAFE), the national co-ordinating body for refuges in England, had introduced an additional aim that refuges should provide specific support for children. This was followed in 1990 by the funding of a national children's officer post. The same year an evaluation was carried out of children's workers in nine WAFE refuges, which highlighted the value of their role as children's advocates and in offering support to children who had been physically or sexually abused (Ball 1990). The children themselves were positive about the children's workers and enjoyed the activities and play sessions provided. The main area of difficulty, identified by the children's workers themselves, was the lack of time to explore children's feelings and anxieties more fully on a one to one basis (a lack confirmed in Saunders' retrospective study of adults who spent time in refuges as children – see Saunders 1994 and 1995).

By the 1990s most refuges saw the provision of services to children as an important priority, and this was accompanied by the production of an information pack on work with children in refuges (WAFE 1992). In 1993 WAFE adopted a policy for children's rights in refuges (see Debbonaire 1994:164-169). Despite these developments, funding limitations mean that a small, but significant number of refuges lack facilities for children, and almost one third have no designated children's worker (Hague, Kelly, Malos and Mullender 1996).

Against this backdrop of financial constraints and uncertainties, refuges have been determined to provide improved services and facilities for children.

Higgins (1994) and Debbonaire (1995) have indicated that some of the reasons for this commitment to separate work and advocacy for children have been as follows:

■ children constitute two-thirds of refuge populations

■ coming into a refuge can be a traumatic experience for children

■ living in a crowded refuge can be stressful

■ children will often have experienced physical and/or sexual abuse themselves

■ children have different needs to their mother's needs

■ children's and mother's wishes may be in conflict.

A variety of age-appropriate work and activities has been developed over the years to meet the needs of children in refuges. These have been underpinned by the two key principles of a commitment to promoting the rights of children living with domestic violence and a belief in the healing value of play (Debbonaire 1994). Some of the work provided by children's workers is summarised by Debbonaire below:

Types of work being done with children in women's aid groups

There is no single job description that reflects the range of work going on with children in refuges but most children's workers will provide all or some of the following:

■ Play sessions for different age groups, including painting and other messy play, cooking

■ Outdoor activities, e.g. trips to park and further afield

■ Holidays for children, e.g. outward bound, outings to seaside, camping in France

■ Provision of advice and information specifically for children

■ Encouraging and helping children to help each other, through developing peer support, holding separate children's meetings, discussions on refuge rules e.g. why women only

■ One to one support sessions with children

■ Organising parties for birthdays and religious festivals

■ Holiday play and activity schemes

■ Work with mothers and children on a range of matters: problems in parent–child relationships, non violent punishment

■ Information on local advice and counselling services, youth and sporting activities etc.

■ Advocacy – supporting women in getting school and nursery places, access to health care for children, statements for children with special needs

---

> ■ Involvement in case conferences or giving evidence in court in
> support of child/mother
>
> ■ Liaison with local schools about general domestic violence issues,
> confidentiality, security
>
> *From Debbonaire (in Saunders 1995: 63).*

Hague, Kelly, Malos and Mullender's (1996) survey of children's work in
refuges categorised the work undertaken by child workers as involving:

■ play work

■ working with and through mothers

■ direct work with children (including formal and informal one to one work
children's meetings and groupwork)

■ advocacy work for children.

Higgins (1994) suggests that much of the work with children has been
innovative, and that this is especially so in relation to the development of
structured work with individual children. The aim of such individual work is to
help children recognise and understand their experiences of domestic
violence by supporting them in talking about it and in dealing with the
complexity of their emotions. Such work is carefully undertaken with an
agreement between mother, child and worker and with clear policies on limits
to confidentiality should there be any disclosures of abuse.

In all these areas, attempts are made to ensure that the work is age-
appropriate and flexible in approach, and that it reflects WAFE's commitment
to anti-racist and anti-discriminatory practice (see WAFE 1992). Higgins
(1994) explains how this is achieved by means of a multi-cultural playroom, by
sharing other languages and cultures and by discussing race awareness in
children's meetings. This is supplemented by working with children in a way
which is supportive of difference and diversity and encouraging equality of
treatment for boys and girls, and for children with impairments and learning
disabilities. At Hammersmith Women's Aid the children have produced their
own anti-discriminatory policies, which are reproduced below:

> **This is our Anti-Racism Statement!**
>
> 1. Do not make fun of other people's accents.
>
> 2. Do not make fun of their religion
>
> 3. Do not make fun of other people's food, and make noises about it.
>
> 4. Do not make fun of people's hair and what they look like, calling
> names etc.
>
> *From Higgins 1994: 173*

Anti-Sexism Statement!

1. We want boys and girls to play together.

2. Don't make fun of boys when they play with dolls and stuff.

3. Boys are not to take over the playroom.

4. Girls for football and rugby

5. Club for both girls and boys

From Higgins 1994: 173

Hague and her colleagues (1996) conclude that much sensitive and effective work with children is being carried out by children's workers in refuges with a level of expertise that is not found amongst other professionals:

> ... the valuable work they [*children's workers*] were already found to be doing can be publicised and celebrated through this report, especially as professionals in other settings who do undertake counselling and therapy are typically profoundly ignorant about woman abuse and often about wider anti-oppressive agendas too. (Hague, Kelly, Malos and Mullender 1996: 59)

This would appear to be a strong argument for the continued expansion and development of children's work within refuges, and for adequate long-term resources to be provided. This might also include the provision of services to children who are in temporary accommodation because the refuge has been unable to house them. Currently, some children's workers are funded via the local authorities through the provision of the Children Act Section 17(10), empowering local authorities to fund work with 'children in need'. But, as Thangam Debbonaire points out:

> With few exceptions, local authorities in England still do not specifically fund the work done in refuges with children, despite the fact that it clearly comes under this definition. (Debbonaire 1994: 159)

9.19 Preventative work with children in schools

> The final frontier in dealing with violence in our society which most often leaves women and children as victims is the potential role of primary prevention programmes ... Hope may lie in primary prevention programmes within school systems which ensure that children ... are made aware of this issue (Jaffe, Hurley and Wolfe 1990: 469)

Primary prevention relates to the prevention of violence before it occurs by examining and changing the attitudes, beliefs and behaviour which lead to violent behaviour. Such primary prevention mainly occurs in schools, and has been particularly developed in Canada, Australia and New Zealand. Such innovative work in schools is now beginning to become more widespread in the UK.

9.20 Violence prevention in Canada

Mullender (1994b: 256-265 and 1996a: 162-163) has summarised the development of violence prevention work in schools in Canada, where such work is particularly advanced. It began there around 1988, partly due to the presence and influence of Peter Jaffe on the Board of Education for the City of London, Ontario. Following a conference on the issue, a decision was taken that violence prevention should be addressed in schools. Training was given to school heads and designated teachers before five pilot schools each held a day long event on the issue, including plays, films and speakers. Counsellors were also made available for children who made disclosures or who found the material distressing.

This was followed in 1989 by a large day workshop on violence, which was attended by 680 secondary school pupils and staff from 21 school boards across the region. Subjects covered at the workshop included:

- rape and violence in teenage dating relationships

- where to turn for help

- breaking down the isolation

- the establishment of student-run hotlines

- supporting and helping others

- the need for more teacher awareness and concern.

The success of the workshop proved school to be an appropriate environment in which to tackle and prevent violence. This was coupled with an acceptance by the Ontario Ministry of Education that domestic violence had an impact on children's learning, thereby making it an issue of concern for education. Thus, the work was soon expanded. By 1991 all secondary schools in London (Ontario) had held similar workshops. This was followed by local and regional developments and initiatives including:

- a set of procedures to use for teachers when children disclose living with violence

- the distribution of resource kits and videos to every school

- the publication of a monthly violence prevention newsletter

- the distribution of leaflets on domestic violence for students and for teachers

- information sessions for classes or staff groups

- presentations in school for pupils, staff and parents

- a violence awareness week.

Some of the initiatives were aimed at elementary and kindergarten schools as well as secondary schools. A violence awareness week, for example, might include age-specific activities, such as 11-year-olds helping 6-year-olds to draw anti-violence posters and kindergarten children being given information by shelter workers on how to call for help if their mother was being attacked. Gamache and Snapp (1995) provide a more detailed account of violence prevention programmes for elementary schools, and Sudermann, Jaffe and

Hastings (1995) of such programmes for secondary schools, which have been used in the US. In effect, such work has provided a combination of both prevention and intervention.

In addition to these developments, the Ontario Ministry of education promoted a policy of no tolerance of violence in schools, and requiring every school to develop a violence-free policy. This was accompanied by active co-operation with women's organisations such as the Women's Community House in London, described above. Loosley (1994) describes how, since 1989, part of the children's program of this organisation has been to provide schools with a violence awareness program. This was initially aimed at 6 to 12-year-olds and has now been expanded to include the 4 to 18 age range, and covers a number of issues related to attitudes and beliefs about violence, particularly in relation to violence against women. Through discussion groups, puppet shows and plays, children are encouraged to think about safety planning, and to identify alternatives to the misuse of power and control in relationships:

> It is through mutual community efforts like this program, and the promotion of an open awareness and understanding of woman abuse and issues of violence, that those involved with children can make a difference in their lives. (Loosley 1994:186)

As the violence prevention work has developed there have been increasing attempts to integrate this work into the general school system. In London (Ontario) this has resulted in the production of a video and training pack, entitled A *School-based Anti-violence Programme* (ASAP). This comprehensive pack covers a wide range of issues, including:

■ the need to involve the whole school and local community in violence prevention

■ prevention and intervention strategies for elementary and secondary schools

■ how to create a safer school climate

■ how to promote gender equality

■ positive responses to disclosure (from children and staff)

■ further available resources.

Such a programme is far in advance of anything in existence in Britain. Nevertheless, Mullender (1994b) suggests there are some omissions to the ASAP manual, especially in relation to its lack of integration of racism awareness, and its failure to mention homophobia or the fact that schools and school staff may be abusive. No doubt these are areas for further development. The overriding message remains that the violence prevention work in Canadian schools has generated much excitement and enthusiasm and provides a model for others to follow. Most importantly, evaluation of the work to date has shown that for the majority of pupils it has had a significant impact on their awareness of abuse issues, and on the sources of help available. The children and young people involved are also almost unanimous in their support of the need to address the issue of violence and abuse and of the approaches being used to achieve this.

9.21 *Violence prevention in the UK*

> An exciting amount has been achieved there [*Canada*] and, as a general
> approach, it would be highly transferable to the British context. This makes
> the relative inactivity here look inexcusable and dangerous in comparison.
> (Mullender 1994b: 257)

Mullender (1994b) points out that work in the UK on violence prevention in
schools and in youth work is largely undeveloped and *ad hoc* rather than co-
ordinated. This is beginning to change in some areas as a result of the
influence of inter-agency initiatives, and many more education authorities have
now produced, or are in the process of producing, education packs on
violence prevention. In addition to this, some of the work on conflict
resolution now being carried out in some schools does include an
acknowledgement of domestic violence as an issue.

Much of the impetus for the preventative work that is being carried out has
come from Women's Aid groups, who have given talks in schools and
provided teachers with training to raise their awareness of the issues. In some
cases refuge workers have joined with teachers to plan anti-violence work,
which has also focused on bullying and racism within schools. Higgins (1994)
has described how Hammersmith Women's Aid built strong links with local
schools and has provided workshops for teachers and helpers on the effects
of domestic violence. The refuge was also involved with a joint project on
bullying and ran a workshop with 14 and 15-year-old girls on positive images
for young women, which raised issues concerning sexism, racism and violence
against women. In addition to this, some schools now include aspects of
violence-free conflict resolution in their curriculum (Debbonaire 1994).

Hague, Malos and Dear (1996) have also identified a growing trend for some
of the inter-agency initiatives to develop preventative work in schools and
youth projects. Inter-agency projects in Leeds, Islington and Keighley have
provided support work in schools, which has been further developed by the
production of comprehensive education packs and training modules. In Leeds,
a Home Office funded programme for primary schools was developed and
tested alongside teachers in the classroom. In Keighley, the Home Office
funded the development of a resource pack on gender issues and violence
for use in schools and youth clubs. In Islington, inter-agency initiatives led to
the publication in 1995 of a *Stop Domestic Violence* manual for use in schools.
This is a very thorough and comprehensive manual, including advice and
information, training modules, curriculum material and ideas on awareness
raising. In addition, a few forums have produced plays and workshops for
schools and youth groups.

Clearly, such developments are welcome and useful. Generally, however,
schools and youth and community services in Britain remain an untapped
source of potential for work on violence prevention and education.
Recommendations for the future development of such work have come from
various sources, including research studies (Hague, Kelly, Malos and Mullender
1996) and from a local authority following a conference on domestic violence
and children (Holder, Kelly and Singh 1994). Amongst their recommendations
are the following:

- all schools to develop policies recognising domestic violence

- schools/colleges to have policies on confidentiality and safety

- regular input from refuges to all teachers and youth workers about domestic violence and the work of the refuge

- partnerships between refuges, colleges and youth services to develop curricula/programmes/activities on sexism, power, gender and non-violent relationships

- schools and youth clubs to develop skills work on assertiveness, conflict resolution and problem solving

- schools, colleges and youth services to develop peer networking, advocacy and education to provide support for young people

- educational systems to recognise the impact of domestic violence on children's and young people's learning, which may necessitate additional support.

The implementation of these recommendations would serve to act as both intervention and prevention. The breaking down of the secrecy surrounding domestic violence would enable those children and young people already living with it, or who have lived with it, to gain support and help with safety. All would learn the impact of violent behaviour and hopefully understand that the power and control that such violence exemplifies is not acceptable in any relationship.

9.22 Summary

- Adults in a variety of settings will encounter children who are living with/have lived with domestic violence. This will include doctors, health visitors, solicitors, social workers, family centre workers, foster/adoptive carers, teachers, youth workers and mental health practitioners.

- Whenever children's behaviour raises anxiety of any kind, or where there are child protection concerns, it is important to bear in mind the possibility that the issue of domestic violence may be an important (and key) aspect of the context for the child. This may be particularly so for children who are presenting with emotional or behavioural difficulties.

- Incorporating an awareness and understanding of domestic violence in this way can enhance practice and improve partnership work with parents because it allows a fuller understanding of the overall family picture.

- It is important to ask children about domestic violence whenever this is possible/appropriate, and it may be necessary to find out or ask over a period of time, as children might be fearful of the consequences of disclosure, and/or protective of their parent(s) and/or have learnt to keep the 'family secret' from others.

- When a child discloses experiences of domestic violence, the primary focus must be on safety and protection from abuse.

- The needs of children who have lived with domestic violence are varied and may be affected by factors such as age, race and disability.

- Some children may have learnt to excuse their father and blame their mother for the violence, and may need interventions which are both supportive and challenging.

- Support for children must be provided by professionals who have an understanding of domestic violence dynamics and of the effects of these on children. The continuum of support needed will range from low key interventions consisting of validation and affirmation of children's experiences through to long-term therapy.

- Some children, especially those who have also experienced sexual and/or physical abuse from the perpetrator of the domestic violence, will benefit from individual therapeutic work. This work must include a consideration of basic safety needs, an exploration of some of the confusion and ambivalent feelings the violence has evoked, and ensuring that children learn to understand that they are not responsible for the violence.

- Groupwork is a valuable method of working with children who have experienced domestic violence, especially as children themselves welcome the use of such groups. Such work addresses issues such as breaking the secret, strengthening self-esteem, defining violence and assigning responsibility, protection planning and learning to express feelings.

- In the UK, individual and groupwork for children who have lived with domestic violence developed initially within refuges and is still in its infancy outside refuges. Several of the children's charities (such as the NSPCC, Barnardo's and The Children's Society) have developed, and are in the process of developing, projects to provide these services.

- Primary prevention programmes, which aim to examine and change the attitudes, beliefs and behaviour which lead to violent behaviour are now beginning to become more widespread in schools in the UK.

- In some areas such violence prevention work has been further developed by the production of comprehensive education packs and training modules. For instance, Islington council has published a comprehensive *Stop Domestic Violence* manual for use in schools, which includes advice and information, training modules, curriculum material and ideas on awareness raising.

CHAPTER TEN: INTERVENTION WITH MALE PERPETRATORS OF DOMESTIC VIOLENCE

In social work practice little attention has been paid to challenging the behaviour of the violent man (see Farmer and Owen 1995, Mullender 1996a, Humphreys 1997, O'Hagan and Dillenburger 1995; and see Chapter Eight). Programmes to confront and change the behaviour of men who have been violent are now being developed in the UK, although many are in their infancy and are still in the process of evaluating their success in terms of stopping the men's violent behaviour. It should be noted that many of these programmes do not appear to address the impact of men's behaviour on children, even though most of the men concerned are probably fathers.

10.1 Intervention approaches with perpetrators of male violence

Any interventions which endeavour to change the behaviour of violent men will to some extent be influenced by beliefs about the causes and reasons for this behaviour. There are various theories and explanations as to why men are violent to women (see Hague and Malos 1993 and Jenkins 1990 for overviews), some of which are summarised by Scourfield (1995) as follows:

- seeing the violence as biological (men are 'naturally' violent)

- systems theory (emphasises the 'dysfunctional' family unit as the cause of the violence)

- psychodynamic (violence is caused by problems in the man's past)

- social learning (violence is learnt through observation/modelling)

- social structural (violent men are fulfilling their dominant gender role)

- feminist (violence is rooted in patriarchy and in men's need to have power and control over women). (Scourfield 1995: 5-7)

These different perspectives obviously lead to a number of different approaches to working with violent men, which can be broadly categorised as:

- anger management

- cognitive behavioural work

- individual therapeutic work

- family therapy work

- pro-feminist approach

Some of these approaches will be examined in more detail in the remainder of this chapter. It has to be recognised that work with violent men, whatever the approach, requires specific skills, which may be somewhat different to the usual social work skills. According to Milner (1996), traditional social work practice aims to disperse anger and has not provided skills in confrontation techniques, which are crucial in relation to work with violent men. It is essential, therefore, that adequate training and safety measures are introduced before challenging violent men can occur. O'Hara (1994) points to the need for using only experienced workers for such work. It will also be important to

be aware of existing agencies which offer programmes for violent men, and to make referrals where necessary.

Whoever attempts this work must ensure the centrality of the message that violence is *not* acceptable and must aim to confront/stop/prevent further violence. This will require skilful intervention given that many men deny and/or minimise their violence (Hearn 1996a; and see Chapter One), and will explain it in terms of anger problems. In this respect, there are limitations to the use of anger management techniques when working with violent men. Mullender (1996a) argues that the social learning theory underpinning this approach does not adequately challenge men's assumptions about, and their attempts to use, violence to control and dominate women with whom they have relationships:

> An overall objection to the concept of anger management is that it feeds into men's habitual denial and minimisation of their behaviour. A 'problem with my anger' ... does not sound criminal, unacceptable or commensurate with the physical and emotional damage inflicted on women. (Mullender 1996a: 230)

10.2 *The development of programmes for violent men in the US and Canada*

In the USA and Canada there has been a longer history of agencies providing services to men who are violent to their female partners. The early programmes tended to adopt models of intervention which were mostly informed by the more individualist theories of male violence. Adams (1988) provides a useful overview of these earlier clinical treatment models, which he labels as the 'insight model', the 'ventilation model', the 'interaction model' and the 'cognitive-behavioural' and 'psychoeducational models'. All these models are criticised for not taking gender and power into account, overly empathising with men, and not necessarily placing responsibility for the violence with the man:

> ... some of these approaches *collude* with batterers by not making their violence the primary issue or by implicitly legitimizing men's excuses for violence. (Adams 1988: 177)

These approaches reflect what Dobash and Dobash (1992) refer to as the 'therapeutic society', which they see as prominent in North America, and which is characterised by the belief that all social, economic and political problems are seen to be rooted in individual difficulties which can be solved through therapy. These individualist approaches are seen to be problematic in work with violent men because they are not adequately challenging of men's behaviour:

> Despite their apparent diversity, therapeutic approaches to violent men have a number of common elements ... the basic assumption is that the fundamental cause of violence is faulty personality or psychopathology .... No individual man is accountable for his violence; the family, faulty backgrounds or situational factors are the causes. (Dobash and Dobash 1992: 239)

Mullender (1996a) echoes the Dobash's concern about another individualist model of male violence, used especially in earlier American interventions. This

can be broadly categorised as the intrapsychic model, which is problematic in that it explains men's violence in terms of unresolved past problems and can, therefore, lead to collusion in absolving men of accepting responsibility for their current abusive actions by focusing on past experiences as excuses. This is not to say that issues from the past might not need to be addressed, but that this needs to be done separately from the focus on their violence.

10.3 A co-ordinated community approach to domestic violence and violent men

Because men's denial and minimisation of violence is so entrenched and widespread (Ptacek 1988; Hearn 1996a) and because so many see violence as a legitimate way of dealing with their female partners (Mooney 1994), it is vital that any interventions aimed at changing their behaviour are challenging, confronting and do not allow men to avoid any of the responsibility for their behaviour (for more details of such work with violent men see, for instance, Edleson and Tolman 1992; Russell 1995). This is precisely the philosophy underpinning the pro-feminist model of work with violent men, sometimes combined with empowering groupwork for women. This approach was first developed in 1977 in Boston by EMERGE, which was established in close co-operation with the local women's shelter. This led to the establishment of other profeminist men's programmes, such as RAVEN, and both now have projects across the US. There is much variation as to how such projects are organised with some offering specific programmes, whilst others offer a co-ordinated community approach to domestic violence.

The most well-known example of a co-ordinated approach to domestic violence is the Domestic Abuse Prevention Project in Duluth, Minnesota which combines empowering support services for women with programmes for violent men. This latter, however, remains a component of the project which is fiercely debated, especially as one of Duluth's founders acknowledges:

> ... after all, there is little evidence that batterers' rehabilitation groups are successful. (Pence 1998)

It also co-ordinates the work of the police, the courts, social services and women's shelters and attempts to inform practice and policy initiatives on domestic violence issues (Hague and Malos 1993; Dobash and Dobash 1992). Some now also include parenting groups for violent men as part of their domestic abuse programmes (see Mathews 1995 for a more detailed account of one such group). Thus, such programmes have far-ranging aims, including attempting to educate and inform the wider public, ensuring the safety of women and challenging individual men. (Similar co-ordinated approaches based on the Duluth model have been established in other parts of the world – see Busch and Robertson (1994) for one such example in New Zealand and Frances (1995) for an overview of community programmes in Australia).

10.4 The UK context

> [W]hile there are many agencies involved with men who have been violent to women, few specialize in, or have men's violence to women, as their main concern. (Hearn 1996b: 111)

In the UK the provision of services to men who are violent to their female partners is a relatively recent area of social work and probation provision. This has begun to develop partly as a result of policies aiming to increase the criminalisation of domestic violence, and to a growing recognition that more interventions need to be aimed at men as the cause of domestic violence (Hague and Malos 1993; Mullender 1996a).

Most existing anti-violence counselling programmes in the UK are run by voluntary or independent organisations, sometimes with some statutory funding, and some in partnership with local domestic violence forums, often with funding from probation (Hague, Malos and Dear 1996). Partnerships with the probation service, as the main agency with responsibility for working with offenders, are developing most rapidly. In the future, the probation service is likely to be involved with programmes for men either as service providers, as funders of voluntary projects or as the main referring agency. Where the probation service already provides groupwork for male sex offenders, it is important that it is also recognised that many of these men will also be perpetrators of domestic violence. This will help avoid perpetuating the false dichotomy between abusers of children and abusers of women, and allow such groups the additional opportunity to tackle men's violence on a wider scale, and to make the connections between various misuses of male power. This approach might be useful across all agencies. Hearn (1996b), for instance, asks:

> Would it be appropriate to create (anti-) violence workers who would be able to follow through the inter-agency interventions that are necessary in working against violence? Focusing on men's violence also means taking up the problem of violence in a consistent way throughout agencies. (Hearn 1996b: 111)

It has to be recognised, however, that specialist projects for domestic violence perpetrators being established by the probation service will exclude many domestic violence perpetrators. This is because many men do not appear before the courts, and few are placed on probation (Scourfield 1995; and see Chapter Five). Similar problems arise for those voluntary projects taking only court-mandated referrals.

10.5 UK programmes for violent men

In Britain projects to work with violent men have developed in a variety of ways and adopted a range of models of approaches. Some, such as AGENDA in Nottingham and the Domestic Violence Intervention Project (DVIP) in London have drawn on the ideas of Duluth, and DVIP was the first to provide two linked services for supporting women and for challenging men. There are also several MOVE (Men Overcoming Violence) groups throughout the country as well as other inter-agency and independent schemes, such as the Everyman Centre in Plymouth. This latter project is jointly financed by the local health authority and social services department with some central government funding from the Department of Health rather than from probation partnership funding. It also runs a parallel support service for women, and mostly works with men who self refer.

Some initiatives have stemmed from inter-agency projects. These include the IMPACT project in Derby, which is run directly by the inter-agency forum and is again based on the Duluth model. Similarly, Cleveland domestic violence forum runs groups for male perpetrators, which, like IMPACT, has set up a women's support group to run in tandem with the men's programme (Hague, Malos and Dear 1996). All these projects vary in structure and approach in terms of the source of referrals (self-referral, court-mandated or both), the amount of involvement of and accountability to women survivors and the philosophy which informs their work (see Mullender (1996a) for the current locations and variations of groups in the UK).

10.6 Running programmes for violent men in the UK

Malloch and Webb's (1993) study of intervention and provision for violent men in the UK found variations in the work being carried out. They differentiated the approach of the specialist ('focused') projects from the ('non-focused') statutory sector provision. The latter consisted of social workers or probation officers who worked with male offenders as part of their generic caseload but whose interventions were not designed to deal exclusively with domestic violence. They found that the 'non-focused' workers tended to view domestic violence as a result of individual inadequacies and/or problems within the relationship itself. Therefore, their interventions were aimed at changing individual psychological processes, possibly leading to reconciliation:

> Statutory social work intervention in domestic violence is rarely governed by explicit policies or direct work guidelines ... thus ... the focus of work tends to be directed at improving the functioning of the male abuser or altering the functional dynamics of the relationship through marital therapy. (Malloch and Webb 1993: 125)

In contrast, the 'focused' approach of the specialist projects required interventions with high levels of 'challenging and confronting' of male attitudes about women. This was in marked contrast to the 'curing and caring' approach adopted by the non-focused workers (Malloch and Webb 1993: 140).

In his later survey of 23 UK agencies offering a service to domestic violence perpetrators (15 specialist projects in the voluntary sector and 8 in the statutory sector working with perpetrators as part of a wider caseload), Scourfield (1995) found that the work is primarily undertaken in a group setting. 43% of the agencies had programmes run just by men, whilst 48% involved both men and women, and 9% were run by women only. However, unlike in North America, Scourfield found that few of the men's projects (17%) had formal links with and accountability to refuges. Scourfield also found that practice had moved on from the earlier interventions and that most (57% n=13) of the agencies appeared to be working on a pro-feminist model of challenge and the promotion of male responsibility for the violence.

However, some concerns about men's projects continue, especially those with little or no accountability to women. Mullender (1996a) indicates that some of the men's self-help projects have been criticised for their lack of a strong pro-feminist approach and that, as a result, some have responded by introducing changes. There is also concern about the possibility of male

collusion in all-male groups and of working from 'men's agendas' (Mullender, 1996a: 237). This was typified by the example of one men's group, which includes reconciliation amongst its aims. Mullender considers this to be possibly at odds with, and detracting from, the focus on stopping men's violence and empowering women (Mullender 1996a).

10.7 *The pro-feminist approach to working with violent men*

All the UK agencies working with violent men in Scourfield's (1995) survey, which he characterised as pro-feminist, said they used 'cognitive-behavioural' techniques in their approach, although it is not always clear exactly what is meant by this label. According to Mullender (1996a) and Adams (1988), the pro-feminist model uses cognitive-behavioural techniques in order to achieve individual change and the acceptance of individual responsibility. This is coupled with an educational element which places the violence in a social/structural context in order to challenge assumptions about men and women, whilst maintaining the centrality of power and control issues. Similar approaches have also been developed by therapists doing individual work with violent men where it is required that men take full responsibility for their actions (see, for instance, Jenkins 1990).

Adams (1988) provides a detailed account of how such a groupwork programme would develop. This would involve a very directive approach from the workers, including:

■ initial counselling groups to concentrate on the safety of the woman, with men being asked to devise 'safety plans' to minimise the possibility for further violence

■ separate contact is made with the woman and she is offered support etc.

■ men are confronted about their minimisation or denial of responsibility for the violence, including examining their excuses and reasons for violence

■ men's other controlling and abusive behaviour patterns are identified

■ men are asked to keep 'control logs' to make them more accountable for their behaviour

■ video taped exercises are used to show the controlling behaviour.

Adams also points out that counselling alone is ineffective to achieve change and must be accompanied by legal sanctions.

10.8 *The effectiveness of programmes for violent men*

There are many questions still to be answered about the effectiveness of men's programmes, both in terms of whether they promote the safety of women and children and whether, and in what ways, they can achieve change in the behaviour of violent men. Few services have any systematic means of monitoring their efficacy and there are difficulties in determining what constitutes 'success' and by whom this should be decided (Mullender 1996a; Scourfield 1995). There is also the concern that, whether attendance in such programmes is court-mandated or voluntary, the men attending programmes

represent only a very small fraction of domestic violence perpetrators. Any claims of success or otherwise need to be viewed, therefore, with some caution.

There are also concerns that such programmes might give women false and unsafe hopes about staying or returning, and that attendance at such programmes may be used in some cases in order to enhance men's position in contested residence or contact cases (Mullender 1996a; Morley 1993). Attending such groups may also be used as a manipulative ploy by men to gain reconciliation with their partners – examples of this were found in England and Denmark in Hester and Radford's (1996) study of post-separation contact arrangements in circumstances of domestic violence.

There is also concern that the development of services for men will be at the expense of the funding and provision of supportive and protective services for women (Mullender 1996a; Pringle 1995). Other debates have centred around the use of such men's programmes as a diversion from criminal prosecution, and there is concern that this may be seen as a 'soft' alternative for men, and serves to decrease the seriousness of domestic violence as a crime (Hague and Malos 1993; Mullender 1996a).

10.9 Recent evaluations of UK programmes for violent men

Recently, there has been in-depth, independent evaluation of three UK programmes for violent men, which have increased our knowledge of this work. Dobash, Dobash, Cavanagh and Lewis (1996) have evaluated two such programmes in Scotland – CHANGE[1], established in the former Central Region of Scotland in 1989, and the Lothian Domestic Violence Probation Project (LDVPP), established in Edinburgh in 1990. In England, Burton, Regan and Kelly (1998) have carried out an evaluation of the Domestic Violence Intervention Project (DVIP), based in West London, and which incorporates two separate, but linked projects – the Women's Support Service (WSS) and the Violence Prevention Programme (VPP).

The programmes evaluated by Dobash and his colleagues were both based within the criminal justice system – men attended the programmes on a mandatory basis as a condition of their probation orders, following convictions for violent offences against their female partners. In order to assess the effectiveness of the programmes, they were compared with the outcomes for those offenders who were given traditional sanctions (such as fines, probation or prison sentences). Parallel information was obtained from some of the partners and ex-partners of the offenders, and in all cases data was collected at three stages – at the point of imposition of the criminal justice sanction, at 3 months and at 12 months. Attendance at the programmes occurred every week for a period of 6 to 7 months, and consisted of a structured, challenging, cognitive-behavioural groupwork approach.

Dobash and his colleagues found overall that *all* criminal justice sanctions had some positive effects in terms of the reduction of further violence. However, in comparison to those men given traditional sanctions, the programmes for

---

[1] Since the evaluation CHANGE has stopped operating.

violent men were most successful in changing men's behaviour. According to their partners, this applied in relation to a reduction in men's violent behaviour, in the frequency of violent episodes and to overall improvements in their controlling and intimidating behaviour, all of which led to an enhanced quality of life for the women involved. The aspects of the groupwork which men found most helpful were:

- group discussions focusing on minimisation and denial

- group discussion to identify 'triggers' to violence

- video work to show well-known scenes

- learning to take 'time outs' to prevent a violent episode.

Despite these positive outcomes, Dobash and his colleagues acknowledge that the findings need to be treated with some caution. This is particularly so as the numbers involved are small and are smaller still by the third stage of evaluation, making conclusions about longer-term impacts more tentative. There is also the possibility of some selection bias, both in the sentencing process and in the acceptance of men onto programmes. Furthermore, although there had been a reduction in violence, a third (33%) of the men in the programme had committed at least one further violent act against their partners by the end of the 12 month follow up. Whilst men may benefit from talking explicitly about their violence, and can learn to accept some responsibility for their behaviour, it is clear that women and children cannot be guaranteed their safety during the process of such programmes, or indeed, afterwards.

The DVIP programme in West London, evaluated by Burton and her colleagues (1998) is different in some respects to the programmes outlined above. In particular, men can be accepted onto the Violence Prevention Programme (VPP) on either a court-mandated or voluntary basis. Unlike the Scottish projects, DVIP also runs a linked Women's Support Service (WSS), which aims to offer empowering support work for women in order to maximise their safety. Both the projects were evaluated by the research team by means of a multi-stage approach, using questionnaires and in-depth interviews with violent men, the women partners, probation officers and staff from both projects. This was supplemented by analysis of group sessions and case files.

The pro-active support offered to women through WSS was seen to be a crucial part of the overall programme aims of DVIP, as these are both to stop men's use of violence and increase the safety of women. The work undertaken with women explored issues, such as self-esteem and the impact of violence on children. In fact, an important area of development in DVIP was to integrate children's issues into all areas of its work.

Burton and her colleagues found that for some women involvement with WSS had been 'successful' in a variety of ways, including providing women with the opportunity to end the relationship safely or to re-negotiate their relationships. WSS was also effective in reaching women who tend not to use other domestic violence services, namely, women from ethnic minorities and women with professional qualifications.

The VPP aspect of the project consisted of a two stage programme of groupwork over a 32 week period, focusing firstly on men's physical violence,

followed by exploration of other aspects of men's abusive and violent behaviours.

There was tentative evidence of the programme achieving some 'success' in that *some* women reported that the violence stopped. Men who completed the programme also appeared to have undergone changes in their behaviour and in their understanding of, and attitudes to, domestic violence. However, there was concern that the attrition rate for both voluntary and court mandated attendance was extremely high with less than a third of the men referred to the programme completing it.

On the basis of their evaluation Burton and her colleagues make some suggestions on work with violent men, including:

- the safety of women and children must be central to any programmes for violent men

- separate parallel support programmes for women are vital

- 'voluntary' referrals to programmes are important in that such men may be the most motivated and and may have a positive influence on other men in the group. Voluntary referrals are also important for women, who can require attendance at such programmes in order to try to end the violence in their relationship.

There is still much to learn about how, and if, violent men's behaviour can change. There are indications that this might best be achieved in co-ordinated, multi-faceted responses to domestic violence. However successful these might appear, it is important that work with men is not used as an alternative to a criminal justice response, as this would ultimately lead to the down-grading of domestic violence as a crime, thus further endangering women and children.

10.10 Summary

- Programmes to confront and change the behaviour of men who have been violent to female partners are mostly in their infancy in the UK. As yet, many do not appear to specifically address the impact of men's behaviour on children.

- Programmes alone may be ineffective in achieving change in the behaviour of violent men, and must not be seen as a diversion from effective legal sanctions.

- There are various theories and explanations as to why men are violent to women, leading to a number of different approaches to working with violent men, particularly cognitive behavioural work, a pro-feminist approach and anger management.

- Men's denial and minimisation of violence is entrenched, as is the notion that violence is a legitimate way for men to deal with their female partners.

- Whatever the approach adopted, work with violent men requires specific skills, which may be somewhat different to the usual social work skills. A central feature of this work must be the message that violence is *not* acceptable and must aim to confront/stop/prevent further violence.

■ In the UK, most anti-violence counselling programmes are run by voluntary or independent organisations, some with statutory funding, and some in partnership with local domestic violence forums. Projects vary in structure and approach in terms of the source of referrals, the amount of involvement of and accountability to women survivors and the philosophy which informs their work.

■ Recent, independent evaluations of three UK programmes for violent men have shown that they have some success in changing men's behaviour and in increasing women's safety in a variety of ways, although the numbers involved are too small to make generalisations.

■ Women's and children's safety need to be central to any programmes for violent men and parallel support programmes for women should be offered.

CHAPTER ELEVEN: MULTI-AGENCY INVOLVEMENT AND CO-OPERATION IN DOMESTIC VIOLENCE

> At present education, health and social services departments and the family justice system work in considerable ignorance of each other's skills, strengths and weaknesses. There is a need for initiatives ... to improve services for troubled children. (Harris Hendriks, Black and Kaplan 1993: 174)

Women and children who are experiencing domestic violence will be in contact with a variety of service providers (see Chapter One). It is important, therefore, that all these services provide a co-ordinated approach to domestic violence in order to ensure that women and children are protected and supported. Historically, the abuse of women and the abuse of children in the family (and by the same man) have been viewed as separate issues. This has led to the development of separate services and policies to address the needs of each group (Atkinson 1996).

This separation has tended to be replicated in the inter-agency initiatives, which have developed in Britain over the last few years. These include the establishment of domestic violence forums, which have focused mostly on the experiences of women, whilst multi-agency Area Child Protection Committees (ACPCs) have the explicit function of focusing on children and their protection. The issue of children and domestic violence has been mostly absent from inter-agency policies at national level, both in relation to ACPCs and domestic violence forums.

To provide the most effective response to domestic violence, it is essential that these two multi-agency bodies develop ways of working in partnership, and ways of giving weight to the voices of the women and, especially, the children concerned. This may be partly possible through collaboration between them with regard to children's services plans. This will help to create an integrated and strategic approach to services for children experiencing domestic violence.

This chapter examines both the work of ACPCs in relation to domestic violence and the work of inter-agency forums on domestic violence with regard to children, drawing lessons for further development.

11.1 The development of multi-agency ACPCs and their responses to domestic violence

Atkinson (1996) has shown that in the field of child protection, inter-agency co-operation has been operating since 1974, but was established in a more consistent and co-ordinated way in the wake of *Working Together Under The Children Act* guidance (Home Office 1991). There are now approximately 150 ACPCs (covering every local authority in England), which vary considerably in structure, funding and effectiveness.

More recently, ACPCs have provided annual reports, which in part summarise current issues and concerns. In the reports from 1992 onwards there is evidence of an increasing awareness of domestic violence as an issue of concern for children, though less evidence concerning effective intervention (Atkinson 1996; Mullender 1998). Mullender (1998) argues that ACPCs have

been quite late in recognising the needs of children who have lived in circumstances of domestic violence, and need to develop more child-centred, co-ordinated responses along the lines of those already in existence in Canada and the USA. Some ACPCs are beginning to develop initiatives to address this issue. These have included multi-agency training events, which have drawn on the expertise of children's workers in refuges as well as on a range of other professional and academic sources.

11.2 The development of inter-agency domestic violence forums

Hague and Malos (1993) and Hague, Malos and Dear (1996) have charted the development of inter-agency responses to domestic violence in Britain. They show that such work is not new – in fact, from the beginning of the refuge movement in the 1970s Women's Aid groups attempted to work with the support of the statutory agencies. More co-ordinated and formal approaches to multi-agency developments began in the 1980s, mostly at local authority level. By the end of the 1980s, local innovative inter-agency projects had been established in several areas, notably Leeds, Nottingham, Wolverhampton and Hammersmith and Fulham. These have since become model examples for others to follow.

Developments at a national level in inter-agency domestic violence work date from the mid 1980s onwards, and in the 1990s were particularly influenced and promoted by several important policy documents and reports, including:

■ the National Inter-Agency Working Party Report on Domestic Violence (Victim Support 1992)

■ the Home Office Circular 60/90 encouraging an improved police response to domestic violence and the establishment of local Domestic Violence Forums (1990)

■ the Home Affairs Select Committee Inquiry into Domestic Violence (1993)

■ a Home Office Circular on inter-agency work and domestic violence (1995)

■ a Department of Health (1997) circular on the responsibilities of local authorities in relation to the *Family Law Act 1996* noted the importance of inter-agency co-operation with regard to domestic violence and child protection, and recommended the setting up of domestic violence forums where these do not already exist.

All of this activity has led to the establishment of many local inter-agency initiatives, some of which have been further developed by means of Crime Prevention and Safer Cities projects. However, there are many variations in ethos, practices and policies amongst the different inter-agency bodies, many of which operate in the form of domestic violence forums.

11.3 The work of inter-agency domestic violence forums

Hague, Malos and Dear (1996), in the only national study in the UK of inter-agency responses to domestic violence, focused on the structure of the agencies, on the work done and on power and equality issues. The study also

assessed the role of Women's Aid refuges and examined the involvement of domestic violence survivors. Children were not the main focus of the study, but there were some findings in relation to their welfare which will be discussed.

The study identified the existence of around 200 inter-agency domestic violence initiatives, which varied considerably in structure and in the extent and nature of their activities. A few had funding to employ co-ordinators, whilst others had no funding at all, leading to difficulties with continuity and effective development work. There were also differences in the range of agencies represented.

Inter-agency forums provide an opportunity in various ways to develop a co-ordinated approach to domestic violence. These may include the following:

- liaison, networking and the sharing of information, including each agency educating the other agencies on their work in relation to domestic violence

- co-ordinating local services, including the production of good practice guidelines, resource directories and carrying out monitoring exercises across agencies of responses to domestic violence

- improving local service practice and delivery of services

- initiating and developing domestic violence training

- involvement in public education and awareness work, such as the production of leaflets and posters, and through plays, exhibitions and Zero Tolerance campaigns

- the establishment of direct services for women and children, including telephone information and help lines, and self-help groups and drop-in sessions for women and children.

11.4 Inter-agency initiatives and work with children

As outlined in Chapter Nine, in some localities services for children who have lived with domestic violence have developed directly from the inter-agency forums. These include violence prevention programmes in schools and support groups for children. In addition, Hague, Malos and Dear (1996) found that some domestic violence forums have children's needs sub-groups which engage in joint work, usually with social services and local children's charities. Cleveland's multi-agency domestic violence forum had such a sub-group, which worked with local children's charities, refuge workers, social services and education departments to develop innovative work with and for children. This included the production of policies on children and domestic violence and inter-agency procedures and practice guidance for the local ACPC. The group also worked to improve the funding and provision of children's workers in refuges. Similar initiatives on domestic violence and child protection are now in progress elsewhere in the country. Generally, however, issues relating to children who have lived with domestic violence tend to be overlooked by the forums. It is essential that forums take on these issues rather then ignoring them.

11.5 *The involvement of social services departments in inter-agency forums*

Social services have a vital role to play in providing support to women and children who have experienced domestic violence. Their role in this respect is discussed in detail elsewhere in this book (see Chapter Eight). Despite this, Hague, Malos and Dear (1996) found that social services were often absent at inter-agency domestic violence forums. Though they were active in a large number of forums, this tended to be representation at basic grade social worker level rather than at management or policy maker level. Mullender (1998) points out that increasing specialisation, the purchaser/provider spilt, as well as the child protection and community care functions of social services may present difficulties about who should join a forum. However, there were indications that social services were beginning to become more involved in inter-agency forums as a result of the growing recognition of the adverse impacts for children of living with domestic violence, and of the links between domestic violence and the direct abuse of children.

Where there is active commitment to the forums from social services this has contributed to the development of good practice guidelines, and to the inclusion of domestic violence in children's services plans. Mullender (1996a and 1998) has argued that best practice in social work departments has occurred in the context of inter-agency work, where co-operation between agencies has led to a more co-ordinated and effective response. Examples of these include the Leeds and Cleveland inter-agency forums which have been successful in maintaining social services involvement and in developing practice responses and training initiatives across the spectrum of social work provision.

11.6 *The involvement of housing departments/associations, the education service and health services in inter-agency forums*

Access to safe, affordable and decent accommodation is essential if women and children are to be empowered to leave violent relationships. Hague, Malos and Dear (1996) found housing departments to be very active in some domestic violence forums, often via the involvement of those responsible for homelessness. In some cases, such as Greenwich and Bristol, policies specifically relating to domestic violence housing policy and practice have been developed.

Generally, education and health services were notable by their absence at inter-agency forums. As mentioned in Chapter Nine, some education departments have been involved in the production of training packs for schools. Health visitors and Accident and Emergency personnel were quite active in forums, but other primary care staff did not attend, and this was seen by other agencies to be a significant lack, given the fundamental role of health care providers for women and children experiencing domestic violence:

11.7 *The involvement of Women's Aid refuges in inter-agency forums*

Women's Aid play a central role in providing support and safety for women and children experiencing domestic violence. One of the difficulties faced by

inter-agency forums, according to Hague, Malos and Dear (1996), is how to maintain this centrality within the forums, especially in relation to more powerful statutory agencies. This is compounded by the fact that refuge participation is not always possible due to small staffing ratios and underfunding. This can lead to statutory agencies 'taking over' the inter-agency work and to refuges and other women's' support services being marginalised. This may be even more so in relation to specialist refuges for Black and Asian women, which tend to be more under-funded than most (Hague and Malos 1993; Mama 1996). In some cases, refuges were not involved at any level in the domestic violence forums, whilst in others their specialist expertise and knowledge were not recognised.

Some inter-agency projects, such as those in Sheffield, Greenwich, Derby and Cleveland, have adopted various methods to try to overcome this problem of the marginalisation of women-centred organisations. Amongst these have been:

- agreed principles that refuges take a leading role

- refuges always take the chair of the forum

- a reserved place for a refuge delegate on the steering committee.

However, differences in politics and attitudes often remain between refuges and the statutory agencies, which can lead to tensions and misunderstandings. These are important issues which need to be addressed if they are not to restrict the effectiveness and development work of some domestic violence forums. All agencies need to ensure that Women's Aid groups are not isolated and marginalised, and Women's Aid may need to consider producing guidelines and strategies to aid refuge involvement in inter-agency domestic violence work.

11.8 The involvement of the police in inter-agency forums

The police force plays a vital role in responding to domestic violence, and in intervening to protect those who are experiencing it. Though much of their work in this respect focuses on the woman in relation to prosecution and the criminal processes, it is also clear that effective intervention from them can have important implications for the safety and well-being of the children involved. Policy developments over the last few years have meant that the police are expected to play a very active role in domestic violence forums.

Home Office Circular 60/90 marked the beginning of a more comprehensive and sensitive approach by the police to domestic violence (for more details see Chapter Five). Amongst the recommendations of the circular was the need for liaison with statutory and voluntary agencies to provide long term support for women and children. Chief Constables were urged to liaise with a wide range of agencies in order to develop and implement domestic violence policies. They were advised that all officers likely to be involved in incidents of domestic violence should receive training in their powers under the law, and in understanding force policies and procedures, particularly in relation to working with other agencies.

The result has been a gradual improvement in the approach of the police to dealing with domestic violence. There are now more positive reports on

police practices filtering through from refuges and from women themselves. In particular, the establishment of Domestic Violence Units (DVUs) has been seen as a crucial element in these changes, as specialist domestic violence officers are able to develop better working relationships with local Women's Aid groups, thereby offering an improved service to women and children.

In the survey by Hague, Malos and Dear (1996) the police were found to be one of the agencies most often involved within the domestic violence forums. In the eight areas studied in some depth, they found the involvement of the police to be mostly sensitive, though there were difficulties expressed in some forums where the police took a very active initiating role, which could sometimes be perceived as dominating. There was some tentative evidence to suggest that such issues were less frequent in those areas with DVUs or dedicated police officer posts. However, there still remained a problem in some police forces of domestic violence work being seen as 'social work' rather than 'real' police work. Other difficulties also emerged in relation to the involvement of the police in domestic violence forums, especially concerning the social control function of the police and accusations of racism. This led some women's groups and Black women's groups to view their involvement with suspicion and as inappropriate. Morley and Mullender (1994) suggest that the Victim Support report (1992) found that this problem could be resolved in some areas (such as Leeds, Nottingham, Wolverhampton, Hammersmith and Fulham) by forums being led by local councils or the voluntary sector so as to avoid the problem of the agenda being seen to have been set by the police. This led to more agencies being brought together and to the police having a positive role.

11.9 The involvement of legal services in inter-agency forums

A variety of legal and court personnel were found by Hague, Malos and Dear's (1996) survey to attend domestic violence forums, though not with any consistency.

The probation service took an active role in many forums, partly as a result of the importance given to domestic violence in probation work by government inquiries (Home Affairs Committee 1993) and by an internal position statement (the Association of the Chief Officers of Probation 1992 and 1996). Involvement may be in relation to their probation work with offenders or to their role as court welfare officers in civil proceedings. There were, however, variations in the response of probation services to the forums and to the issue of domestic violence generally. Attendance at the forums had resulted in some services developing, or being in the process of developing, practice guidelines on domestic violence, whilst in other areas individual officers who attended the forums were finding it difficult to have domestic violence taken seriously by their services. Hester, Pearson and Radford's (1997) national survey of the practice of court welfare officers in relation to domestic violence found similar differences across the country in terms of practice and policy developments and in the extent to which domestic violence was being addressed as an important issue.

Other court personnel, judges, magistrates and the Crown Prosecution Service rarely attended the domestic violence forums during the period of Hague, Malos and Dear's (1996) study. Despite this, some forums have

developed training packs for magistrates and court personnel, whilst others have developed projects to support women through the criminal justice processes.

11.10 Anti-discriminatory practice in domestic violence forums

Hague, Malos and Dear (1996) found that many forums had not begun to deal with issues of diversity concerning race, religion, sexuality, disability and class. There were examples, however, of some forums beginning to address such issues, especially in relation to race, racism and disability, and of attempts being made to integrate these into the practice of inter-agency work. The main focus of this, however, would appear to relate to women rather than there being any specific consideration of the needs of children. Such anti-discriminatory practice include:

■ the establishment of specialist sub-groups

■ the production of literature and resource material in different languages and formats

■ the production of information and literature for specific groups

■ the provision of interpreting services

■ ensuring fully accessible venues for all events/activities

■ developing projects for specific groups of women and children

■ ensuring that the forum and its management have representatives from different groups.

Despite some developments and progress in domestic violence forums to address equal opportunity issues in their work, most acknowledge that this remains a difficult area of development. It is important that forums take on these issues as an integral part of their role, and that they look to involve smaller grass roots organisations, including community based groups from minority ethnic communities, as well as the more established community organisations. It is equally important that any such developments also include the needs and perspectives of the children.

In Derby, the Domestic Violence Action Group routinely produces all its material in large print and on audio-tape and also has this material translated into the most widely used local community languages. Translation and interpretation are key issues in providing an effective service to women and children who do not speak or read English. However, these need to be carried out in ways that are sensitive to culture and aware of gender issues, especially as interpreters are in a potentially powerful position. Use of interpreters, in particular, should be underpinned by the following principles:

■ an understanding of the need for, and issues concerning, confidentiality

■ offer the choice of a female interpreter

■ the inappropriateness of using children or relatives as interpreters

■ check that the interpreter is fluent and that the language/dialect is the same as the woman's.

For those who are communicating with a woman via an interpreter, it is important to consider the following points:

■ try to communicate directly with the woman, making as much use as possible of the English they can speak or understand

■ think of ways to ensure that the interpreter reflects completely and honestly what the woman has said

■ ensure that the interpreter informs you of any difficulties or reluctance with translating particular issues.

11.11 Ways forward for improved multi-agency practice

> Where they work well [*inter-agency forums*] are a constructive way of improving the services abused women receive, by pressing each member agency to be more rigorous in its response to the issue and by co-ordinating overall responses to women, children and men. At their best they can ... highlight practice that needs to improve and points at which responses fall down between agencies. (Mullender 1996a: 250)

There is no doubt that well co-ordinated multi-agency collaboration has the potential to improve services to women and children experiencing domestic violence and to maximise their continual safety and well-being. It is also clear that working in partnership with a range of agencies with different remits and roles presents a number of difficulties and challenges. There are issues concerning the relative power positions of agencies both within and between the voluntary and statutory sectors. There is a need to address issues concerning `ownership' and accountability of the inter-agency work carried out, and a need to ensure that partnership policies and decisions can be translated into effective practice. Such work also faces major challenges from re-organisations in local authorities, health and education and the continuing purchaser/provider split, which can be seen to undermine the ethos of co-operation between agencies.

Despite these difficulties, there are clear indications from child protection inquiries and part 8 reviews (for example, the report concerning Sukina Hammond as discussed in Chapter Two) of the dangers of the failure to work together in practice, particularly in relation to children living with domestic violence. Atkinson (1996) and Mullender (1998) both suggest that the most positive way to develop multi-agency collaboration is in the creation of working partnerships between ACPCs and domestic violence forums. This is an area of development which has also been emphasised in a recent Department of Health consultation paper on inter-agency co-operation (1988):

> In view of our increased understanding of the links between domestic violence and child protection, we need to think further about how ACPCs and Domestic Violence Fora can work together more effectively. (Department of Health 1998: 11)

This will not necessarily be an easy task, given the different responsibilities involved. Debbonaire (1998) has pointed out that liaison between these two networks, therefore, will need to be clear in order to avoid any duplication of resources and work, and to ensure consistency of response across all agencies involved.

According to Mullender(1996a) this co-operation is already occurring in some areas (such as Sheffield and Birmingham) where the local ACPCs and domestic violence forums have brought people together at conferences and seminars to share expertise and experience. These have led professionals to consider what needs to change in practice in order to meet the needs of children living with domestic violence.

In addition to this, Atkinson (1996) suggests that there is further scope for collaboration between ACPCs and domestic violence forums in relation to the production of children's services plans, which are now statutory for all local authorities, and which aim to improve the delivery of services to children. The more recent (1996) Department of Health updated guidance on such plans emphasises the need for planning services to children in an integrated way. This includes a focus on inter-agency co-operation and collaboration as a means to view children and families in a broader context. This provides an opportunity to include children's experiences of domestic violence on the agenda when planning children's services. The requirement to consult children in the plans would also give children who have experienced domestic violence a voice in the services they need. Children's services plans are now already agreed and in place, and it is important that the issue of children and domestic violence is reviewed and audited, as an essential part of service delivery to children. Where necessary, attention should be given to adding domestic violence to those plans which do not already include this on their agenda for children's services.

Thus, if children's needs in domestic violence situations are to be addressed it is essential that there is effective inter-agency co-ordination between domestic violence forums, and ACPCs, and that children's services plans include services for children experiencing domestic violence. Ways in which this might be achieved in order to provide effective practice include:

- support from senior managers and policy makers for inter-agency work and co-ordination between domestic violence forums and ACPCs

- the inclusion in job specifications of inter-agency activity between domestic violence forums and ACPCs

- ensuring that issues taken up in domestic violence forums and ACPCs are fed back into agency policy and practice

- ensuring that children and domestic violence is a regular, specific agenda item on both domestic violence forums and ACPCs.

Such co-operation can assist in developing the establishment of formal policies and in promoting best practice in relation to domestic violence. It can also provide creative steps forward towards innovative service co-ordination, involving intervention and both preventative and educative work.

11.12 Summary

- Women and children who are experiencing domestic violence will be in contact with a variety of service providers, who need to provide a co-ordinated approach in order to maximise the continual safety and well-being of these women and children.

- In the past, the abuse of women and the abuse of children in the family (usually by the same man) have been viewed as separate issues. This has led to the development of separate services and policies to address the needs of each group.

- The separation of the abuse of women and children has tended to be replicated in the development of multi-agency initiatives – domestic violence forums have focused mostly on the experiences of women, and ACPCs have an explicit focus on children and their protection. At a national level, the issue of children and domestic violence has been mostly absent in the policies of both of these groups.

- Co-operation between ACPCs and domestic violence forums is already occurring in some areas, leading to a more co-ordinated and effective response, and to a more integrated response to the needs of children living with domestic violence.

- To provide the most effective response to domestic violence ACPCs and domestic violence forums need to develop ways of working in partnership, giving weight to the voices of the women and, especially, the children concerned.

- It is important in multi-agency work to promote anti-discriminatory practice and address equal opportunity issues. This will include a recognition of the relative power positions of the different agencies involved, and active involvement of Women's Aid and other community based groups, including those from minority ethnic communities.

- ACPCs and domestic violence forums should collaborate together to produce children's services plans to create an integrated and strategic approach to services for children experiencing domestic violence. Within such plans the issue of children and domestic violence needs to be regularly reviewed and audited, as an essential part of service delivery to children.

BIBLIOGRAPHY

Abrahams, C. (1994) *The Hidden Victims – Children and Domestic Violence*. London: NCH Action for Children.

Adams, D. (1988) 'Treatment models of men who batter: A profeminist analysis' in K. Yllo and M. Bograd (eds.) *Feminist Perspectives on Wife Abuse*. Newbury Park: Sage.

Ahluwalia, K. and Gupta, R. (1997) *Circle Of Light*. London: Harper Collins.

Alessi, J.J. and Hearn, K. (1984) 'Group treatment of children in shelters for battered women', in A.R. Roberts (ed) *Battered Women and Their Families*. New York: Springer.

Alexander, P.C., Moore, S. and Alexander, E.R. (1991) 'What is transmitted in the intergenerational transmission of violence', *Journal of Marriage and the Family*, 53, 657-668.

Anderson, L. (1997) *Contact Between Children and Violent Fathers: In Whose Best Interests?*. London: Rights of Women.

Andrews, B. and Brown, G.W. (1988) 'Marital violence in the community: a biographical approach', *British Journal of Psychiatry*, 153, 305-312.

Armstrong, H. (1994) *ACPC: National Conference: Discussion Report: Annual Reports ACPCs 1992-93*. London: DOH.

Association of Chief Officers of Probation (1992 revised 1996) *Position statement on domestic violence*. London: ACOP.

Atkinson, C. (1996) *'Partnership Working – Supporting those who Work with the Children of Domestic Violence'*. Paper given at the Behind Closed Doors Seminar – The effects of Domestic Violence on Children and Vulnerable Young People, Thames Valley.

Ball, M. (1990) *Children's Workers in Women's Aid Refuges: Report on the Experience of Nine Refuges in England*. London: National Council of Voluntary Childcare Organisations.

Ball, M. (1995) *Domestic Violence and Social Care: A report on two conferences held by the Social Services Inspectorate*. London: Department of Health.

Barron, J. (1990) *Not Worth the Paper...? The Effectiveness of Legal Protection for Women and Children Experiencing Domestic Violence*. Bristol: Women's Aid Federation of England.

Barron, J., Harwin, N. and Singh, T. (1992) *Women's Aid Federation England Written Evidence to House of Commons Home Affairs Committee Inquiry into Domestic Violence*. Bristol: WAFE.

Bhatti-Sinclair, K. (1994) 'Asian women and violence from male partners' in C. Lupton and T. Gillespie (eds.) *Working With Violence*. Basingstoke: Macmillan Press.

Binney, V., Harkell, G. and Nixon, J. (1988 reprint of 1981 text) *Leaving Violent Men: A Study of Refuges and Housing for Battered Women*. Bristol: Women's Aid Federation England.

Borkowski, M., Murch, M. and Walker, V. (1983) *Marital Violence: The Community Response*. London: Tavistock.

Bourlet, A (1990) *Police Intervention in Marital Violence*. London: Open University Press.

Bowker, L.H., Arbitell, M. and McFerron, J.R. (1988) 'On the relationship between wife beating and child abuse' in K. Yllo and M. Bograd (eds) *Feminist Perspectives on Wife Abuse*. Newbury Park: Sage.

Bowstead, J, Lall, D. and Rashid, S. (1995) *Asian Women and Domestic Violence: Information for Advisers*. London: London Borough of Greenwich Women's Equality Unit.

Brandon, M. and Lewis, A. (1996) 'Significant harm and children's experiences of domestic violence', *Child and Family Social Work*, 1 (1), 33-42.

Bridge Child Care Consultancy Service (1991) *Sukina: An Evaluation of the Circumstances Leading to her Death*. London: Bridge Child Care Consultancy Service.

British Crime Survey (1996) London: Home Office.

Browning, D.H. and Boatman, B. (1977) 'Incest: children at risk', *American Journal of Psychiatry*. 134 (1), 69-72.

Bull, J. (1993) *Housing Consequences of Relationship Breakdown*. London: HMSO

Burge, S. (1989) 'Violence against women as a health care issue', *Family Medicine*, 21, 368-373.

Burton, S., Regan, L. and Kelly, L. (1998) *Supporting Women and Challenging Men: Lessons from the Domestic Violence Intervention Project*. Bristol: Policy Press.

Busch, R. and Robertson, N. (1994) "Ain't no mountain high enough (to keep me from getting to you)": An analysis of the Hamilton Abuse Intervention Pilot Project' in J. Stubbs (ed) *Women, Male Violence and the Law*. Sydney: University of Sydney Law School.

Carlson, B.E. (1990) 'Adolescent observers of marital violence', *Journal of Family Violence*, 5, 285-299.

Carroll, J. (1994) 'The protection of children exposed to marital violence', *Child Abuse Review*, 3, 6-14.

Catchpole, A. (1997) 'Working with children who have been abused' in M. John (ed) *A Charge Against Society. The Child's Right to Protection*. London: Jessica Kingsley.

Children Act (1989). London: HMSO.

Children's Subcommittee of the London Coordinating Committee to End Woman Abuse, London, Ontario (1994) 'Make a difference: how to respond to child witnesses of woman abuse' in A. Mullender and R. Morley, R. (eds.) *Children Living with Domestic Violence: Putting Men's Abuse of Women on the Child Care Agenda*. London: Whiting and Birch.

Christensen, L. (1990) 'Children's living conditions. An investigation into disregard of care in relation to children and teenagers in families of wife maltreatment', *Nordisk Psychology*, 42, Monograph 31, 161-232.

Christopoulos, C., Cohn, A.D., Shaw, D.S., Joyce, S., Sullivan-Hanson, J., Kraft, S.P., and Emery, R.E. (1987) 'Children of abused women: 1. Adjustment at time of shelter residence', *Journal of Marriage and the Family*, 49, 611-619.

Cleaver, H. and Freeman, P. (1995) *Parental Perspectives in Cases of Suspected Child Abuse*. London: HMSO.

Cleaver, H., Unell, J. and Aldgate, J. (forthcoming) 'Children and Families Where Adult Mental Health, Alcohol, and Substance Abuse and Domestic Violence are Issues'.

Cockett, M. and Tripp, J. (1994) *The Exeter Family Study. Family Breakdown and its Impact on Children.* Exeter: University of Exeter Press.

Criminal Justice Act 1967. HMSO: London.

Criminal Justice Act 1988. HMSO: London.

Cummings, E. M., Zahn-Waxler, C. and Radke-Yarrow, M. (1984) 'Developmental changes in children's reactions to anger in the home', *Journal of Child Psychology and Child Psychiatry,* 25, 63-74.

Davis, L.V. and Carlson, B.E. (1987) 'Observations of spouse abuse. what happens to the children?', *Journal of Interpersonal Violence,* 2 (3), 278-291.

Debbonaire, T. (1994) 'Work with children in Women's Aid refuges and after', in A. Mullender and R. Morley (eds.) *Children Living with Domestic Violence.* London: Whiting and Birch.

Debbonaire, T. (1995) 'Children in refuges – the picture now' in A. Saunders with C. Epstein, G. Keep and T. Debbonaire (1995) *It Hurts Me Too: Children's Experiences of Domestic Violence and Refuge Life.* Bristol: WAFE/Childline/NISW.

Debbonaire, T (1997) *Briefing Paper on Child Contact.* Bristol: WAFE.

Debbonaire, T. (1998) 'Domestic violence and inter-agency child protection work – an overview of recent developments' in N. Harwin, G. Hague and E. Malos (eds) *Domestic Violence and Multi-Agency Working: New Opportunities, Old Challenges?.* London: Whiting and Birch.

Department of Health (1998) *Working Together to Safeguard Children: New Government Proposals for Inter-Agency Co-operation. Consultation Paper.* London: DOH.

Department of Health (1997), Local Authority Circular LAC(97) 15 *Family Law Act 1996. Part IV Family Homes and Domestic Violence.* London: DOH.

Department of Health, Department for Education and Employment (1996) *Children's Services Planning: Guidance.* London: DOH and DEE.

Dietz, C.A. and Craft, J.L. (1980), 'Family dynamics of incest: a new perspective', *Social Casework,* 61, 602-609.

Dobash, R.E. and Dobash, R.P. (1980) *Violence Against Wives: A Case Against the Patriarchy.* Sussex: Open Books.

Dobash, R.E. & Dobash, R.P (1984) 'The nature and antecedent of violent events', *British Journal of Criminology,* 24 (3), 269-288.

Dobash, R.E. and Dobash, R.P. (1992) *Women, Violence and Social Change.* London: Routledge.

Dobash, R.E. and Dobash, R.P. and Cavanagh, K. (1985) 'The contact between battered women and social and medical agencies' in J. Pahl (ed) *Private Violence and Public Policy.* London: Routledge.

Dobash, R., Dobash, R.E., Cavanagh, K. and Lewis, R. (1996) *Research Evaluation of Programmes for Violent Men.* Edinburgh: HMSO.

Dobash, R., Dobash, R.E., Cavanagh, K. and Lewis, R. (1995) 'Evaluating criminal justice programmes for violent men' in R.E. Dobash, R.P. Dobash and L. Noaks (eds) *Gender and Crime.* Cardiff: University of Wales Press.

Dominy, N. & Radford, L. (1996) *Domestic Violence in Surrey: Towards an Effective Inter-Agency Response.* London: Roehampton Institute/Surrey Social Services.

Dunhill, C (1989) *The Boys In Blue: Women's Challenge to the Police.* London: Virago.

Edleson, J.L. (1995) 'Mothers and children: understanding the links between woman battering and child abuse', Paper presented at the Strategic Planning Workshop on Violence Against Women. Washington: National Institute of Justice.

Edleson, J.L. and Tolman, R.M. (1992) *Intervention for Men Who Batter. An Ecological Approach.* Newbury Park: Sage.

Edwards, S .(1989) *Policing domestic violence.* London: Sage.

Emery, R.E. and O'Leary, D.K. (1982) 'Children's perceptions of marital discord and behaviour problems of boys and girls' *Journal of Abnormal Child Psychology,* 10 (1), 11-22.

Epstein, C. and Keep, G. (1995) 'What children tell Childline about domestic violence', in A. Saunders with C. Epstein, G. Keep, and T. Debbonaire *It Hurts Me Too: Children's Experiences of Domestic Violence and Refuge Life.* Bristol: WAFE/Childline/NISW.

Evans, A. (1991) *Alternatives to Bed and Breakfast, Temporary Housing Solutions for Homeless People.* London: National Housing and Town Planning Council.

Evans, A. and Duncan, S. (1988) *Responding to Homelessness: Local Authority Policy and Practice.* London: HMSO.

Evason, E. (1982) *Hidden Violence: A Study of Battered Women in Northern Ireland.* Belfast: Farset Press.

Family Law Act (1996) London: HMSO.

Fantuzzo, J.W., DePaola, L.M., Lamber, L., Mariono, T., Anderson, G. and Sutton, S. (1991) 'Effects of interpersonal violence on the psychological adjustment and competencies of young children', *Journal of Consulting and Clinical Psychology,* 59, 258-265.

Fantuzzo, J.W. and Lindquist, C.U. (1989) 'The effects of observing conjugal violence on children: A review and analysis of research methodology', *Journal of Family Violence,* 4 (1), 77-94.

Farmer, E. and Owen, M. (1995) *Child Protection Practice: Private Risks and Public Remedies.* London: HMSO.

Farmer, E. and Pollock, S. (1998 forthcoming) *Substitute Care for Sexually Abused and Abusing Children.* Chichester: Wiley.

Finkelhor, D. (1996) *Long-term Effects of Sexual Abuse.* Paper presented to Child Abuse and Neglect Conference, Dublin: August.

Fonagy, P., Steele, M., Steele, H., Higgitt, A. and Mayer, L.S. (1994) 'the Emmanuel Miller Memorial Lecture 1992: the theory and practice of resilience', *Journal of Child Psychology and Psychiatry,* 35 (2), 231-258.

Forman, J. (1995) *Is There a Correlation Between Child Sexual Abuse and Domestic Violence? An Exploratory Study of the Links Between Child Sexual Abuse and Domestic Violence in a Sample of Intrafamilial Child Sexual Abuse Cases.* Glasgow: Women's Support Project.

Forsstrom-Cohen, B. and Rosenbaum, A. (1985) 'The effects of parental marital violence on young adults: An exploratory investigation', *Journal of Marriage and the Family,* 47, 467-471.

Frances, R. (1995) 'An overview of community-based intervention programmes for men who are violent or abusive in the home' in R.E. Dobash, R.P. Dobash and L. Noaks (eds) *Gender and Crime*. Cardiff: University of Wales Press.

Gamache, D. and Snapp, S. (1995) 'Teach your children well. Elementary schools and violence prevention' in E. Peled, P. Jaffe, and J.L. Edleson *Ending the Cycle of Violence. Community Responses to Children of Battered Women*. Thousand Oaks: Sage.

Garmezy, N. (1985) 'Stress-resistant children: in search of protective factors' in J. Stevenson (ed) *Recent Research in Development Psychopathology*. Oxford: Pergamon.

Gelles, R.J. and Loseke, D.R. (1993) *Current Controversies on Family Violence*. ??

Gibbons, J., Conroy, S. & Bell, C. (1995) *Operating the Child Protection System: A Study of Child Protection Practices in English Local Authorities*. London: HMSO.

Glaser, D. and Prior, V. (1997) 'Is the term child protection applicable to emotional abuse?', *Child Abuse Review*, 6, 315-329.

Goddard, C.R. and Carew, R. (1988) 'Protecting the child: Hostages to fortune?', *Social Work Today*, 20 (16), 12-14.

Goddard, C and Hiller P. (1993) 'Child sexual abuse: assault in a violent context', *Australian Journal of Social Issues*, 28 (1), 20-33.

Grace, S. (1995) *Policing Domestic Violence in the 1990s*. Home Office Research Study No.139. London: HMSO.

Graham, P., Rawlings, E. & Rimini, W. (1988) 'Survivors of terror: battered women, hostages and the Stockholm Syndrome' in K. Yllo & M. Bograd (eds.) *Feminist Perspectives on Wife Abuse*. London: Sage.

Grotberg, E. (1997) 'The International Resilience Project' in M. John (ed) *A Charge Against Society. The Child's Right to Protection*. London: Jessica Kingsley.

Grusznski, R.J., Brink, J.C, Edleson, J.L. (1988) 'Support and education groups for children of battered women', *Child Welfare*, 67 (5), 431- 444.

Hague, G., Harwin, N., McMinn, K., Rubens, J. and Taylor, M. (1989) 'Policing Male Violence in the Home' in C. Dunhill, C. *The Boys In Blue: Women's Challenge to the Police*. London: Virago

Hague, G., Kelly, L., Malos, E., Mullender, A. with Debbonaire, T. (1996) *Children, Domestic Violence and Refuges: A Study of Needs and Responses*. Bristol: Women's Aid Federation (England).

Hague, G. and Malos, E. (1993) *Domestic Violence: Action for Change*. Cheltenham: New Clarion Press.

Hague, G. and Malos, E (1994) 'Domestic violence, social policy and housing', *Critical Social Policy*, 42.

Hague, G., Malos, E. and Dear, W. (1996) *Multi-agency work and Domestic Violence*. Bristol: The Policy Press

Hallett, C (1995) 'Child abuse: an academic overview' in P. Kingston and B. Penhale (eds) *Family Violence and the Caring Professions*. Basingstoke: Macmillan.

Hanmer, J. (1989) 'Women and policing in Britain' in J. Hanmer, J. Radford and E. Stanko (eds) *Women, Policing and Male Violence*. London: Routledge.

Hanmer, J. and Saunders, S (1993) *Women, Violence and Crime Prevention*. Aldershot: Avebury.

Hanmer, J., and Saunders, S. (1984) *Well-Founded Fear: A Community Study of Violence to Women.* London: Hutchinson

Harne, L. and Rights of Women (1997) *Valued Families. The Lesbian Mother's Legal Handbook.* London: The Women's Press.

Harris Hendriks, J., Black, D. and Kaplan, T. (1993) *When Father Kills Mother. Guiding Children Through Trauma and Grief.* London: Routledge.

Harwin, N. (1997a). *Briefing paper: Stalking and the 1997 Protection from Harassment Act.* Bristol: Women's Aid Federation of England.

Harwin, N. (1997b). *Briefing paper: The 1996 Family Law Act – continuing concerns.* Bristol: Women's Aid Federation of England

Harwin, N. (1997c). *Briefing paper: Response to Working Party on Vulnerable Witnesses.* Bristol: Women's Aid Federation of England

Harwin, N. and Barron, J. (1998 forthcoming), 'Domestic violence and social policy: perspectives from Women's Aid' in C. Itzin and J. Hanmer, J. (eds) *Home Truths.* London:(pub)

Hearn, J. (1996a) 'Men's violence to known women': historical, everyday and theoretical constructions by men' in B. Fawcett, B. Featherstone, J. Hearn, & C. Toft (eds.) *Violence and Gender Relations.* London: Sage.

Hearn, J. (1996b) 'Men's violence to known women: men's accounts and men's policy developments' in B. Fawcett, B. Featherstone, J. Hearn, & C. Toft (eds.) *Violence and Gender Relations.* London: Sage.

Hershorn, M. and Rosenbaum, A. (1985) 'Children of marital violence: a closer look at unintended victims', *American Journal of Orthopsychiatry,* 55, 260-266.

Hester, M., Humphries, J., Pearson, C., Qaiser, Radford, L. and Woodfield. K. (1994) 'Separation, divorce, child contact and domestic violence', in A. Mullender and R. Morley (eds.) *Children Living with Domestic Violence.* Whiting and Birch.

Hester, M., Kelly, L. and Radford, J. (eds) (1996) *Women, Violence and Male Power.* Buckingham: Open University Press.

Hester, M. and Pearson, C. (1998 forthcoming) *From Periphery to Centre – Domestic Violence in Work with Abused Children.* Bristol: Policy Press.

Hester, M. and Pearson, C. (1997) 'Domestic violence and children – the practice of family court welfare officers', *Child and Family Law Quarterly,* 9 (3), 281-290.

Hester, M., Pearson, C., and Radford, L. (1997) *Domestic Violence: A National Survey of Court Welfare and Voluntary Sector Mediation Practice.* Bristol: Policy Press.

Hester, M. and Radford, L. (1992) 'Domestic violence and access arrangements for children in Denmark and Britain', *The Journal of Social Welfare and Family Law,* 1.

Hester, M and Radford, L. (1996) *Domestic Violence and Child Contact Arrangements in England and Denmark,* Bristol: Policy Press.

Higgins, G. (1994) 'Hammersmith Women's Aid childhood development project' in A. Mullender and R. Morley (eds.) *Children Living with Domestic Violence.* London: Whiting and Birch.

Hilberman, E. and Munson, K. (1977) 'Sixty battered women', *Victimology,* 2, 460-470.

Hilton, N.Z. (1992) 'Battered women's concerns about their children witnessing wife assault', *Journal of Interpersonal Violence*, 7 (1), 77-86.

Hoff, L. (1990) *Battered Women As Survivors*. London: Routledge.

Holden, G.W. and Ritchie, K.L. (1991) 'Linking extreme marital discord, child rearing, and child behaviour problems: evidence from battered women', *Child Development*, 62, 311-327.

Holder, R., Kelly, L. and Singh, T. (1994) *Suffering in Silence: Children and Young People Who Witness Domestic Violence*. London: Hammersmith and Fulham Domestic Violence Forum.

Home Affairs Select Committee (1993) *Report of Inquiry into Domestic Violence*. London: HMSO.

Home Office (1990) Circular 60/90, *Domestic Violence*. London: Home Office.

Home Office (1994) *National Standards for Probation Service Family Court Welfare Work*, London: Home Office.

Home Office (1995) *Inter-agency circular work: inter-agency co-ordination to tackle domestic violence*. London: Home Office.

Home Office (1995) *Child Protection – Messages from Research*. London: Home Office.

Home Office, Department of Health, DES, and Welsh Office (1991) *Working Together Under the Children Act 1989: A Guide to Arrangements for Inter-Agency Co-operation for the Protection of Children from Abuse*. London: HMSO.

Homer, M., Leonard, A., & Taylor, P. (1984) *Private Violence: Public Shame. A Report on the Circumstances of Women Leaving Domestic Violence in Cleveland*. Cleveland: Cleveland Refuge and Aid for Women and Children.

Hooper, C.-A. (1987) 'Getting him off the hook: the theory and practice of mother blaming in child sexual abuse', *Trouble and Strife*, 12, 20-25.

Hooper, C.-A. (1992) *Mothers Surviving Child Sexual Abuse*. London: Routledge.

Hooper, C.-A. (1995) ' Women's and their children's experiences of domestic violence: rethinking the links', *Women's Studies International Forum*, 18 (3), 349-360.

House of Commons Home Affairs Select Committee (1993) *Report of Inquiry into Domestic Violence*. London: HMSO.

Housing Act (1996) London: HMSO.

Housing Act 1985. HMSO: London

Housing (Homeless Persons Act) 1977. HMSO: London.

Hughes, H. (1992) 'Impact of spouse abuse on children of battered women', *Violence Update*, 1, 9-11.

Hughes, H.M. (1988) 'Psychological and behavioural correlates of family violence in child witnesses and victims', *American Journal of Orthopsychiatry*, 58 (1), 77-90.

Hughes, H. and Barad, S. (1983) 'Psychological functioning of children in a battered women's shelter', *American Journal of Orthopsychiatry*, 53 (3), 525-531.

Hughes, H.M., Parkinson, D. and Vargo, M. (1989) 'Witnessing spouse abuse and experiencing physical abuse: a "double whammy"?', *Journal of Family Violence*, 4 (2), 197-209.

Humphreys, C. (1997) *Case Planning Issues Where Domestic Violence Occurs in the Context of Child Protection.* Coventry: University of Warwick.

Humphreys, C. (1997b) 'Child sexual abuse allegations in the context of divorce: issues for mothers', *British Journal of Social Work,* 27, 529-44.

Humphreys, C and Kaye, M. (1997) 'Third party applications for protection orders: opportunities, ambiguities and traps', *Journal of Social Welfare and Family Law,* 19 (4), 403-421.

Humphreys, C, Kaye, M. and Harwin, N. (1997) *Third Party Orders.* Bristol: WAFE.

Hurley, D.J., and Jaffe, P. (1990) 'Children's observations of violence: II. Clinical implications for children's mental health professionals', *Canadian Journal of Psychiatry,* 35 (6), 471-476.

Hyden, M. (1994) *Woman Battering As Marital Act.* Oslo: Scandinavian University Press.

Hyman, C.A. (1978) 'Some characteristics of abusing families referred to the NSPCC' *British Journal of Social Work,* 8 (2), 171-179.

Imam, U.F. (1994) 'Asian children and domestic violence' in A. Mullender and R. Morley (eds.) *Children Living with Domestic Violence.* London: Whiting and Birch.

Jaffe, P. (1996) 'Children of domestic violence: Special challenges in custody and visitation dispute resolution', *Special Challenges in Custody and Visitation,* 24, 19-30.

Jaffe, P., Hurley, D., and Wolfe, D. (1990) 'Children's observations of violence: I. Critical issues in child development and intervention planning', *Canadian Journal of Psychiatry,* 35 (6), 466-469.

Jaffe, P., Wilson, S. and Wolfe, D. (1986) 'Promoting changes in attitude and understanding of conflict among child witnesses of family violence', *Canadian Journal of Behavioural Science,* 18, 356-380.

Jaffe, P., Wolfe, D. A., and Wilson, S. K. (1990) *Children of Battered Women.* California: Sage.

Jaffe, P., Wolfe, D. A., Wilson, S. K. and Zak, L. (1985) 'Critical issues in the assessment of children's adjustment to witnessing family violence', *Canada's Mental Health,* 33 (4), 14-19.

Jaffe, P., Wolfe, D. A., Wilson, S. K. and Zak, L.(1986a) 'Similarities in behavioural and social maladjustment among child victims and witnesses to family violence', *American Journal of Orthopsychiatry,* 56 (1), 142-146.

Jaffe, P., Wolfe, D. A., Wilson, S. K. and Zak, L (1986b) 'Family violence and child adjustment: A comparative analysis of girls' and boys' behavioural symptoms', *American Journal of Psychiatry,* 14 (1), 74-77.

Jaffe, P., Wolfe, D. A., Wilson, S. K. and Zak, L (1986c) 'Emotional and physical health problems of battered women', *Canadian Journal of Psychiatry,* 31, 625-629.

James, G. (1994) *Study of Working Together Part 8 Reports.* London: DOH.

Jenkins, A. (1990) *Invitations to Responsibility. The Therapeutic Engagement of Men who are Violent and Abusive.* Adelaide: Dulwich Centre Publications.

Johnston, J. (1992) *High Conflict and Violent Divorcing Families: Findings on Children's Adjustment and Proposed Guidelines for the Resolution of Disputed*

Custody and Visitation: Report of the Project. California: Centre for the Family in Transition.

Jolly, S. (1995) 'Implacable hostility, contact and the limits of law', *Child and Family Law Quarterly,* 7 (4), 228-235.

Jones A. (1980) *Women Who Kill.* New York: Fawcett Columbine.

Jouriles, E.N., Barling, J. and O'Leary, K.D. (1987) 'Predicting child behaviour problems in maritally violent families', *Journal of Abnormal Child Psychology,* 15, 165-173.

Jouriles, E.N., Murphy, C.M. and O'Leary, K.D. (1989) Interspousal aggression, marital discord, and child problems', *Journal of Consulting and Clinical Psychology,* 57, 453-455.

Kalmuss, D. (1984) 'The intergenerational transmission of marital aggression', *Journal of Marriage and the Family,* 46, 11-19.

Kaye, M. (1996) 'Domestic violence, residence and contact', *Child and Family Law Quarterly,* 8 (4) pp??

Kelly, L. (1988) *Surviving Sexual Violence.* Cambridge: Polity Press.

Kelly, L. (1992) 'Disability and child abuse: a research review of the connections', *Child Abuse Review,* 1, 157-167.

Kelly, L. (1994) 'The interconnectedness of domestic violence and child abuse: Challenges for research, policy and practice', in A. Mullender and R. Morley (eds.) *Children Living with Domestic Violence.* London: Whiting and Birch.

Kelly, L. (1996) 'When woman protection is the best kind of child protection: Children, domestic violence and child abuse', *Administration,* 44 (2), 118-135

Kelly, L. and Radford, J. (1996) 'Nothing really happened: the invalidation of women's experiences of sexual violence' in M. Hester, L. Kelly and J. Radford (eds) *Women, Violence and Male Power.* Buckingham: Open University Press.

Kelly, L., Regan, L. and Burton, S. (1991) *An Exploratory Study of the Prevalence of Sexual Abuse in a Sample of 1200 16 to 21 Year Olds.* Final report to the ESRC. London: Child Abuse Studies Unit, University of North London.

Kirkwood, C. (1993) *Leaving Abusive Partners.* London: Sage.

Kolbo, J., Blakely, E.H., and Engleman, D. (1996) 'Children who witness domestic violence: a review of empirical literature', *Journal of interpersonal violence,* 11 (2), 281-293.

Law Commission (1992) *Family Law: Domestic Violence and the Occupation of the Family Home.* Report No 207. London: HMSO.

Levine, M.B. (1975) 'Interparental violence and its effect on the children: a study of 50 families in general practice', *Medicine, Science and the Law,* 15 (3), 172-176.

Lobel, K. (ed.) (1986) *Naming the Violence – Speaking Out About Lesbian Battering.* Seal Press.

London Borough of Greenwich (1987) *A Child in Mind: Protection of Children in a Responsible Society. Report of the Commission of Inquiry into the Circumstances Surrounding the Death of Kimberley Carlile.* London: London Borough of Greenwich.

London Borough of Hackney (draft 1998) *Responding to Domestic Violence. Hackney Inter-agency Guidelines.* London: London Borough of Hackney Strategic Policy Unit.

London Borough of Hackney (1994) *Good Practice Guidelines: Responding to Domestic Violence*. London: London Borough of Hackney Women's Unit.

London Borough of Hackney (1993) *The Links Between Domestic Violence and Child Abuse: Developing Services*. London: Hackney Council Press and Publicity Team

Loosley, S. (1994) 'Women's Community House children's programme: a model in perspective' in A. Mullender and R. Morley (eds.) *Children Living with Domestic Violence*. London: Whiting and Birch.

Lord Chancellor's Department (1996) *Marriage and the Family Law Act 1996: The New Legislation Explained*. London: HMSO.

Malloch, M.S. and Webb, S.A. (1993) 'Intervening with male batterers – A study of social workers' perceptions of domestic violence', *Social Work and Social Sciences Review*, 4 (2), 119-147.

Malmquist, C. (1986) 'Children who witness parental murder: post traumatic aspects', *Journal of the American Academy of Child and Adolescent Psychiatry*, 25 (3), 320-325.

Malos, E. and Hague. G (1993a) *Domestic Violence and Housing – Local Authority Responses to Women and Children Escaping from Domestic Violence*. Bristol: Women's Aid Federation and University of Bristol.

Malos, E. and Hague. G (1993b) 'Homelessness and domestic violence: the effect on children and young people', *Childright*, 99, 15-19.

Mama, A. (1996) *The Hidden Struggle: Statutory and Voluntary Sector Responses to Violence Against Black Women in the Home*. London: Whiting and Birch.

Mathews, D.J. (1995) 'Parenting groups for men who batter' in E. Peled, P.G. Jaffe, and J.L. Edleson (eds.) *Ending the Cycle of Violence*. Thousand Oaks: Sage.

Mayhew, P., Aye Maung, N. and Mirrlees-Black, C. (1993) *The 1992 British Crime Survey*. Home Office Research Study No. 132. London: HMSO.

Maynard, M. (1985) 'The Response of Social Workers to Domestic Violence', in J. Pahl (ed.) *Private Violence and Public Policy*. London: Routledge.

McGee, C (1996) 'Children's and mother's experiences of child protection following domestic violence', paper given at Violence, Abuse and Women's Citizenship International Conference, Brighton.

McGee, C. (forthcoming) *Children's and Mother's Experiences of Child Protection Following Domestic Violence*. London: NSPCC.

McGibbon, A., Cooper, L. and Kelly, L. (1989) *What Support?* Hammersmith and Fulham Council Community Police Committee Domestic Violence Project: Polytechnic of North London

McKay, M.M. (1994) 'The link between domestic violence and child abuse: assessment and treatment considerations', *Child Welfare*, 73 (1), 29-39.

McWilliams, M. and McKiernan, J. (1993) *Bringing It All Out Into The Open: Domestic Violence In Northern Ireland*. Belfast: HMSO.

Mezey, G.C. and Bewley, S. (1997) 'Domestic violence and pregnancy', *British Medical Journal*, 314.

Milner, J.(1996) ' Men's resistance to social workers' in B. Fawcett, B. Featherstone, J. Hearn, & C. Toft (eds.) *Violence and Gender Relations*. London: Sage.

Mirrlees-Black, C. (1995) 'Estimating the extent of domestic violence: findings from the 1992 British Crime Survey', *Home Office Research Bulletin*, 37, pp.1-18.

Mooney, J. (1994) *The Hidden Figure: Domestic Violence in North London*. London: Islington Police and Crime Prevention Unit.

Moore, J.G. (1975) 'Yo-yo children – victims of matrimonial violence', *Child Welfare*, 54 (8), 557-66.

Moore, J.G., Galcius, A. and Pettican, K. (1981) 'Emotional risk to children caught in violent marital conflict – the Basildon treatment project', *Child Abuse and Neglect*, 5, 147-152.

Moore, T., Pepler, D., Weinberg, B., Hammond, L., Waddell, J. and Weiser, L. (1990) 'Research on children from violent families', *Canada's Mental Health*, 19-23.

Morley, R. (1993) 'Recent responses to 'domestic violence' against women: A feminist critique', in R. Page and J. Baldock (eds) *Social Policy Review*, 5, 175-206.

Morley, R. and Mullender, A (1994) *Preventing Domestic Violence to Women*. Crime Prevention Unit Series, Paper 48. London: Home Office Police Department.

Mullender, A. (1994a) 'Groups for child witnesses of woman abuse: learning from North America', in A. Mullender and R. Morley (eds) *Children Living with Domestic Violence: Putting Men's Abuse of Women in the Child Care Agenda*. London: Whiting and Birch.

Mullender, A. (1994b) 'School-based work: education for prevention', in A. Mullender and R. Morley (eds) *Children Living with Domestic Violence: Putting Men's Abuse of Women on the Child Care Agenda*. London: Whiting and Birch.

Mullender, A. (1996a) *Rethinking Domestic Violence: The Social Work and Probation Response*, London: Routledge.

Mullender, A. (1996b) 'Children living with domestic violence', *Adoption and Fostering*, 20 (1), 8-15.

Mullender, A. (1997) 'Domestic violence and social work: The challenge to change', *Critical Social Policy*, 50, 53-78.

Mullender, A. (1998) 'Social service responses to domestic violence: the inter-agency challenge' in N. Harwin, G. Hague and E. Malos (eds) *Domestic Violence and Multi-Agency Working: New Opportunities, Old Challenges?*. London: Whiting and Birch.

Mullender, A., Hague, G., Kelly, L. and Malos, E. (forthcoming) *Child and Family Social Work*.

Mullender, A., Kelly, L., Hague, G., Malos, E. and Imam, U.F. (forthcoming) *Children's Needs, Coping Strategies and Understanding of Woman Abuse*.

Mullender, A. and Morley, R. (eds.) (1994) *Children Living with Domestic Violence: Putting Men's Abuse of Women on the Child Care Agenda*. London: Whiting and Birch.

National Children's Bureau (1993) *Investigation into Inter-Agency Practice Following the Cleveland Area Child Protection Committee's Report Concerning the Death of Toni Dales*. London: National Children's Bureau.

Nazroo, J. (1995) 'Uncovering gender differences in the use of marital violence: the effect of methodology', *Sociology*, 29 (3), 475-94.

NCH Action for Children (1994) see Abrahams, C. (1994).

O'Hagan, K. and Dillenburger, K. (1995) *Abuse of Women Within Childcare Work*. Buckingham: Open University Press.

O' Hara, M. (1994) 'Child deaths in the context of domestic violence: Implications for professional practice' in A. Mullender and R. Morley (eds.) *Children Living with Domestic Violence: Putting Men's Abuse of Women on the Child Care Agenda*. London: Whiting and Birch.

O'Leary, K.D. and Curley, A.D. (1986)'Assertion and family violence: correlates of spouse abuse', *Journal of Marital and Family Therapy*, 12, 281-289.

Pagelow, M.D. (1981) 'Factors affecting women's decisions to leave violent relationships', *Journal of Family Issues*, 2, 391-414.

Pagelow, M.D. (1982) 'Children in violent families: direct and indirect victims', in S. Hill and B.J. Barnes (eds) *Young Children and Their Families*. Lexington: Lexington Books.

Pahl, J. (ed.) (1985) *Private Violence and Public Policy*. London: Routledge.

Parton, N. (1990) *Taking child abuse seriously*', in The Violence Against Children Study Group Taking Child Abuse Seriously. London: Unwin Hyman.

Parker, R. (1995) 'Introduction' in E. Farmer and M. Owen (1995) *Child Protection Practice: Private Risks and Public Remedies*. London: HMSO.

Peake, A. and Fletcher, M. (1997) *Strong Mothers. A Resource for Mothers and Carers of Children who have been Sexually Assaulted*. Lyme Regis: Russell House Publishing.

Peled, E. (1997) 'Intervention with children of battered women: a review of current literature', *Children and Youth Services Review*, 19 (4), 277-299.

Peled, E. and Davis, D. (1995) *Groupwork with Children Of Battered Women: A Practitioner's Manual*. Sage: Thousand Oaks.

Peled, E. and Edleson, J.L. (1992) 'Breaking the secret: multiple perspectives on groupwork with children of battered women', *Violence and Victims*, 7 (4), 327-46.

Peled, E., Jaffe, P. and Edleson, J.L. (eds) (1995) *Ending the Cycle of Violence. Community Responses to Children of Battered Women*. Thousand Oaks: Sage.

Pence, E.(1988) *Batterer's programs: Shifting from Community Collusion to Community Confrontation*. Duluth, MN: Duluth Domestic Violence Intervention Project.

Pence, E. (1998) 'A coordinated community response to domestic violence' in N. Harwin, G. Hague and E. Malos (eds) *Domestic Violence and Multi-Agency Working: New Opportunities, Old Challenges?*. London: Whiting and Birch.

Pfouts, J.H., Scopler, J.H. and Henley, H.C. (1982) 'Forgotten victims of family violence', *Social Work*, 367-368.

Pringle, K. (1995) *Men, Masculinities and Social Welfare*. London: UCL Press.

Porter, B.K. and O'Leary, K.D. (1980) 'Marital discord and childhood behaviour problems', *Journal of Abnormal Child Psychology*, 8, 287-295.

Protection from Harassment Act (1997) London: HMSO

Ptacek, J. (1988) 'Why do men batter their wives?' in K. Yllo and M. Bograd (eds.) *Feminist Perspectives on Wife Abuse*. Newbury Park: Sage.

Pynoos, R.S. and Eth, S. (1985) 'Children traumatized by witnessing acts of personal violence; homicide, rape or suicide behaviour' in S. Eth and R.S. Pynoos (eds.) *Post Traumatic Stress Disorder in Children*. Washington: APA.

Radford, J., Kelly, L. and Hester, M. (1996) 'Introduction' in M. Hester, L. Kelly and J. Radford (eds) *Women, Violence and Male Power*. Buckingham: Open University Press.

Re O (Contact: Imposition of Conditions) (1995) 2 FLR 124.

Re F (Minors) (Contact: Mother's Anxiety) (1993) 2 FLR 830.

Rosenbaum A. and O'Leary, K. (1981) 'Children: the unintended victims of marital violence', *American Journal of Orthopsychiatry*, 51 (4), 692-699.

Rosenberg, M.S. (1984) *Inter-generational Family Violence: A Critique and Implications for Witnessing Children*, Paper presented at the 92nd annual convention of the American Psychological Association, Toronto.

Rosenberg, M. and Simmons, R. (1971) *Black and White Self-esteem: the Urban School Child*. Washington DC: American Sociological Association.

Ross, S.M. (1996) 'Risk of physical abuse to children of spouse abusing parents', *Child Abuse and Neglect*, 20 (7), 589-598.

Russell, M.N. (1995) *Confronting Abusive Beliefs. Group Treatment for Abusive Men*. Thousand Oaks: Sage.

Rutter, M. (1985) 'Resilience in the face of adversity: protective factors and resistance to psychiatric disorder', *British Journal of Psychiatry*, 147, 598-611.

Saradjian, J. (1997) 'Typical and atypical female perpetrators of child sexual abuse', Paper presented at BASPCAN conference. London: 9 December.

Saunders, A. (1994) 'Children in women's refuges: a retrospective study' in A. Mullender and R. Morley (eds.) *Children Living with Domestic Violence: Putting Men's Abuse of Women on the Child Care Agenda*. London: Whiting and Birch.

Saunders, A. with Epstein, C., Keep, G. and Debbonaire, T. (1995) *It Hurts Me Too: Children's Experiences of Domestic Violence and Refuge Life*. Bristol: WAFE/Childline/NISW.

Saunders, D.G. (1988) 'Wife abuse, husband abuse, or mutual combat?' in K. Yllo and M. Bograd (eds) *Feminist Perspectives on Wife Abuse*. Newbury Park: Sage.

Scourfield, J. (1995) *Changing Men*. Norwich: University of East Anglia.

Silvern, L. and Kaersvang, L. (1989) 'The traumatised children of violent marriages', *Child Welfare*, 68 (4), 421-436.

Silvern, L., Karyl, J. and Landis, T. (1995) 'Individual psychotherapy for the traumatized children of abused women' in E. Peled, P. Jaffe, and J.L. Edleson *Ending the Cycle of Violence. Community Responses to Children of Battered Women*. Thousand Oaks: Sage.

Sinclair, D. (1985) *Understanding Wife Assault: A Training Manual for Counsellors and Advocates*. Toronto: Ontario.

Skuse, D. (forthcoming) Institute of Child Health. London: DOH.

Smart, C. (1995) 'Losing the struggle for another voice: the case of family law', *Dalhousie Law Journal*, 18 (2)

Smith, G. (1997) 'Psychological resilience' in *Turning Points*. London: NSPCC.

Smith, L. (1989) *Domestic Violence: An Overview of the Literature*. Home Office Research Studies 107. London: HMSO

Stagg, V., Wills, G.D. and Howell, M. (1989) 'Psychopathology in early childhood witnesses of family violence', *Topics in Early Childhood Special Education*, 9, 73-87.

Stanko, E.A., Crisp, D., Hale, C. and Lucraft, H. (1998) *Counting The Costs: Estimating the Impact of Domestic Violence in the London Borough of Hackney.* London: Crime Concern.

Stanley, J., Goddard, C. (1993) 'The association between child abuse and other family violence', *Australian Social Work*, 46 (2), 3-8.

Stark, E. and Flitcraft, A. (1985) 'Woman-battering, child abuse and social heredity: what is the relationship?' in N.K. Johnson (ed) *Marital Violence.* London: Routledge and Kegan Paul.

Stark, E. and Flitcraft, A.H. (1988) 'Women and children at risk: A feminist perspective on child abuse', *International Journal of Health Studies*, 18 (1), 97-119.

Straus, M., Gelles, R.J. and Steinmetz, S.K. (1980) *Behind Closed Doors: Violence in the American Family.* Newbury Park: Sage.

Sudermann, M., Jaffe, P. and Hastings, E. (1995) 'Violence prevention programs in secondary (high) schools' in E. Peled, P. Jaffe, and J.L. Edleson *Ending the Cycle of Violence. Community Responses to Children of Battered Women.* Thousand Oaks: Sage.

Taylor, J. and Chandler, T. (1995) *Lesbians Talk: Violent Relationships.* London: Scarlet Press.

Tayside Women and Violence Group (1994) *Hit or Miss: An Exploratory Study of the Provision for Women Subjected to Domestic Violence in Tayside Region.* Dundee: Tayside Regional Council, Equal Opportunities Unit.

Telch, C.F. and Lindquist, C.U. (1984) 'Violent versus non-violent couples: a comparison of patterns', *Psychotherapy*, 21, 242-248.

Thoburn, J., Lewis, A. and Shemmings, D. (1995) *Paternalism or Partnership? Family Involvement in the Child Protection Process.* London: HMSO.

Thomas, A., Chess, S. and Birch, H. (1968) *Temperament and Behaviour Disorders in Children.* New York: New York University Press.

Thomas, A. and Niner, P. (1989) *Living in Temporary Accommodation: A Survey of Homeless People.* London: HMSO.

Thurston, R. and Beynon, J. (1995) 'Men's own stories, lives and violence; research as practice' in R.E. Dobash, R.P. Dobash and L. Noaks (eds) *Gender and Crime.* Cardiff: University of Wales Press.

Tormes, Y. (1972) *Child Victims of Incest.* Denver Colorado: American Humane Association.

Truesdell, D.L., McNeil, J.S. and Deschner, J.P. (1986), 'Incidence of wife abuse in incestuous families', *Social Work*, Mar-Apr, 138-140

Ulbrich, P. and Huber, J. (1981) 'Observing parental aggression: distribution and effects', *Journal of Marriage and the Family*, 43, 623-631.

Victim Support (1992) *Domestic Violence: Report of a National Inter-Agency Working Party on Domestic Violence.* London: Victim Support.

Violence Against Children Study Group (1990) *Taking Child Abuse Seriously.* London: Unwin Hyman.

Wagar, J.W. and Rodway, M.R. (1995) 'An evaluation of a group treatment approach for children who have witnessed wife abuse', *Journal of Family Violence*, 10, 295-306.

Walker, L. (1984) *The Battered Woman Syndrome.* New York: Springer Press

Weinehall, K. (1997) 'To grow up in the vicinity of violence: young people's stories about domestic violence', Akademiska avhandlingar vid Pedagogiska institutionen, Umea universitet, 45, 328-342.

Wilson, S.K., Cameron, S., Jaffe, P. and Wolfe, D. (1986) *Manual for a Group Program for Children Exposed to Wife Abuse*. London, Ontario: London Family Court Clinic.

Wilson, S.K., Cameron, S., Jaffe, P. and Wolfe, D. (1989) 'Children exposed to wife abuse: an intervention model', *Social Casework*, 70, 180-184.

Westra, B.L. and Martin, H.P. (1981) 'Children of battered women', *Maternal-Child Nursing Journal*, 10, 41-51.

Wolfe, D.A., Jaffe, P., Wilson, S. and Zak, L. (1985) 'Children of battered women: The relation of child behaviour to family violence and maternal stress', *Journal of Consulting and Clinical Psychology*, 53 (5), 657-665.

Wolfe, D.A., Jaffe, P., Wilson, S. and Zak, L (1988) 'A multivariate investigation of children's adjustment to family violence' in G.T. Hotaling, D. Finkelhor, J.T. Kirkpatrick and M.A. Straus (eds) *Family Abuse and its Consequences: New Directions in Research*. Newbury Park: Sage.

Wolfe, D.A., Zak, L, Wilson, S. and Jaffe, P. (1986) 'Child witnesses to violence between parents: Critical issues in behavioural and social adjustment', *Journal of Abnormal Child Psychology*, 14 (1), 95-104.

Women's Aid Federation England (1989) *Breaking Through: Women Surviving Male Violence*. Bristol: WAFE.

Women's Aid Federation England (1992) *A Women's Aid Approach to Working with Children*. Bristol: WAFE.

Women's Aid Federation England (1996) *Report from Annual Survey of Refuges and Helpline Services* (unpublished)

Women's Aid Federation England (1997) *Annual Report*. Bristol: WAFE

Women's Coalition Against Family Violence (1994) *Blood on Whose Hands?: The Killing of Women and Children in Domestic Homicides*. Brunswick Victoria: Women's Coalition Against Family Violence